Elementary Teacher's _New_ Complete Ideas Handbook

Previous P-H Books by Authors

Contemporary English in the Elementary School, 2nd ed., 1975.
Elementary Teacher's Complete Ideas Handbook, 1965.
The Language Arts Handbook
Teaching Writing in K-8 Classrooms

Elementary Teacher's
New Complete Ideas Handbook

Iris McClellan Tiedt
and
Sidney Willis Tiedt

Prentice-Hall, Inc.
Englewood Cliffs, New Jersey

Elementary Teacher's New Complete Ideas Handbook
by Iris M. Tiedt and Sidney W. Tiedt

Prentice-Hall International, Inc., *London*
Prentice-Hall of Australia, Pty. Ltd., *Sydney*
Prentice-Hall Canada, Inc., *Toronto*
Prentice-Hall of India Private Ltd., *New Delhi*
Prentice-Hall of Japan, Inc., *Tokyo*
Prentice-Hall of Southeast Asia Pte. Ltd., *Singapore*
Whitehall Books, Ltd., Wellington, *New Zealand*
Editora Prentice-Hall do Brasil Ltda., *Rio de Janeiro*

© 1983 by

PRENTICE-HALL, INC.

Englewood Cliffs, N.J.

Third Printing . . . . . March 1988

Library of Congress Cataloging in Publication Data

Tiedt, Iris M.
  Elementary teacher's new complete ideas handbook.

  Rev. ed. of: Elementary teacher's complete ideas
handbook / by Sidney W. Tiedt and Iris M. Tiedt. [1965]
  Includes index.
  1. Elementary school teaching—Handbooks, manuals,
etc. 2. Elementary school teachers—Handbooks, manuals,
etc. 3. Tiedt, Sidney W. II. Tiedt, Sidney, W.
Elementary teacher's complete ideas handbook. III. Title.
LB1555.T537 1983   372.11′02   83-8611
ISBN 0-13-260695-X

Printed in the United States of America

About the Authors

Iris McClellan Tiedt, a graduate of Northwestern University, earned her masters degree from the University of Oregon and her doctorate from Stanford University. Having taught in Illinois, Alaska, Oregon, California, Washington, and Utah, Dr. Tiedt is presently the director of the South Bay Writing Project at San Jose (California) State University. Known nationwide as an expert speaker and consultant, Dr. Tiedt has also authored many articles and publications, including *The Language Arts Handbook* (Prentice-Hall), *The Writing Process: Composition and Applied Grammar* (Allyn & Bacon), and *Teaching Writing in K-8 Classrooms* (Prentice-Hall).

Sidney Willis Tiedt, also a graduate of Northwestern University, received his masters degree from Northwestern and his doctorate from the University of Oregon. Having been a teacher, administrator, director and consultant throughout the West Coast, Dr. Tiedt has written many publications and articles, including material for *The Elementary School Journal, Elementary English, The Social Studies, Journal of Teacher Education,* and *Instructor.* Dr. Tiedt is presently a professor of education at San Jose (California) State University.

902645

To the Teacher

"How can I make teaching the basics more fun?"
"Where can I find ideas to improve student writing?"
"What can I do to enrich my reading program?"

Newly revised, the *Elementary Teacher's New Complete Ideas Handbook* provides answers to your questions. This successful handbook has been used by thousands of teachers since it was first published in 1965.

As we prepared this book for you, we tried to include refreshing ideas, sources, and strategies for teaching in all areas of the K-8 curriculum. We describe teacher-tested instructional strategies clearly so that you can use them in your classroom immediately. These ideas can be used with children of all ability levels and with both small and large group instruction—you decide how they best meet the needs of the children you teach.

Basic skills are at the heart of this handbook. We have selected powerful, teacher-tested methods that you can easily carry out without complicated preparation. The ideas will stimulate your thinking and will suggest modifications that fit your particular class. Thus, your teaching will become more effective and your students will increase their achievements, making teaching and learning more exciting!

The first chapter, "You're in Charge!" will help you get off to a good start in September. Included are suggestions for the very first day of school as well as for the last day before summer vacation. You will find help for dealing with student problems (discipline), working with parents (communication), and planning for calendar-related activities. These practical ideas will aid you in organizing and managing the classroom so that learning can take place.

Ten chapters focus on the basic elementary school curriculum, the teaching you do every day of the year. These ideas reflect current concerns: gifted students, working with ESL and bilingual children, evaluation, and multicultural teaching. Because of renewed interest in teaching the basics, we have expanded the number of chapters in the handbook from ten to twelve, enabling us to add a chapter on oral language development to support the reading and writing programs and a chapter on spelling and handwriting, important components of the writing program. Throughout this handbook, we have emphasized the importance of teaching reading and writing across the total curriculum.

Of special interest to the classroom teacher is the final chapter, "Resources for Teaching." Here are a variety of up-to-date tools that will not only improve your teaching abilities but also introduce you to more creative teaching materials.

Here is information at your fingertips. Good luck and good teaching!

Iris McClellan Tiedt
Sidney Willis Tiedt

Table of Contents

Basic Decoding Skills • 118

Identifying Letters • Comparing Symbols, Letters and
Words • First-Day Reading • Sight Words • Initial
Consonants • Consonant Blends • Word Wheels • Vowel
Sounds • Wordlists • Making Words • Word Basketball

Emphasizing Comprehension in Reading • 128

Comic Strip Reviews • Bulletin Board Display • Reporting
Unusual Information • Books Featuring Handicapped Children
• Reading Across the Curriculum • A Class Motto • Uninterrupted
Sustained Silent Reading • Book Reporting • Responding to Books
• Sharing Magazines • A Background of Stories • Understanding
Others • Getting to Know Authors • Cutting a Title • A Book Fair

Beginning Mathematical Concepts • 136

Math Awareness • Numbers in Our Language • The Numbers in
My Life • Math-Related Words • Beginning Work with Numerals
• Recognizing Numerals • Writing Numbers • Number Concepts
• The Sequence of Numbers • More Work with Numbers • Share
a Number Poem

The Math Center • 144

Number Language • Addition and Subtraction Facts • Multiplication
and Division Facts • Timer Tasks • Listening and Math

Puzzles and Intrigue • 150

Food for Thought • Challenges • Interesting Patterns with
Numbers • A Math Board • Five-Minute Math • Real-Life
Math • Writing Math Stories • Math Words • Math and Women
• Mystifying Your Friends • Challenging Gifted Students

Stimulating Thinking • 159

Brainstorming • Critical Thinking • Categorizing and
Classifying • Lively Discussions • A Class Motto • An
Exercise in Logic • Educated Guesses • Limited Information •
• Memory Training • Asking Questions • Levels of Questioning
• "Scientific" Poetry

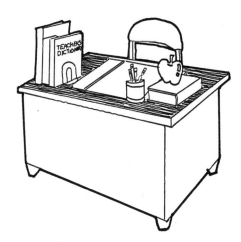

1. You're in Charge!

As you enter a classroom for the first time as a teacher, you are probably overwhelmed by the thought of being in charge of planning and carrying out instruction for 15, 20, or even 30 children. You can do a great job, however, with careful thought and planning.

In this chaper we will examine ways of making the classroom situation function more smoothly. You will find suggestions for working with students, handling discipline, evaluating progress, as well as having a good time. You will also find suggestions for improving your teaching skills and making your classroom more attractive.

At the end of this chapter is a handy collection of calendars. Use them to provide stimulating ideas that reinforce the learning of language skills and to add content in the various subject areas, art and music activities, and games and physical exercise.

"You're in Charge!" sets the stage for the chapters that follow. While focusing on the different areas of the elementary school curriculum, each chapter will present teaching ideas to be used with a specific subject. Several chapters are devoted to teaching reading and the language arts, for these subjects occupy more than half of the total curriculum. In each chapter, however, we have included activities that relate the various content areas, because teaching in the elementary school *should* be correlated—art, music, science, mathematics, and social science can be integrated with the development of the language skills of listening, speaking, reading, and writing.

Browse through the chapters now to see what you can use in

your classroom. Jot down notes in the margins; add titles to booklists; insert variations that occur to you as you read. Make this book your own.

REMEMBER: STUDENTS ARE HUMAN

By assuming a positive attitude toward students and their needs, you will enjoy your work and be a more effective teacher. The ideas presented in this section help you to work with students as learners, and to establish a classroom climate that is both cooperative and productive.

Learning Student Names

Names are very personal, so you must learn to pronounce each name correctly. Practice, if necessary, until you can say each student's name without hesitation. When students come from other countries and you find their names more difficult to pronounce, ask them to say the name slowly as you repeat it carefully until they tell you, "That's right."

Ask students what they prefer to be called. Do not arbitrarily decide to call one boy "Robert" while the next Robert becomes "Bob," "Bobby," or "Robbie." If Charles prefers to be called "Chuck," remember the nickname.

Nameplates

To help you and the other students learn the names of the members of the class, have them make nameplates to place on their desks for the first few days. One folded type of sign is made from a 9″ × 12″ sheet of colored construction paper. Use light colors so the printing will show up clearly. The paper is folded into equal thirds; students can approximate or use rulers to be exact. Have students lightly pencil the letters in place first to permit them to erase if the spacing is not right. Then, crayons or felt pens can be used to make the letters stand out. When the lettering is completed, tape the bottom edges together.

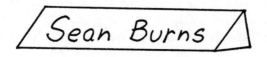

For primary youngsters, you or an aide might make the name-plates before the students arrive. Seeing the names in print helps children to read a variety of names. You can use the names at times to reinforce knowledge of spelling or phonics. For example: ask students what words begin with the same sound as Tommy's name.

Name Tags

Have students cut out leaf shapes to use as name tags. Provide patterns like the one outlined here, so students have enough room to print their first names. If students pin these name tags on their clothing, they can wear them to lunch or the playground as they gradually get acquainted.

Play a game using the tags. Have students leave their name tags on your desk as they go home. The next morning, read each tag and see who can pin the tag on the right person.

You may want to have a NAME TREE in the classroom on which students can pin their leaves before going home.

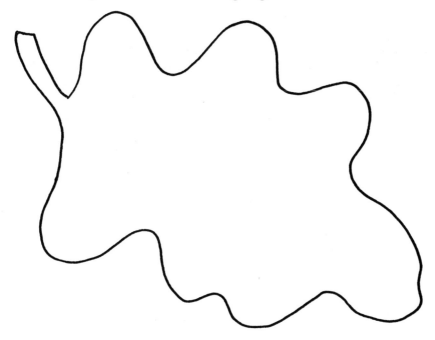

Class Directory

Children (and parents) will enjoy having a list of the students in the class, which includes both first and last names, addresses, and telephone numbers. Make multiple copies of the directory for your own use, too, as this list proves handy on many occasions as you check in books, log permission slips for a field trip, or determine which children have done special jobs. The list is also useful in letter-writing activities, so make copies available in February for Valentine's Day.

Talking with Students

Students enjoy talking with their teacher if the teacher is responsive. Many informal times—at recess, while students are working independently, during individual conferences—can be used to become acquainted with each student.

Another kind of talking can be accomplished through a TALK-ING BOOK in which students write, and you write back to encourage the dialogue. Have students write daily for ten minutes while you respond about once a week.

Personal Recognition

At the end of the day, read through the list of students in the class. Have you had some sort of direct contact with each student? If you notice that there are one or two students to whom you have not spoken directly, make a point of touching them casually and talking to them: "Margaret, you certainly worked hard today. Keep up the good work." "I'd like you to pass out some paper for me tomorrow morning, Paul. Will you remind me?"

A Change of Pace

Even the best students get bored doing the same type of activity over a long period of time. Plan for "breaks" that relieve tension and give students a chance to move around. Consider the following:

• *Attention span.* Plan reasonable lengths of time for any activity. Do not expect first-graders to sit still for 40 minutes.

• *Independent study.* Elementary school children should not be expected to work totally independently for long periods of time. Combine independent work with group work (whole class or small groups). A writing assignment, for example, should usually consist of (1) prewriting—large group discussion or other stimulus for writing;

(2) independent writing—trying out what was presented; and (3) follow-up—sharing in pairs or small groups.

- *Active learning.* Students will learn more from hands-on activities that engage them actively in the learning process than from "lecture-type" lessons.

Children will usually learn better if you alternate seatwork with active music or art periods. Have a quick game of "Simon Says" as a seventh-inning stretch before moving into a more taxing job, such as long division. (More suggestions are offered in Chapter 11, "Games and Activities: Indoors and Outdoors.")

Handling Problems

Students' behavior problems often indicate their need for attention, so try to make each student feel accepted and that he or she is a valuable member of the classroom. The child who is involved and has a sense of responsibility for what goes on in the classroom will tend to be cooperative.

To encourage students to begin working on a specific task, begin walking around the room slowly. Students are more visible to you and will tend to get their materials together and settle down to work if they see you. Occasionally, write numbers on the students' papers as you walk, indicating the number of minutes it took that particular student to get the first writing on paper: 1 (began immediately), 3 (a little slow), 5 (much too slow, wasting time). Conversely, you can use the "magic hand" and simply put a hand on the shoulder of a student who is working efficiently.

Students who get into mischief are usually controlled by simple techniques. Looking directly at a student may be helpful. Another simple method is to work at the back of the room while students are studying. If they cannot see you, they do not know whether or not you are watching them. More direct methods of quieting students who disturb others include:

- Having the student come to your desk for a conference
- Helping the student analyze the reasons for not being able to work quietly
- Asking the student to move his or her desk to a far corner at the back of the room. In this way, the student cannot show off for the others.

Make sure you provide positive reinforcement when the student behaves well, and help the student quietly resume a normal place in the classroom.

Teaching for Self-Esteem

Perhaps the most important thing we teach in the elementary school is self-esteem. Our teaching strategies can either build up or tear down children's feelings of self-esteem, that is, the way they see themselves.

Share this story that emphasizes the importance of diversity.

There's Nobody Like You!

The French poet Jean Cocteau found out early in life why diversity is better than uniformity.

As a young man, M. Cocteau was designing a stage set which required a tree as background. He spent night after night in the theater basement cutting out individual leaves for his creation.

Then, a wealthy friend whose father owned a factory approached him with another idea.

"Give me the design of the leaf," he said, "and in three days you will have thousands of them here."

After his friend's return, they pasted the multitute of identical leaves onto the branches.

The result, M. Cocteau recalled, was "the most boring package of flat, uninteresting forms one can see."

At last he understood why each leaf of a tree and each man in the world are different from any other.

Christopher News Notes, no. 187, May 1971.

Emphasize evaluation techniques that show children how you feel about them. If you really like and respect children, you will not mark their papers angrily with a red pencil or harangue them about mistakes they make. Instead, you will use positive reinforcement.

The following suggestions appear in "Building Positive Concepts of Self and Others" in *Multicultural Teaching: A Handbook of Activities, Information, and Resources* by Pamela and Iris Tiedt (Boston: Allyn & Bacon, 1979).

Supportive Evaluation Techniques

- *Self-evaluation.* As much as possible, have students check their own work. Provide answer sheets so they can discover mistakes immediately. Stress reading items over again as needed, and correcting errors. If you eliminate yourself from this kind of "grading," you cease to be the ogre who has all the "right" answers.

- *Individual conferences.* Have a short conference with each student once a week, if possible. Five minutes of individual attention does a lot for children who need support. This is a good time for examining children's writing or talking about the library book they are currently reading.

- *Send a letter to parents.* Several times during the year, send a letter to each parent commending at least one thing their child has accomplished. Children will be glad to take a Good Work Letter home. Be sure to write this letter in the language spoken at the student's home even if you have to prepare several translations.

- *Accentuate the positive.* Count up what students *do* accomplish, not what they fail to achieve or the mistakes they make. Compare:
"Wow, you spelled thirteen words out of fifteen correctly!"
"Too bad, you missed two words out of fifteen today."

BE A BETTER TEACHER

Think about the job of teaching; you may sometimes feel like a juggler trying to keep everything balanced while appearing calm, smiling, and in charge. Gradually, you really will have everything under control so that you can enjoy teaching. For the experienced teacher, some of these tips are taken for granted, but for the beginning teacher, they may prove invaluable.

Establishing a Daily Schedule

Although no schedule should be inflexible, children need to know what to expect at different times of the day. Print a copy of the schedule on posterboard and read it along with the students. Discuss the need for such a schedule, and realize that the schedule should be changed as needed. Your classroom timing will be influenced by the starting time of the school, of course, and such set times as lunch or recess that are shared with others.

Certain Routines

Students will be comfortable complying with procedures that you establish if they know and understand them. Some teachers have personal ways of asking the class to come to order, for example:

flicking the overhead lights
playing a chord on the piano
ringing a bell
writing directions on the board

Often, teachers want students to head their papers in specific ways. Prepare a chart that reminds students of an acceptable form. For example:

Student Responsibilities

Use contracts for student work so that students understand what they have to do and assume responsibility for undertaking specific learning tasks. A contract can be written for any subject assignment or for jobs in the room or on the playground.

```
Date begun:_____
Progress check 1:_____
Progress check 2:_____
Completed:_____
Signed:_____
```

Involving Students

As much as possible, have students assume responsibility for tasks done around the classroom. Here are twenty things students can do. You can probably think of many more!

1. Distribute paper for art and language activities.
2. Return corrected work to students.
3. Lead the Pledge of Allegiance and opening song.
4. Care for chalkboards and erasers.
5. Be official pencil sharpener at specific times.
6. Be host/hostess when guests visit the classroom.
7. Act as messenger to other classes or office.
8. Take care of windows and shades.
9. Feed pets.
10. Water flowers.
11. Arrange displays (committee).
12. File material in instructional materials file (committee).
13. Be friends for new students.
14. Empty wastebasket.
15. Lead students en route to lunch, recess, dismissal.
16. Be classroom librarian; work in central library.
17. Check attendance.
18. Be class officer.
19. Keep routine records (milk money, charity contributions).
20. Be student editor; assistant teacher.

Talking Less

Teachers tend to dominate the classroom with talking—giving directions and lectures, asking questions. Step back and let students do more of the active learning. Set up situations in which students can initiate the talking and interact with each other directly. IDEA: Try having an occasional period of NO TALKING.

Move yourself out of the dominant role by trying these ideas:

• Let a puppet or mascot do the talking. This "friend" can scold the children, teach the children, or praise them.

• Write key words on the board without saying anything: RECESS in five minutes. Are you ready for lunch?

• Introduce abbreviations: CU = Clean Up; SSS = Stand, Stretch, Sit.

Using Displays to Teach Skills

The bulletin board can be used to present procedures that students can follow. You might, for example, use the bulletin board as part of a Learning Center to show directions for completing a project. The directions given here are for writing a letter, but they might include a variety of other activities, such as origami (Japanese paper folding), math processes, compiling a social studies booklet, or writing a research report.

Using Time Efficiently

As a teacher, you must be constantly aware of how you use student learning time. Naturally, you want to make sure that students are not wasting time and that they are engaged in purposeful learning activities most of the time they are in the classroom. Students who are actively involved, furthermore, are less likely to present discipline problems, so always have activities planned that students can work on if they complete an assigned project.

Frequently assess the activities to make sure students are really *learning* something—many workbook or duplicated sheets are merely busy work. Free reading of magazines or books and writing projects are good activities that do not waste the students' time. (Look for independent activities in the chapters that follow.)

Filling Transition Time

Often, you will find short periods of time—before lunch, before recess, before dismissal—during the day's schedule when it is impractical to begin a new activity. Have a number of enjoyable but worthwhile activities that make use of this time.

- Build up a repertoire of songs that your students enjoy singing. Say, "We have a few minutes until lunch. Let's sing 'I've Been Working on the Railroad.'" In this way, you can slip in a little more time for music than you would normally schedule.

- Introduce the game of "Password" to students for use during any free time. Ask one or several students to be player(s). They can turn their heads while you print the word on the board for the other students to see, and then erase it. The class will be intrigued by the clues given and the efforts to guess the word. You can also have students play this game in pairs, in which players take turns being LEADER and LISTENER as they try to pass the word by giving verbal clues.

- Students will love to follow your directions mentally in "Mental Math," and see if they can come up with the correct answer. "Take 6; multiply it by 5; divide by 3; add 4; divide by 2. What is your answer?" Include any mathematical processes that your students know. This is excellent practice for students who are still learning arithmetical facts. You might ask students to write the answer on paper before you say it aloud.

- "Brainstorm" a list of titles that you can use later for writing topics. "Let's see how many good titles we can think of in five minutes." After lunch, students can choose one of the titles to talk or write about.

Beginning School Upon Arrival

See that children know exactly what to do when they enter the classroom. If students (such as those who are bused) come into the

suggestions realistic in terms of parent obligations. Suggest that parents try the following:

1. Encourage your children to talk to you. Listen to their sharing of what happened at school that day.
2. Touch children—hug them, put your arm around them, put your hand on their shoulder—even when you have to "reach up" to do it. Children of all ages need to feel loved to develop a feeling of self-esteem.
3. Read to your children. Let them read to you as much as they want. Children learn to read by reading; quantity will lead to quality.
4. Regulate your children's television watching time. School-work should come first. Television should not replace other experiences—reading, talking, family outings.

MAKE YOUR ROOM APPEALING

Students will enjoy thinking of ways to make their classroom more attractive. Students can create a Reading Center, hang mobiles from the ceiling, and plan appealing and informative displays on the bulletin board. This brainstorming of ideas is a good class project for the start of the new school year.

Forming Display Committees

Students learn organizational as well as research skills as they prepare a bulletin board display. Provide a list of HINTS FOR GOOD DISPLAYS to assist students in producing an attractive and informative bulletin board.

Hints for Good Displays

1. Choose a theme or one main idea for your display.
2. Use only a few key words for the caption.
3. Select two or three attractive contrasting colors.
4. Make sure lettering can be seen across the room. Pin the letters in place and check before attaching them more permanently.
5. Line up letters and other display materials by using a meter stick.
6. Avoid a cluttery appearance by using a limited number of display items.

Brainstorming Display Captions

Stimulate student interest in constructing displays by discussing the types of displays you might use. Brainstorm a number of captions and list the suggestions on the chalkboard:

A WAY WITH WORDS

ARE YOU "BOARD" WITH SCHOOL?

FLYING HIGH IN READING

Other reference materials will help students, too, as they search for ideas. *Bulletin Board Captions* (Contemporary Press) suggests a number of versatile captions that can be adapted to varied topics simply by changing the underlined word.

TIME TO WRITE

Preparing Sets of Letters

Show students how to construct block letters by drawing patterns on graph paper.

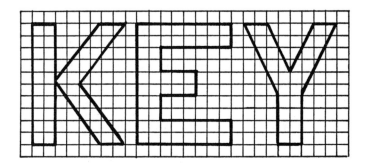

One set of letters can be constructed from each of these colors—black, white, red—to supply you with letters for any display. Other colors can be used also, as desired. A set of letters should include the following numbers of each letter:

10   A, I, E, O, S

6   B, C, D, G, H, L, M, N, P, R, T, U, Ẏ

2   F, J, K, Q, V, W, X, Z

Interesting Backgrounds

Often, the brown cork of the bulletin board serves as an effective background for a display, but for the sake of variety try other colors and textures. To avoid the task of pinning numerous small sheets of colored construction paper on a board, obtain several large sheets of paper or cloth which will cover the board in one operation. There are many possibilities that can be explored; listed here are just a few.

1. Colored burlap
2. Discarded drapes, tablecloths
3. Wrapping papers, grasscloth, rice paper, crepe paper
4. Upholstery, drapery remnants
5. Patterned cloth (stripes, small figures, flowers)
6. Colored corrugated cardboard
7. Net or mesh (either cloth or screening)
8. Newspaper

There are several distinct advantages to the use of these types of large coverings. The chief one is that you can cover the board quickly by inserting a few strategic pins or staples. The cloth has another advantage—storage; it can be used repeatedly, stored easily, and will not show pin or staple marks.

CALENDAR EVENTS

The calendar offers a stimulating source of ideas the whole year round. You will find ideas related to every area of study in the curriculum.

History—dates of historical events; birthdates of presidents
Science—discoveries; scientists' birthdates
Reading—authors' birthdates
Writing—topics related to history; current events

IMPORTANT: *The calendars shown here must be adapted for the current year.* The events listed in these calendars have been collected over a period of years as interesting and motivating.

The creative teacher will think of many ways of introducing this information to students. Use the material to make a large calendar on the bulletin board each month. You might also try some of these ideas:

Feature an event or person in a display.
Read the writings of a noted author.
Sing a song related to an event.
Prepare plays related to an event.
Have students read about a period of time or a famous person.
Have students research information about one person.
Each day have a student report on one item featured that day.

SEPTEMBER

SUN	MON	TUE	WED	THUR	FRI	SAT
Flower: Aster or Morning Glory. Birthstone: Sapphire		**1** Child Labor Act, 1916. World War II began, 1939. Commercial TV authorized, 1940	**2** US Treasury Dept est 1789. Eugene Field 1850-1895. **V-J Day**, 1945	**3** Henry Hudson discovered Manhattan, 1609. Treaty of Paris ended American Revolution, 1783	**4** Los Angeles, CA founded, 1781. First transcontinental TV, 1951	**5** Continental Congress convened in Philadelphia, 1774. Jesse James 1847-1882
6 Marquis de Lafayette, 1757-1834. Jane Addams 1860-1935. President McKinley shot. Died 9/14, 1901	**7 Labor Day** (varies) Elizabeth I 1533-1603. Brazilian Independence from Portugal, 1822. Elinor Wylie 1885-1928	**8** Richard the Lion-Hearted 1157-1199. Antonin Dvorak 1841-1904	**9** Cardinal Richelieu 1585-1642. California (31), 1850	**10** Battle of Lake Erie, 1813. Elias Howe invented sewing machine, 1846. Mother Seton first U.S.-born saint, 1975	**11 Defender's Day** in Maryland. Jenny Lind's first concert in U.S. 1850. William Sydney Porter (O. Henry) 1862-1910	**12** H.L. Mencken 1880-1956. First Russian rocket to moon, 1959
13 Grandparent's Day (varies). Dr. Walter Reed 1851-1902. John J. Pershing 1860-1948	**14** Francis Scott Key wrote **The Star Spangled Banner,** 1814. Ivan Pavlov 1849-1936	**15** Pilgrims left Eng. on **Mayflower,** 1620. James Fenimore Cooper 1789-1851. William Howard Taft (27th Pres.) 1857-1913	**16 Mexican Independence Day.** Alfred Noyes 1880-1958	**17 Von Steuben Day Citizenship Day.** Adoption of U.S. Constitution, 1787	**18** Capitol cornerstone laid by George Washington, 1793	**19** George Washington's **Farewell Address,** 1796. Lajos Kossuth 1802-1894
20 Alexander the Great, 356-323 B.C. Magellan sailed, 1519. USS Constitution (Old Ironsides) launched, 1797	**21** First daily newspaper published in U.S. 1784. H.G. Wells 1866-1946	**22 Autumn begins** 10:05 p.m. EST. First French Republic est. 1792	**23** Benedict Arnold found guilty of treason, 1780	**24** Zachary Taylor (12th Pres.) 1784-1850. Supreme Court created, 1789. **Black Friday,** 1869	**25 American Indian Day.** Columbus began second trip to America, 1493. First American newspaper published, 1690	**26** T.S. Eliot 1888-1965. George Gershwin 1898-1937
27 Senior Citizen's Day in Indiana. Samuel Adams 1722-1803. First railroad steam locomotive (England), 1825	**28** William the Conqueror invaded England, 1066	**29 Rosh Hashanah Michaelmas** (varies). Enrico Fermi 1901-1954	**30** First use of ether, 1842. Munich Pact 1938		**Second Week** National Hispanic Week. **Third Week** Constitution Week	**Fourth Week** National 4-H Club Week. National Pet Week

OCTOBER

SUN	MON	TUE	WED	THUR	FRI	SAT
Flower: Calendula or Cosmos **Birthstone:** Opal or Tourmaline	**First Week:** Employ the Physically Handicapped Week National Clean Air Week	**Second Week:** Fire Prevention Week **Third Week:** National Business Women's Week		**1** First World Series. First Model-T Ford sold. 1908	**2** Mohandas K. Gandhi 1869-1948 First meeting of Pan-American Union. 1889	**3** George Bancroft 1800-1891 Thomas Wolfe 1900-1938
4 Jean Francois Millet, 1814-1875 Rutherford B. Hayes (19th Pres). 1822-1893 Sputnik I (USSR), first satellite. 1957	**5** Child Health Day Chester A. Arthur (21st Pres.) 1830-1886 Joshua Logan 1908-	**6** Jenny Lind 1820-1887 Le Corbusier 1887-1965 **The Jazz Singer,** first talking movie. 1927	**7** James Whitcomb Riley 1849-1916 Niels Bohr 1885-1962	**8** Yom Kippur (varies) Chicago Fire. 1871 Eddie Rickenbacker 1890-1973	**9** Lief Ericsson Day Camille Saint-Saëns 1835-1921 John Lennon 1940-1980	**10** Giuseppe Verdi 1813-1901 US Naval Academy opened. 1845 Helen Hayes 1900-
11 Pulaski Memorial Day Eleanor Roosevelt 1884-1962 Francois Mauriac 1885-1970	**12** Columbus Day (varies) Christopher Columbus sighted land. 1492	**13** White House construction began. 1792 Rudolf Virchow 1821-1902	**14** William Penn 1644-1718 Dwight D. Eisenhower (34th Pres). 1890-1969 e.e. cummings 1894-1962	**15** World Poetry Day Virgil 70-19 B.C.	**16** Noah Webster 1758-1843 David Ben-Gurion 1886-1973 Eugene O'Neill 1888-1953	**17** First transatlantic wireless service. 1907 Albert Einstein came to the US. 1933
18 US flag officially raised in Alaska. 1867	**19** Sandwich invented. 1744 American Revolution ended when Cornwallis surrendered. 1781	**20** Sir Christopher Wren 1632-1723 John Dewey 1859-1952	**21** Samuel Coleridge 1772-1834 Alfred Nobel 1833-1896 U.N. founded in San Francisco. 1945	**22** Franz Liszt 1811-1886 Sam Houston first president of Republic of Texas. 1836	**23** Swallows depart Capistrano, CA today	**24** United Nations Day First telegram sent across US. 1861
25 Geoffrey Chaucer 1340-1400 Pablo Picasso 1881-1973 Richard E. Byrd 1888-1957	**26** Erie Canal opened. 1825 Mahalia Jackson 1911-1972	**27** Niccolo Paganini 1782-1840 Theodore Roosevelt (26th Pres) 1858-1919 Dylan Thomas 1914-1953	**28** Harvard College founded. 1636 Statue of Liberty unveiled. 1886 Jonas Salk 1914-	**29** John Keats 1795-1821 Stock Market crashed. 1929	**30** John Adams (2nd Pres.) 1735-1826 Ballpoint pen patented. 1888	**31** Halloween Reformation Day Jan Vermeer 1632-1675 Nevada (36). 1864

NOVEMBER

SUN	MON	TUE	WED	THUR	FRI	SAT
1 All Saints' Day, Benvenuto Cellini 1500-1571, Stephen Crane 1871-1900	**2** James K. Polk (11th Pres) 1795-1849, Warren G. Harding (20th Pres) 1865-1923, N. Dakota (39), 1889; S. Dakota, (40),1889	**3** Election Day (varies), Geo. Washington disbanded army, 1783, William Cullen Bryant 1794-1878	**4** Erie Canal opened, 1825, Will Rogers 1879-1935	**5** First auto patent issued, 1895, Shirley Chisholm (NY), first black woman elected to House of Representatives, 1968	**6** John Philip Sousa 1854-1932, First performance of Peter Pan, 1903	**7** Marie Curie 1867-1934, Albert Camus 1913-1960, Bolshevik Revolution, 1917
8 Montana (41), 1889, Edward Brooke (MA), first black senator in 85 yrs, elected 1966	**9** W. C. Handy 1873-1958	**10** Frederich von Schiller 1759-1805, US Marine Corp est. 1775, Stanley found Livingstone, 1871	**11** Veterans Day, Washington (42), 1889, Armistice signed to end World War I, 1918	**12** Elizabeth Cady Stanton Day, Dr. Sun Yat-sen 1866-1925	**13** Robert Louis Stevenson 1850-1894	**14** Sadie Hawkins Day, Robert Fulton 1765-1815, Moby Dick published, 1851
15 Zebulon Pike discovered Pike's Peak, 1806, Felix Frankfurter 1882-1965	**16** Paul Hindemith 1895-1963, Oklahoma (46), 1907	**17** Congress first used the Capitol building, 1800, Suez Canal opened 1869	**18** Louis Jacques Daguerre 1789-1851, US Standard Time est. 1883, Panama Canal Treaty signed, 1901	**19** James A. Garfield (20th Pres) 1831-1881, Abe Lincoln's Gettysburg Address 1863	**20** Robert F. Kennedy 1925-1968	**21** Mayflower Compact signed, 1620, Voltaire 1694-1778, North Carolina (12), 1789
22 Charles de Gaulle 1890-1970, John F. Kennedy assassinated, 1963	**23** Franklin Pierce (14th Pres) 1804-1869	**24** Zachary Taylor (12th Pres) 1784-1850, Toulouse-Lautrec 1864-1901	**25** Andrew Carnegie 1835-1919, Carrie Nation 1864-1911, Joe DiMaggio 1914-	**26** Thanksgiving Day (varies), First official Thanksgiving, 1789, Sojourner Truth died, 1883	**27** Charles Beard 1874-1948	**28** William Blake 1757-1827, First auto race, 1895
29 Louisa May Alcott 1832-1888, Richard E. Byrd first to fly over the South Pole, 1929	**30** Mark Twain 1835-1910		**Flower:** Chrysanthemum **Birthstone:** Topaz	**Second Week:** Cat Week	**Third Week:** American Education Week	

DECEMBER

SUN	MON	TUE	WED	THUR	FRI	SAT
Flower: Holly or Narcissus; **Birthstone:** Turquoise		**1** Mary Martin 1914-	**2** Napoleon crowned himself emperor. 1804. Monroe Doctrine. 1823. Georges Seurat 1859-1891	**3** Illinois (21). 1818 First successful heart transplant performed by Dr. Christiaan Barnard. 1967	**4** George Washington bade farewell to his officers at Fraunces Tavern, NY. 1783 Vasili Kandinsky 1855-1944	**5** Martin Van Buren (8th Pres.) 1782-1862 Walt Disney 1901-1967 21st Amendment repealed 18th. 1933
6 St. Nicholas Day in Europe Thomas Edison made first sound recording 1877 Dave Brubeck 1920-	**7** Delaware (1). 1787 Pearl Harbor attacked. 1941	**8** Eli Whitney 1765-1825 James Thurber 1894-1961	**9** John Milton 1608-1674 Christmas Seals first sold in US 1908	**10** Mississippi (20). 1817 Emily Dickinson 1830-1886 US acquired Cuba, Guam, Puerto Rico and Philippines. 1898	**11** Indiana (19). 1816 Robert Koch 1843-1910	**12** Pennsylvania (2). 1787 First radio signal crossed the Atlantic. 1912
13 New Zealand discovered. 1642	**14** George Washington died. 1799 Alabama (22). 1819 Ronald Amundsen reached South Pole. 1911	**15** Bill of Rights Day First 10 amendments ratified as Bill of Rights 1791	**16** Ludwig van Beethoven 1770-1827 Boston Tea Party. 1773 Noel Coward 1899-1973	**17** John Greenleaf Whittier 1807-1892 Wright brothers first flight at Kitty Hawk, NC. 1903	**18** New Jersey (3). 1787 Ratification of 13th Amendment ended slavery. 1865	**19** George Washington led Continental Army into Valley Forge, PA. 1777
20 Louisiana Purchase. 1803 Cherokees forced off their land in Georgia because of gold strike. 1835	**21** Winter begins at 5:51 p.m. EST Hanukkah (varies) Pilgrims landed at Plymouth, MA 1620	**22** Puccini 1858-1924 Edwin A. Robinson 1869-1935	**23** US Federal Reserve System est. 1913 Transistor invented. 1947	**24** Kit Carson 1809-1868	**25** Christmas Isaac Newton 1642-1727 Clara Barton 1821-1912	**26** Maurice Utrillo 1883-1955
27 Louis Pasteur 1822-1895 Branch Rickey 1881-1965	**28** Iowa (29). 1846 Woodrow Wilson (28th Pres.). 1856-1924 Chewing gum patented. 1869	**29** Charles Goodyear 1800-1860 Andrew Johnson (17th Pres.) 1808-1875 Texas (28) 1845	**30** Rudyard Kipling 1865-1936	**31** New Year's Eve Official end of World War II. 1946		**Second Week:** Human Rights Week

JANUARY

SUN	MON	TUE	WED	THUR	FRI	SAT
	Birthstone: Garnet	**Flower:** Carnation or Snowdrop			**1** New Year's Day, Paul Revere 1735-1818, Betsy Ross 1752-1836, Emancipation Proclamation, 1863	**2** James Wolfe (conqueror of Quebec) 1727-1759, Georgia ratified Constitution 1788
3 Lucretia Mott 1793-1880, Alaska (49), 1959	**4** Jakob Grimm 1785-1863, Louis Braille 1809-1852, Utah (45), 1869	**5** Stephen Decatur 1779-1820, George Washington Carver 1864-1943	**6** Feast of Epiphany (varies), Joan of Arc 1412-1431, Carl Sandburg 1878-1967, New Mexico (47), 1912	**7** First national election, 1789, Millard Fillmore (13th Pres) 1800-1874	**8** Battle of New Orleans, 1815, Elvis Presley 1935-1977	**9** Carrie Chapman Catt 1859-1947, Simone de Beauvoir 1908-, Richard M Nixon (37th Pres) 1913-
10 League of Nations founded, 1920, First U.N. General Assembly, London, 1946	**11** Alexander Hamilton 1755-1804, Amelia Earhart began solo flight across Pacific, 1935	**12** John Hancock 1737-1793, Jack London 1876-1916	**13** Emile Zola published J'accuse, a defense of Alfred Dreyfus, 1898	**14** Albert Schweitzer 1875-1965, John Dos Passos 1896-1971	**15** Moliere 1622-1673, Martin Luther King Jr 1929-1968	**16** Prohibition Amendment effective, 1920
17 Benjamin Franklin 1706-1790, Anton Chekov 1860-1904	**18** Daniel Webster 1782-1852, Versailles Peace Conference opened, 1919, Muhammad Ali 1942-	**19** Robert E. Lee 1807-1870, Edgar A Poe 1809-1849, Paul Cezanne 1839-1905	**20** First basketball game played, 1892	**21** General Stonewall Jackson 1824-1863, First atomic submarine, Nautilus, launched, 1954	**22** Sir Francis Bacon 1561-1626, Lord Byron 1788-1824, U Thant 1909-1974	**23** Edouard Manet 1832-1883, 24th Amendment barred poll tax in Federal elections, 1964
24 Gold discovered in CA 1848 / **31** Franz Schubert 1797-1828	**25** Robert Burns 1759-1796, Transcontinental telephone service inaugurated in US, 1915	**26** Douglas MacArthur 1880-1964, Michigan (26), 1837	**27** Wolfgang Mozart 1756-1791, Lewis Carroll 1832-1898, Vietnam conflict ended, 1973	**28** Auguste Piccard 1884-1962, Arthur Rubinstein 1887-	**29** Thomas Paine 1737-1809, William McKinley (25th Pres) 1843-1901, Kansas (34), 1961	**30** Franklin D. Roosevelt (32nd Pres), 1882-1945, Adolf Hitler became Chancellor of Germany, 1933

FEBRUARY

SUN	MON	TUE	WED	THUR	FRI	SAT
	1 National Freedom Day US Supreme Court first met. 1790 Victor Herbert 1859-1924	**2 Candlemas Day Groundhog Day** James Joyce 1882-1941	**3** Felix Mendelssohn 1809-1847 Elizabeth Blackwell 1821-1910 **Luna 9**, USSR, first soft landing on moon. 1966	**4** Confederate States of America formed, 1861 Charles A Lindbergh 1902-1974	**5** Roger Williams 1603-1683 Adlai Stevenson 1900-1965	**6** George (Babe) Ruth 1895-1948 Senate ratified treaty ending Spanish-American War, 1899
7 Sir Thomas More 1478-1535 Charles Dickens 1812-1870 Sinclair Lewis 1885-1951	**8** Jules Verne 1828-1905 Boy Scouts of America founded. 1910	**9** William Harrison (9th Pres.), 1773-1841 US Weather Service est. 1870 Amy Lowell 1874-1925	**10** End of French & Indian War, 1763 Charles Lamb 1775-1834 Leontyne Price 1927-	**11** Thomas A. Edison 1847-1931	**12** Abraham Lincoln (16th Pres.) 1809-1865 Charles Darwin 1809-1882 Yalta Agreement signed, 1945	**13** Boston's Latin School (oldest US public school) est. 1635 Grant Wood 1892-1942
14 Valentine's Day Thomas Malthus 1766-1834 Frederick Douglass 1817-1895 Oregon (33), 1859 Arizona (48), 1912	**15** Galileo Galilei 1564-1642 Susan B. Anthony 1820-1906 Battleship **Maine** destroyed. 1898	**16** Henry Adams 1838-1918 Ulysses S. Grant forced surrender of Confederate troops at Fort Donelson, 1862	**17** Marion Anderson 1902-	**18** Alessandro Volta 1745-1827 Wendell Willkie 1892-1944 Pluto discovered 1930	**19** Nicolaus Copernicus 1473-1543	**20** US Mail Service est. 1792 Col John Glenn's orbital space flight. 1962
21 W. H. Auden 1907-1973 Malcolm X 1925-1965	**22** George Washington (1st Pres.) 1732-1799 Frederic Chopin 1810-1849 Edna St. Vincent Millay 1892-1950	**23** George Frederick Handel 1685-1759 Siege of the **Alamo** began. 1836	**24 Ash Wednesday** (varies) Wilhelm Grimm 1786-1859 Winslow Homer 1836-1910	**25** Pierre Renoir 1841-1919 Hiram Revels (Miss.), first black congressman, 1870 16th Amendment passed, 1913	**26** Victor Hugo 1802-1885 William Cody (Buffalo Bill) 1846-1917 22nd Amendment passed, 1951	**27** Henry Wadsworth Longfellow 1807-1882 John Steinbeck 1902-1969
28 Montaigne 1533-1592 Republican Party began, 1854 Nijinsky 1890-1950		**Flower:** Violet or Primrose	**Birthstone:** Amethyst		**Black History Week** includes birthdays of Lincoln and Douglass	**Brotherhood Week** includes birthday of Washington

MAY

SUN	MON	TUE	WED	THUR	FRI	SAT
Flower: Lily of the Valley **Birthstone:** Emerald	**National Music Week** begins first week **World Trade Week** begins second week	**Senior Citizens Month Mental Health Month**			**1** May Day Law Day Loyalty Day Empire State building opened 1931	**2** Hudson Bay Company chartered in England, 1670 Bing Crosby 1904-1977 First jetliner passenger service, 1952
3 Machiavelli 1469-1527 First US medical school founded in Philadelphia, 1765	**4** Horace Mann 1796-1859 Thomas Huxley 1825-1895	**5** **Children's Day** in Japan **Cinco de Mayo** Karl Marx 1818-1883 First US manned sub-orbital space flight, 1961	**6** First postage stamp issued by England, 1840 Sigmund Freud 1856-1939 Robert E. Peary 1856-1920	**7** Robert Browning 1812-1889 Johannes Brahms 1833-1897 Peter Tchaikovsky 1840-1893 **Lusitania** sunk, 1915	**8** **Red Cross Day** Harry S. Truman (33rd Pres.) 1884-1972 **V-E Day,** 1945	**9** James Barrie 1860-1937 Byrd & Bennett flew over North Pole, 1926 First eye bank opened in NYC, 1944
10 **Mother's Day** (varies) First transcontinental railroad completed at Promontory, Utah, 1869	**11** Minnesota (32), 1858 Irving Berlin 1888- Salvador Dali 1904-	**12** Edward Lear 1812-1888 Florence Nightingale 1820-1910 Henry Cabot Lodge 1850-1924	**13** Jamestown, Virginia settled, 1607 Congress declared war on Mexico, 1846 Joe Louis 1914-	**14** Gabriel Fahrenheit 1686-1736 State of Israel proclaimed, 1948 Warsaw pact, 1955	**15** Pierre Curie 1859-1906 Final **Mercury** space flight, 1963	**16** **Armed Forces Day** William H. Seward 1801-1872
17 Edward Jenner 1749-1823 Supreme Court declared racial segregation in public schools unconstitutional, 1954	**18** Hispanic Society of America founded, 1904 Dame Margot Fonteyn 1919- **Apollo 10** flight, May 18-26, 1969	**19** **I Am an American Day** Johns Hopkins 1795-1873 Malcolm X 1925-1965	**20** Lindbergh's solo flight from New York to Paris, 1927 Amelia Earhart first woman to fly Atlantic solo, 1932	**21** Albrecht Durer 1471-1528 First bicycles imported from England, 1819 Clara Barton 1821-1912	**22** **National Maritime Day** Richard Wagner 1813-1883 Sir Arthur Conan Doyle, 1859-1930 Sir Laurence Olivier, 1907-	**23** Karl von Linne (Linnaeus) 1707-1778 South Carolina (8), 1788
24 Manhattan bought for $24, 1626 / **31** Walt Whitman 1819-1892	**25** **Memorial Day African Freedom Day** Ralph Waldo Emerson 1802-1882 Beverly Sills 1925-	**26** Suzette la Flesche died, 1903 Battle of Dunkirk May 26-June 4, 1940	**27** Amelia Bloomer 1818-1894 Julia Ward Howe 1819-1910 Georges Rouault 1871-1958 Isadora Duncan 1878-1927	**28** Jean Louis Agassiz 1807-1873 Dionne quintuplets born, 1934	**29** Patrick Henry 1736-1799 Rhode Island (13), 1790 Wisconsin (30), 1848 John F. Kennedy 1917-1963	**30** Joan of Arc burned at stake, 1431 Fernando de Soto landed in Florida, 1539

JUNE

SUN	MON	TUE	WED	THUR	FRI	SAT
	1 Kentucky (15), Tennessee (16), 1796. Brigham Young 1801-1877	**2** Martha Washington 1732-1802. Thomas Hardy 1840-1928. First US soft landing on the moon of Surveyor 1, 1966	**3** Jefferson Davis 1808-1889. Raoul Dufy 1877-1953	**4** Roquefort cheese supposedly discovered in a cave near Roquefort, France, 1070	**5** Joseph & Jacques Montgolfier's balloon ascent, 1783	**6** Nathan Hale 1755-1776. **YMCA** organized in London, 1844. Thomas Mann 1875-1955. **D-Day, 1944**
7 Paul Gauguin 1848-1903. Gwendolyn Brooks first black to receive Pulitzer Prize 1917.	**8** First ocean-going steamboat, 1809. Frank Lloyd Wright 1869-1959. First vacuum cleaner, 1869	**9** John Howard Payne 1791-1852. Cole Porter 1893-1964	**10** Prince Philip of England 1921. Italy formally became a republic, 1946	**11** Kamehameha Day in Hawaii. John Constable 1776-1837. Richard Strauss 1864-1949	**12** Charles Kingsley 1819-1875	**13** Alexander the Great died, 323 B.C. William B. Yeats 1865-1939
14 Flag Day. Children's Day. Trinity Sunday (varies). Harriet Beecher Stowe 1811-1896	**15** Magna Carta, 1215. Benjamin Franklin's kite flying experiment, 1752. Arkansas (25), 1836	**16** Alaskan Gold Rush, 1897. Flight of Valentina V. Tereshkova (first woman in space), June 16-19, 1963	**17** Bunker Hill Day in Massachusetts. Discovery of Mississippi River, 1673. Igor Stravinsky 1882-1971	**18** War declared against Great Britain, 1812. Napoleon's defeat at Waterloo, 1815	**19** Emancipation Day in Texas. Statue of Liberty arrived in NYC harbor, 1885	**20** Great Seal of US adopted, 1782. Start of French Revolution, 1789. Jacques Offenbach 1819-1880. West Virginia (35), 1863
21 Father's Day (varies). First day of Summer. New Hampshire (9), 1788. Rockwell Kent 1882-1971	**22** Slavery abolished in Great Britain, 1772. Julian Huxley 1887-1975. Anne Morrow Lindbergh 1906-	**23** US forces entered Korean War, 1950. International Treaty for Scientific Cooperation, 1961	**24** San Juan Day in Puerto Rico. Midsummer Day (Old English Holiday)	**25** Virginia (10), 1788. Custer's Last Stand, 1876	**26** Pearl S. Buck 1892-1973. United Nations Charter signed, 1945	**27** Charles Parnell 1846-1891. Paul Dunbar 1872-1906. Helen Keller 1880-1968
28 Assassination of Archduke Ferdinand triggered WWI, 1914. Peace Treaty signed at Versailles, 1919	**29** Peter Paul Rubens 1577-1640. First African church in US dedicated in Philadelphia, 1794	**30** Democratic Republic of the Congo (now Zaire) est. 1960. 26th Amendment lowered voting age to 18, 1971		**Flower:** rose or honeysuckle. **Birthstone:** pearl, agate or moonstone	**National Recreation Month** **First full week:** National Humor Week	**Second full week:** National Little League Baseball Week. National Flag Week

help students increase their listening efficiency. You might discuss the following topics:

"Listening is to speaking as reading is to writing."
"Listening means more than just hearing."
"Nature has given us one tongue, but two ears so that we may hear from others twice as much as we speak."

Time and Listening

Studies estimate that half of a child's time in school is spent in listening. Have students keep a diary or log for several days to record the amount of time spent in listening, speaking, reading, and writing. Included will be time spent in physical activities, eating, and sleeping.

A discussion of these findings should be revealing. Students might compile individual graphs showing how their time is used in a 24-hour period. Here is one sample:

A Sound Vocabulary

As children listen to sounds, they expand their vocabularies. Make a large chart on which these words are listed.

LISTEN TO SOUNDS	
harsh	melodious
tinkling	murmuring
creaking	booming
scratching	whining
tapping	scraping

Other charts might focus on Sounds That Animals Make, Sounds Made by the Wind, Soft Sounds, or Loud Sounds.

Listening to Directions

Students need to be able to listen to directions, to hear them accurately, and then to follow them. Talk about the skills involved and practice following oral directions in a variety of ways.

• "Do As I Say" is a game in which the students listen carefully to a set of directions and then try to follow them exactly. Try these types of directions:

(Say the whole paragraph while everyone listens—no writing or questions.)

Write your name on the last line of your paper.
Write the numbers from 1 to 10 all on line 4.
Write the colors of our flag on line 10.

(Repeat the directions twice; then have students write.)

All boys with blue eyes are to line up against the back wall.
All girls with brown eyes stand near the windows.
Boys with brown eyes line up near the door.
Girls with blue eyes stand in front of the chalkboard.

• The tape recorder can assist you in preparing material to provide practice in listening. Make a tape of a story that people know very well, but make some slight changes. See if the students can spot them. You might also tape a story that you play once and then play halfway through again. See if students can finish the story after having heard it only once.

• Folded paper projects offer another opportunity for following oral directions. Begin with simple folding of paper into fourths and eighths. Combine this folding with cutting to make boxes and baskets. More advanced students can try origami (oriental paper folding) or figures such as polyhedrons.

• "Listen, Think, Act" is another game for following directions. Say, "Listen," and then give directions (before calling an individual student's name) while all listen. Then say, "Think," while all try to remember the directions. Last, call one student's name, "Joe, Act." The class watches carefully to see if the person is able to follow the oral directions exactly. This activity can be played with teams. The child who carries out the directions then gives a set of directions in the same way (the number of items included each time should be set according to the ability level of the group). Here is an example of directions to be given at one time:

> Walk to the door. Turn around three times. Touch the teacher's desk. Write your name on the left side of the chalkboard.

• Mental math is excellent for providing this practice in listening as well as using arithmetical skills. According to the ability level of your group, give students oral problems to which they can write the answer (or give it orally).

> Take 3; add 2; subtract 4; double your answer; add 5. What's your answer? (7)

> Take 10; add 5; divide by 3; add 7; multiply by 2; divide by 6. What's your answer? (4)

NOTE: In school we tend to emphasize reading, writing, speaking and listening, in that order. This order of emphasis should be reversed.

Read Aloud

Reading aloud is one of the best instructional strategies for teaching listening skills. Students hear "book language" and learn new concepts and vocabulary. You may be surprised to know that students learn grammar through hearing you read aloud as they listen to the varied structures of English sentences used by the author.

Choose good books to share with students, many of which are listed throughout this handbook. Books about friendship and getting along with other people are especially valuable.

Cohen, Miriam. *Best Friends.* New York: Macmillan, 1971. (PS-1)
Cohen, Miriam. *Will I Have a Friend?* New York: Macmillan, 1967. (K-1)
Roche, P.K. *Good-Bye Arnold!* New York: Dial, 1979. (PS-2)
Sherman, Ivan. *I Do Not Like It When My Friend Comes to Visit.* New York: Harcourt Brace Jovanovich, 1973. (K-1)
Zolotow, Charlotte. *Janey.* New York: Harper & Row, 1973. (PS-3)

Blume, Judy. *Superfudge.* New York: Dutton, 1980. (3-6)
Burch, Robert. *Queenie Peavy.* New York: Viking, 1966. (4-7)
Clifton, Lucille. *The Times They Used to Be.* New York: Holt, Rinehart and Winston, 1974. (3-7)
Coles, Robert. *Dead End School.* Boston: Little, Brown, 1968. (3-7)
Corcoran, Barbara. *Sam.* New York: Atheneum, 1967. (5-9)
Fox, Paula. *Portrait of Ivan.* Scarsdale, NY: Bradbury, 1969. (5-7)

SPEAKING EFFECTIVELY

Most children know how to speak, and some children are highly verbal! The reason for focusing on speaking, however, is to assist children in communicating more effectively and to provide them with varied types of speaking.

Children need to develop self-confidence and self-esteem so that they can speak easily and with some authority, and so that others can understand. Planning a variety of oral activities will help students become more at ease in expressing themselves.

• Have students prepare a tape to accompany a series of photographs or pictures clipped from a magazine. Students can also draw or paint illustrations for this purpose. A script can be written to accompany the pictures used, or each student can speak about his or her own picture. Focus the set of pictures on one theme, such as Winter Sports, with each child telling about one sport or describing the activity pictured. The contribution might also be a short story based on the picture. The pictures can be held by each child as the taped message is heard, or the pictures can be mounted (in the order taped) on a continuous strip of paper to be used in a Scroll Theater.

• Have students send messages to other children. The class with whom you exchange tapes can be across the hall, in another city, or across the ocean. Students can prepare stories, poems, or plays that they have written. At times, they can tape material individually or they can tape some things as a group. Illustrations and written materials can also be sent in conjunction with the tape. You might want to write for information about sending tapes abroad:

World Tape Pals
Box 9211
Dallas, Texas 79015

How We Communicate

Talk about the many ways we have of communicating to one another. Students might list: writing a letter, using the telephone, drawing a picture, talking together, singing a song.

To probe further, ask these questions:

1. How can you communicate with someone who cannot hear?
2. How do you communicate with a person who does not speak the same language you do?
3. What helps you to understand what a person means even if no words are spoken?

You might develop interesting studies of such topics as body language, sign language, and pantomime. Share this quotation with your students.:

"Speech is civilization itself. The word, even the most contradictory word, preserves contact—it is silence which isolates." (From *The Magic Mountain* by Thomas Mann.)

Developing Confidence with Props

If children are shy about speaking before large groups, help them develop more assurance by giving them props to manipulate as they speak. "How to" speeches are successful because the student demonstrates while explaining. Topics might include:

how to cut a snowflake
how to make a book cover
how to fold a paper airplane

Students forget their self-consciousness as they explain and show the class the process described.

Providing a Speaker's Stand

Use a speaker's stand to give students a sense of security, something to support them while speaking. They might stand behind a table or a desk or a simple podium constructed from a cardboard carton.

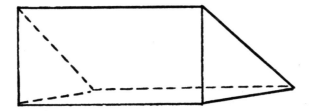

Assisting the Shy Student

Students who continue to have difficulty speaking before a large group may benefit from working in small speaking groups, such as four or five students who recite a poem together. As they become more confident, plan experiences with only one or two other speakers. Soon, students will gain enough confidence to present something short to the class individually. Ways of helping these shy students include:

having them give very brief talks
assigning familiar material—a known joke or a memorized poem
establishing definite guidelines for a short talk

Reading Aloud Effectively

A type of oral presentation that is easier for the shy child is reading orally. Discuss with the class the *art of reading well* and interpreting without exaggeration. Help them list suggestions to follow:

Know the material well, so your eyes can look at the audience.
Read in sentences rather than words.
Use expression according to the material—excitement, softness, speed, pauses.

Various types of material can be read. Poetry, excerpts from books read, short stories—all lend interesting variety to oral presentations. Let each child plan to read aloud to the class after recess, assigning one or two children to each day. At times, have each student select his or her best piece of writing to read to the class. Tape these presentations for use during Open House.

Suggest that students choose their favorite poems, too, to share orally. A good selection is "Who Has Seen the Wind?" by Christina Rossetti.

Who has seen the wind?
Neither I nor you:
But when the leaves hang trembling
The wind is passing thro'.
Who has seen the wind?
Neither you nor I:
But when the trees bow down their heads
The wind is passing by.

Show and Tell

Often used in primary grades, Show and Tell is a good method for providing oral language experiences. Like most activities, sharing of experiences should be a varied method, for any technique becomes dull and uninteresting if overworked. Here are some suggestions for varying the routine to maintain a high level of interest and participation:

Don't have Show and Tell every day or always at the same time.

Select a theme for the sharing period—My Best Friend, Was I Scared!, Work Can Be Fun, An Exciting Moment. Announce the theme the day before.

Use an unusual seating arrangement—circle, semicircle, sitting on the floor.

Tape the speaking occasionally for evaluation by students.

You listen, too, and comment with interest. (Don't be obviously busy with paperwork.)

If a child has something exciting to share, let the child do so, even if sharing is not on your schedule. Take advantage of this show of interest.

Tongue-Twisters

The word for tongue-twister in Spanish is *trabalengua.* Challenge students to say the following example:

Tres tristes tigres trillaron trigo en un trigal.
(Three sad tigers threshing wheat in a wheat field.)

Collect examples of tongue-twisters from different languages. Share some interesting ones in English, too, for the benefit of all students.

Six silent snakes slithering slowly southward.
Eight gray geese grazing gaily into Greece.

The sun shines on shop signs.
Thrice times three; twice times two.

An interesting source of varied tongue-twisters is *A Twister of Twists, a Tangler of Tongues* by Alvin Schwartz (Philadelphia: Lippincott, 1972).

Telling Stories

Storytelling is an ancient art, a favorite with everyone. The oral tradition of telling stories is found in all cultures.

Discuss with the class the art of storytelling. Compile a list of statements about what they like about some storytellers, and then have them listen to records of people telling stories. They can compare their reactions to the way the story was told.

Let each child choose a story to tell to the class. They may want to begin with very simple familiar fairy tales or nursery stories. Each child should be encouraged to tell his or her story freely, even briefly, in order to achieve a feeling of success with storytelling. Mentioning something complimentary about each presentation not only boosts the morale of the speaker, but also points out aspects of storytelling that are considered desirable.

Storytelling can also be taped and used to send to other students. Encourage the selection of longer stories by those who are more able. Never try to have the whole class tell their stories on one day. Rather, arrange to have a few each day at a specified time until all have had a chance to participate.

You, too, can enjoy storytelling with the class. Your telling of stories will lead the way to student enthusiasm. Students can form a Storyteller's Club that presents stories to children in lower grades.

Conversing

Conversation is a type of oral language that we take for granted. Yet, there are skills of conversing that should be taught in the classroom that will enable students to operate more successfully as they engage socially with other people.

Set up conversation situations in which several children play roles and participate in a conversation together. Students can write short descriptions like this to use in practicing conversations:

Matthew, Joe, and Rich are talking about baseball. Each one talks about his favorite player or team.

Terry, Silvia, and Bobby talk about a party they plan to give. They talk about whom they will invite and the games they will play.

Students can have informal conversations in groups similar to discussion groups. For several weeks have students participate in talking time. Write the letters TT on the chalkboard to signal to students that it is time to put away their work and move into talking groups (limited to five students each). The first time you should help the students through the procedure of moving to specified areas for conversation. Arrange seating less formally for this purpose. Discuss how a conversation progresses. Make a list of topics that can be discussed and note that anyone may initiate a subject about which others will comment. After the first conversation experience, discuss any problems or questions that students have, and ask the students to suggest ways of improving the conversation next time.

Participating in a Discussion

Discussion is one of the most common types of oral discourse. We discuss subjects informally with friends, and we work formally on an organized committee. Children need to learn the skills involved in discussion. Talk about discussion with the class—note that you are having a discussion right at that moment. List the qualities of a good discussion on the chalkboard:

Everyone participates.
You need a leader.
People talk one at a time so everyone can hear.

In the classroom, you may sometimes have trouble involving all students in discussion activities. You may need to support shy children, while at the same time teach the highly verbal child to participate more effectively. To encourage the quiet child to partici-pate, try these methods:

Address a question to the child (not to embarrass): "Paul, did you ever know anyone who had an experience like that?"

Ask a general question, then call on someone who has not been active: "How many of you have ever been on a boat or a ship?" (Pause for response; select a quiet student first.)

"What kind of boat were you on, Joan?"

Watch for signs of interest and desire to respond; take advantage of these responses by calling on that child: "Did you have something to add, Sue?"

Make it clear that each response is valued. Make a point of praising the contributions of the child who needs encouragement.

The extremely verbal child, on the other hand, can at times monopolize discussions in such a way that less aggressive children are discouraged. Try to control his or her participation, while at the same time not discouraging it.

Ignore the waving hand part of the time to call on others.

Give the child something else to do as part of the discussion, such as recording ideas expressed.

Let the child act as Discussion Leader (after discussing the qualities of a good leader).

Ask the child to call on someone else.

Limit the child's answers: "Karen, will you tell us one more thing we can add to our list?"

Explore with the class the art of discussing so that they become conscious of their roles in a discussion. Examine the types of questions to be asked. Have them observe discussions on television. Discussion topics might include:

Comparing two characters in a story

Solving a classroom problem—entering the classroom, turning in work

What life was like in a particular period of history

Plans to write a skit teaching the class something—how to introduce a friend to parents; the origin of an interesting word

Working in Groups

Children need help in working effectively' in small groups, independent of the teacher. As you plan experiences to teach discussion skills, have clear objectives in mind, and specifically tell students what they are to work on.

Today we are to work in small groups to discuss ways of making our classroom more attractive. You will talk together for 15 minutes, and I would hope that each group will have at least three suggestions. I want you to select the best suggestion from your group to present to the whole class.

As you work today, I want you to remember how to be a good group member. Let's operate with the rule: Everyone in the group must speak once before a person can speak a second time.

Each group will have a Leader and a Recorder. It is the job of the Leader to see that people take turns speaking and that everyone gets a chance to participate in the discussion. The Recorder will write the suggestions made by the group on a sheet of paper that I will collect.

Now, we will count off by fours to form our groups. (Do so.) Will the members of Group 1 hold up their hands? Maria will be the Leader and Corey will be the Recorder. Group 1 will meet at the Reading Table. Do not move yet. (Follow the same procedure for each group.) Move to your places ready to discuss.

Providing guidelines for discussion is also helpful. Each group may be given a list of three to five questions to answer, or the statement of a problem for which they are to brainstorm solutions. Being as specific as possible and limiting the amount of time to be used aids students in discussing effectively.

Puppetry

Puppetry permits students to lose their identity in that of the character they are portraying. Shy students are encouraged, more verbal children are challenged, and all students are stimulated to use oral language through the use of varied kinds of puppets.

Try a variety of puppets, none of which need to be time-consuming projects. Easily constructed puppets for instant use are stick puppets that consist of paper figures pasted on one end of a tongue depressor or some other kind of flat wood or cardboard. (See Chapter 10, "Art in the Classroom," for making other varieties of puppets suitable for classroom use.)

With puppets, use some of the techniques described earlier in

this section for encouraging children to talk. Role playing is very successful with children manipulating puppets who speak freely about the situation portrayed. Again emphasize free speech rather than lengthy memorization of written scripts.

Addressing a Group

Speaking before a class is frightening to some students. Gradually, they can learn to handle a group presentation with equanimity, but this ease comes only with practice.

Occasionally, have the students speak extemporaneously. Collect a box of small pictures clipped from magazines. Mount these pictures on 4″ × 6″ unlined filing cards for easy storage and reuse with this activity (or creative writing). You may permit each student to select a picture from six laid on your desk, or you may simply have each speaker take the one on top of the pile. Give the speaker 30 seconds to think about what he or she will say and then have the child begin telling the class about the picture. The picture helps the less verbal child to think of something to say.

Before students give their first speeches, have them discuss the techniques of giving a good speech. Make a chart like this to display.

Don't speak until you face the audience.
Look at the people you are speaking to.
Speak so that you can be heard at the back of the room.
Don't read your speech or refer to notes too much.
Speak slowly rather than too fast.

Evaluating Presentations

Teach the students how to help each other by offering positive suggestions. The way you respond to student efforts provides a model that your students will emulate.

Rather than pointing out errors in pronunciation, the way the speaker stood, and the content of the speech, *praise one aspect of the student's presentation.* You might also *suggest one specific area for improvement,* remembering that too many suggestions or criticisms tend to confuse rather than assist the student.

Students will develop greater enjoyment of speaking and will be interested in developing skills in speaking if they have a positive feeling toward oral activities. Any speech impediments and errors in articulation should not be emphasized during these speaking activities; refer these children to the speech specialist, if possible.

When children are speaking to the class, try sitting in the back of the room so the speaker speaks to the group rather than half-turned to the teacher, who is sitting nearby.

Speaking and Listening Relationship

Show students that speaking and listening are independent skills that require the interaction of two people. Display the following quotation and have students discuss it.

"The hearing ear is always close to the speaking tongue."

Ralph Waldo Emerson

ESL AND BILINGUAL STUDENTS

In almost every classroom you will find students who need special help with language learning, with most of these students needing to learn English as a second language. Their language backgrounds differ so widely, however, that we must begin with individual diagnosis.

For students who have only meager ability in speaking English, instruction should be oral. Intensive work in listening to and speaking English will prepare these students to begin writing and reading activities, which are supported by oral language.

The activities described in this section can be used with any student who needs to develop greater facility in using oral English.

Alike and Different: Discrimination

Introduce activities that focus student attention on words that have like elements and help them identify how words differ.

Read groups of words to students who are to designate one word that is different from the rest.

Time, climb, same, lime. (Which word does not rhyme?)
Room, rabbit, bounce, round (Which word does not begin the same?)
Bending, walking, helped, coming. (Which word does not end the same?)

After students become accustomed to such exercises, prepare tapes of these kinds of activities. Students can mark their answers on an answer sheet to be compared with the numbered sheet in a "Big Book of Answers" you have prepared.

Teaching English Patterns

Students who are not fluent in English need to practice the patterns of English sentences. All students can participate in these group activities.

• Give students an opportunity to speak, while at the same time, emphasizing correct usage. The Progressive Conversation is a method we find highly successful. Students respond more positively to this method of studying correct usage than they do to the traditional lengthy written exercise.

To provide practice in the use of *was* and *were,* for example, begin a conversation like this:

Teacher: "Was John late today, Mary?"

Mary: "No, John was not late today. Was the sun shining yesterday, Susan?"

Susan: "Yes, the sun was shining yesterday. Were you at home last night, Jim?"

The Progressive Conversation continues around the room in this fashion with each child constructing a sentence using either *was* or *were.* With large classes, divide the class into two or three conversation groups with a student leader assigned to each group while you walk from group to group guiding progress. If a sentence causes difficulty, write it on the board to discuss the correct usage, and then continue. After all have participated, lead the class to make generalizations about the use of *was* and *were:*

> Both WAS and WERE tell about something in the PAST.
> WAS is used when you are talking about only ONE thing.
> WERE is used when you are talking about MORE than ONE thing.
> WERE is always used with YOU.

• Generalizations about usage can be collected into a Class Book. Refer students to the Class Book when they need to review a problem area. After each discussion about usage, students can be assigned to print the generalizations on a page, such as for DO and DOES. Examples may also be included to illustrate each generalization. Students who commonly make mistakes in oral exercises should be encouraged to check the Class Book when they have questions.

Films Stimulate Talking

Use slides and filmstrips to stimulate speaking in the same fashion. As you show a slide, have students take turns in making some comments about the picture. The filmstrip can be stopped to allow for more comments by the students. Develop a collection of provocative slides—an old house, a child at play, a dog running down the street, a mysterious object—for use in this way.

NOTE: Studies show that aural-oral language abilities affect success in learning to read and write and to learn other subject matter. We need to take time to develop these abilities, therefore, before pushing students into extensive reading and writing assignments.

Using the Opaque Projector

The opaque projector can be used to project a variety of pictures that students can discuss briefly. As you show a picture, call out three or four student names. Each student called is to say a sentence or two about the picture.

Another time, simply ask questions about the picture shown— Why is the dog running? What kind of dress is the girl wearing? Where is she going? Who lives in this house?

Repeat After Me

Repeating what was said is another way of developing listening skills. You may say any series of words, numbers, or names to see if students can repeat them aloud or write them. Say a series of numbers, asking the students to then write the series in reverse order. The number of items will vary with the abilities of the students.

Language Awareness

ESL and bilingual students will benefit if the whole class learns more about the history of English and the diversity of language that exists in the United States.

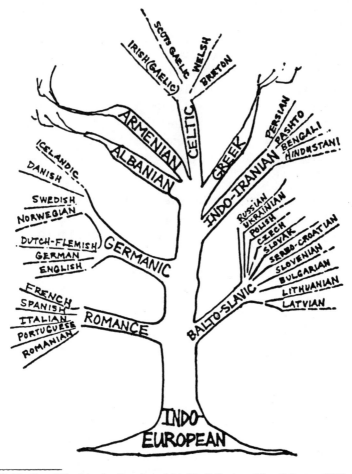

From *Multicultural Teaching* by Pamela and Iris Tiedt. Boston: Allyn & Bacon, 1979.

• Display the family tree of languages to which English belongs. Students will be impressed by the number of languages listed. Furthermore, Indo-European is only one of several large language groupings. You may want to have students research more about languages in the United States.

• Students can compare English with other languages. Here we have *mother* and *father* as spoken in a variety of Indo-European languages.

English	mother	father
Irish	mathair	fathair
Spanish	madre	padre
French	mere	pere
Italian	madre	padre
Portuguese	mae	pai
German	mutter	fader
Russian	maty	otyets
Dutch	moeder	vader
Latin	mater	pater
Greek	meter	pater
Sanskrit	mata	pita

• It is interesting to students to know that we often borrow words from other languages and make them our own simply by using them. Sometimes, however, we spell or pronounce them differently.

Language	*Word*
Malay	ketchup
Arabic	alcohol
German	kindergarten, sauerkraut
French	souvenir, menu, encore
Hindu	shampoo
Spanish	bonanza, mosquito
Dutch	cole slaw, sleigh
American Indian	squash, raccoon
Italian	macaroni, piano
Yiddish	kosher
Japanese	kimono
Scandinavian	smorgasbord

Memorizing Favorite Selections

Although memorization should never be used as a punishment or imposed on students for no real purpose, children do enjoy learning to sing or recite favorite poems or short works. Make memorizing a natural part of enjoying literature together.

Memorization occurs naturally as children pick up words, phrases, or lines when working with choral reading or speaking. Have a Poetry Hour when students can present a poem or just a phrase that they memorized because they liked it. You share your favorites, too, for your participation will enhance the children's appreciation of both poetry and prose.

The Listening Center

Provide a variety of tapes that students can listen to in their free time. Students who need special language assistance should be assigned to listen to and read along with the print and illustrations in a book that you have recorded. Such tapes are readily prepared as you read a story aloud to the class.

Singing Words

Teach children simple songs to sing as a way of reinforcing language development. When introducing these songs to ESL or bilingual students, make sure that they hear the words correctly. Speak the words to the song and then sing it, and have students follow the same procedure.

ORAL LANGUAGE IN OTHER SUBJECTS

Listening and speaking proficiency should be developed throughout the elementary school curriculum. Students can improve their listening skills as they listen to talks on social studies topics, television documentaries on science, and dramatizations presented by other students. Discussion skills, interviews, and ensemble speaking are just a few of the instructional strategies that engage students in speaking English effectively as they learn concepts from social studies, science, mathematics, and so on.

Guided Listening

Present information orally so that students have to "listen to learn," and provide specific directions about the purpose for listening. You might, for example, provide a series of questions that students will be able to answer after listening to an excerpt from "The Bill of Rights."

Play a recorded tall tale about Paul Bunyan as part of a study of the Northwest. Have students first listen to the story to hear and enjoy it. Then, play the tape again as they listen to answer questions you provide.

Taking Listening Notes

Taking notes from taped or recorded material is good practice in listening for a purpose. You can quickly tape a page or two from a textbook that lends itself to outlining. Play the tape first to let the students listen to the content without writing. Then play it again while they take notes without further preparation. Discuss the notes taken; compare by having students write portions of their notes on the chalkboard. Point out good qualities and suggest improvements to be made.

The next day, review the notetaking experience and play the same tape to see whether students are able to take better notes. Provide this type of practice often for upper-grade students as it will benefit their notetaking from printed material also. After notes are taken, *give a test letting each student use notes to help answer the questions.* This activity demonstrates the value of good notes.

Interviewing

Conducting interviews lends interest to study in social studies or other areas. It also provides students with excellent practice in speaking with another person, often an adult. A good method to use as an introduction to the art of interviewing is the Student Interview. Let each student interview someone else in the room so that each student serves as both Interviewer and Interviewee. Some interviews should be conducted in front of the class as a teaching technique; others can then be conducted independently by students as time permits.

Invite a speaker to address the class on a topic of interest. After he or she has spoken, several students (or the entire class) can serve as reporters to interview the person. Interviews should be well planned, with a questionnaire developed before the interview, so that all pertinent questions are covered.

What is your full name?_____

Where do you live?_____

What kind of work do you do?_____

What do you like best about your job?_____

Would you recommend this career to others?_____

How can someone prepare for this career?_____

What do you think about ...?_____

Notice that the questions should be devised to fit the specific person to be interviewed. If a doctor is visiting the class, for example, students will naturally ask questions appropriate to that career.

Oral Histories

Students can interview older people in the community to find out interesting information about how the city has grown. They might ask an older person about his or her specific skills, such as gardening, photography, tatting, or carving. You might contact a senior center near your school which students could visit for the purpose of conducting interviews.

A high school teacher, Eliot Wigginton, used this technique of having his students conduct such interviews in Rabun Gap, Georgia. The students wrote reports of the interviews, which have been since collected into several volumes that include photographs. Aside from being very interesting reading for students, these interviews can serve as models for those your students might write. Entitled *Foxfire* (1, 2, 3, 4, and 5), the books are published by Doubleday and may be found in your local bookstores. A newsletter is also published that you might subscribe to by writing *Foxfire,* Rabun Gap, GA 30568.

This approach is an excellent way of integrating oral language with reading and writing. Students who interview older people in the community will be eager to record what they have learned by writing about it. Other students will want to hear what they have written and also read it. You can publish the students' work informally in a 3-ring notebook that is compiled as students complete their work. Later, you may want to publish the work more formally in a magazine that can be made available to your community.

The Voice Choir (Ensemble Speaking)

Children can enjoy both poetry and prose by speaking it aloud together in a chorus. Work with choric speaking should be informal with emphasis on *pleasure.*

Students will soon learn the lines through repetition. Several poems we have found especially suited to this type of activity are the following, found in May Hill Arbuthnot and Shelton L. Root, Jr.'s *Time for Poetry,* 3rd Edition (Glenview, Illinois: Scott, Foresman, 1968):

> "Jonathan Bing" by Beatrice Brown
> "Macavity: The Mystery Cat" by T. S. Eliot
> "The Owl and the Pussy-Cat" by Edward Lear
> "Puppy and I" by A. A. Milne

Creative Drama

• A good way to introduce students to the possibilities of acting freely is the pantomime which, of course, requires no spoken language on the part of the actor. Let students take turns in portraying through actions only, some type of activity while the class tries to guess what they are doing. Several activities that lend themselves to pantomime are:

Eating a banana	Cutting flowers
Eating spaghetti	Typing a letter
Wrapping a package	Hanging clothes on a line
Sweeping the floor	Jumping rope
Painting a picture	Petting a dog or cat

• Another type of creative drama is role playing in which several children play assigned roles in a given situation. The situation is merely described, the roles assigned, and the action and script develop according to the desires of the actors who may speak freely as they think the person would speak in the given situation. Described here is one situation that can be used as a starter:

> Mr. and Mrs. Carlson have just returned from shopping to find their three children—Mary, Jimmy and Ralph—fighting over a toy while the babysitter, Joan, stands helplessly at one side of the room.

• Familiar stories such as *Red Riding Hood, The Three Bears,* and *The Little Red Hen* can be dramatized by primary students. Older students will know and enjoy dramatizing *Jack and the Beanstalk, Ali Baba and the Forty Thieves,* or *Aladdin and the Wonderful Lamp.* Be sure that all students know the story to be used. If there is any doubt, especially with less common stories, have the students tell the action of the story. Remind them that there are many variations of these tales that have been handed down by word of mouth; this concept will encourage them to add variety to their presentations of the stories.

Rotate the roles and add roles to the story to permit all to participate. No scripts are prepared in written form, however; the dialogue develops as the students explore the story and begin working with it orally. It does not matter if a speech varies slightly every time it is said as long as it serves to move the story action along as needed.

Singing Together

Singing the words of songs is another way of stimulating student speech. Make sure students hear the words accurately by having them say them in sentences without music. Talk about the meaning of the words. Include songs that fit holidays or other subject areas, such as "The Galway Piper" for St. Patrick's Day or a study of Ireland.

The Galway Piper

Irish Folk Song

Ev-ery per-son in the na-tion, or of great or hum-ble. sta-tion,
When the wed-ding bells are ring-ing, his the breath to lead the sing-ing,
When he walks the high-way peal-ing, round his head the birds are wheel-ing,

Holds in high-est es-ti-ma-tion, Pip-ing   Tim   of   Gal-way.
Then in jigs the folks to swing-ing, what   a   splen-did   pip-er!
Tim has car-ols worth the steal-ing, Pip-ing   Tim   of   Gal-way.

Loud-ly he can play or low; he can move you fast or slow,
He will   blow from eve to morn, count-ing sleep a thing of scorn,
Thrush and lin-net, finch and lark, to each oth-er twit-ter, "Hark!"

Touch your heart or stir your toe, Pip - ing   Tim of Gal-way.
Old he   is but not out-worn. Know you such a pip-er?
Soon they sing from light to dark, pip-ings   learned in Gal-way.

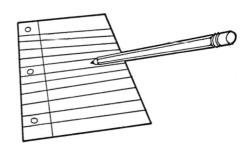

3. Writing Skills

Schools today focus on improving the writing of students at all levels. Primary children begin writing through dictation supported by adults or older students. Middle graders explore the art of storytelling and learn to make statements about their beliefs. Older students continue to grow as they observe the models provided by the authors of literature.

Children's writing progresses with their maturity. Closely co-ordinated with their oral language abilities and their growth in reading, students' early attempts may involve copying what someone else has written. Gradually, however, they become more independent as they express original ideas. This developmental sequence of writing experiences might include:

> talking about ideas and learning new words
> printing isolated letters and words
> copying letters, words, and sentences
> dictating sentences and stories to a mature writer
> transcribing language heard
> writing original sentences and stories
> learning new forms for writing
> growing toward more mature use of language

The ideas presented in this chapter will assist you in guiding student growth at all stages of writing.

BEGINNING WRITING EXPERIENCES

Writing is the most difficult of the language skills because students have to produce thoughts, think about the spelling of words, handle the physical formations of letters, consider how to punctuate and capitalize, and indent appropriately for paragraphs. Every time a child writes a sentence, he or she has hundreds of opportunities to make mistakes. Thus, beginning writers need encouragement and support as they try putting words on paper.

Writing lessons should always begin orally with a stimulus and a warm-up activity. After students think about ideas, they should write as independently as possible. Following the writing period comes sharing, the reward of writing.

Beginning activities should, furthermore, be short. They should be writing activities that students can do because the children want to be successful, to feel good about writing.

Talking About a Film

A short film provides a motivating beginning for writing. "The Red Balloon," for example, tells the enchanting story of a little boy in Paris, a story to which children of all ages respond. Ask questions after viewing the film. Be sure to ask questions that move students into more advanced thinking skills.

Fact: What does the balloon do while the boy is in school?

Inference: How does the boy's life change after the balloon comes to him?

Evaluation: How would you describe the boys who throw stones at the balloon?

Creativity: How does the boy feel when the balloons lift him into the air?

After discussing the film, you might have students write three to five "I wonder" Statements:

I wonder why the balloon came to Pascal's window.
I wonder if the mean boys felt bad after breaking the balloon.
I wonder where the balloons took Pascal.

Other short films that we recommend for this type of activity are:

"Hunter and the Forest" (Encyclopedia Britannica, 8 minutes)
"Clown" (Learning Corporation, 15 minutes)
"Tikki Tikki Tembo" (Weston Woods, 10 minutes)
"The Loon's Necklace" (Canadian Film Board, 11 minutes)
"String Bean" (McGraw-Hill, 17 minutes)

Responding to Books

Talking and writing are great ways to respond to books that you read aloud to students. Choose short books that present interesting concepts as well as outstanding use of language. As students listen to the "book language" that you read, they are learning how to write. Consider using books in a variety of ways. Read, for example, *Sound of Sunshine, Sound of Rain* by Florence Heide (New York: Parents, 1970), a story about a blind black boy. Students might discuss these topics:

Prejudice: When did you know this boy was black? What did Abram mean when he said, "Color don't mean a thing." Describe the sister's feelings during the incident in the store.

Language: List the sound images (there are many because the boy is blind). How did the author describe voices?

Blindness: Describe the boy's attitude toward life. How did he help himself?

Characterization: Compare Abram and the boy's sister. How did you feel about the sister? Did your attitude toward her change in the story?

Every book has something to challenge children's thinking. Have students write questions about this book that can be answered through fact, inference, evaluation, and creativity.

Making Lists

An easy beginning writing activity is making a list, so have students make a list of word associations. Ask them to write the first word that comes to their mind. Then, they quickly write the next word that is suggested by the first, and so on, as shown in these examples:

gold	*horse*
ring	stirrups
circus	feet
elephants	two
jungle	game
trees	playing
monkeys	badminton
chattering	birdie
talking	flying
telephone	sky

An interesting follow-up to this activity is asking students to share the first word they wrote. Observe with students that most of the words are different, an excellent demonstration of the variety in what we are thinking about.

Then ask students to compare the first word they wrote with the last one. Sometimes the two words are related, but often, as in the examples, the mind leaps from idea to idea in a fascinating way. Have a number of students read their lists.

Compiling a Book of Lists

Brainstorm on the chalkboard a long list of topics that interest the students. Ask each student to select a topic that he or she would like to explore, such as:

Cars	Space travel
Gardening	Chemistry
Birds	Wildflowers
Local history	Indian tribes
Florida	Airplanes

Each student prepares one page for a class "Book of Lists." Print the topic in large letters at the top of the page. Then, each student lists words related to that topic. If everyone knows which topics are being explored, students can help each other add intriguing words that are discovered. This project stimulates vocabulary development and may suggest topics for later research.

Journal Writing

A good way to get acquainted with your students at the beginning of the year is to have them keep journals of daily free writing. Students should write every day for a set period of time—ten minutes at first, longer periods for more mature writers. Use small spiral notebooks, a section in a larger ringed notebook, or sheets of paper stapled together. Students should keep journals at school so they are available when it is time to write.

Although journal writing is not evaluated, you might occasionally write a comment to motivate further writing. Students should always feel free to write about any topic that is important to them. To help students who have difficulty thinking of a subject to write about, suggest an optional topic or title:

My Favorite Color
A Time of Day I Like
An Embarrassing Moment
A Person I Admire

Creating a Picture

Give each student a sheet of colored construction paper. Then, pass one colored star to each student. Direct the students to place the star on the page so that it will be part of a picture.

After completing the picture, have students write the first sentence of a story about the picture. They may then exchange pictures and complete the stories.

Group Dictation

Young children who are not yet skilled in writing words will gain much through group dictation as you print the sentences on the chalkboard or on a piece of tagboard (using a felt pen). The dictation may be based on the children's experiences of the day, including sentences like these:

John saw a black dog.
Today is Susan's birthday.

At another time, you may use a large picture to stimulate the construction of interesting sentences that describe the activities in the picture.

Mary is on the way to school.
She is wearing a blue and white dress.
Her dog is following her.

Using Descriptive Language

Write a simple sentence on the chalkboard such as: "A dog ran down the street." How can this sentence be made more interesting? Encourage the students to suggest answers to these questions:

What kind of dog was it?	*size, color, breed*
How did he run?	*scurried, loped, sneaked*
What kind of street was it?	*busy, quiet, crowded, narrow*

Have children share their rewordings of the sentence, which may be something like this: "The little mongrel scurried along the crowded boulevard." Then present other sentences that can be made more interesting in the same way.

The man went into the store.
The woman carried a package.
We saw a child.

DEVELOPING NARRATIVE SKILLS

As students gain confidence in writing, they can focus on developing narrative skills. Storytelling begins orally and proceeds into writing. Narrative forms that elementary students enjoy are jokes or anecdotes, fables, fairy tales, animal stories, fantasy worlds, personal memories, and realistic tales.

Storytelling

Have students think more consciously about storytelling. Working in small groups, they can practice telling stories that they know—jokes or anecdotes and memory stories. Talk about the need for a clear beginning, a middle, and an end in a story.

After students have told their stories, they might write the stories. Having clarified the sentences through oral storytelling, they will be able to write a more fully developed tale.

A Story Chart

As you read stories aloud to students, begin making them aware of the elements that are common to the stories we hear or read. Begin with the common question words that students know and use, and gradually introduce the literature concepts that answer the questions.

Questions	Literature Concepts	Related Ideas
WHO?	Characters	People, Animals, Protagonist, Antagonist, Dialogue
WHERE? WHEN?	Setting	Place, Mood, Time
WHAT? WHY?	Plot	Point of View, Hook, Sequence, Problem, Foreshadowing
HOW?	Conclusion	Solution

Being aware of the beginning, the middle, and the end of a story will help beginning writers develop their content more fully. As they write stories, students can ask the question words to determine if they have supplied the information the reader needs. Have them observe that the beginning of the story reveals the characters and setting; the middle develops the plot; and the end, of course, is the conclusion.

Story Starters

Have students observe the way different authors have begun their stories. Students can make a list of different ways of beginning:

Dialogue
An exciting event
A mysterious setting

Have students write short paragraphs that can be used to begin a story. These story starters can be compiled in a three-ring notebook to which students can refer when they need an idea. To begin this activity, compose several examples with the students on the chalkboard, for example:

> I first heard the sound around five o'clock in the afternoon, but I did not think anything about it then. After dinner, however, I heard it again. It was louder and sounded like something scratching at the back door to get in. When I opened the door, there was nothing there.

Creative Writing and Geography

Foreign countries provide much provocative material to stimulate the imaginations of young writers as they begin learning about these lands and their peoples. Encourage students to write on topics of this nature:

> Write an adventure that includes yourself as you travel in a foreign city.
> What would you do if you suddenly found yourself in Africa? in Japan? in Mexico
> I would like to live in _____because ...
> If I could remake the world, I would ...
> My idea of Utopia would be ..

Developing a Theme

Write five words on the chalkboard around which the students are to write a story. Choose words that are directed toward one type of story—a fairy tale, a mystery, or a space adventure:

> magic, wish, castle, journey, prince
> ghost, hill, storm, tracks, shack
> rocket, planet, craters, cold, gravity

When all children are writing on the same topic, it is interesting to compare the different types of ideas that develop from the same five words. This is a good demonstration of individual differences—

interests, personalities, experiences—all of which influence students' ideas.

Incomplete Drawings

Duplicate the following incomplete drawing. Let the students study the "picture" before they do anything. Then suggest that they write about what the incomplete drawing means to them. Permit students to add lines to the drawing if they wish.

The drawings may later be completed with crayons or colored markers. Some students may contribute other provocative drawings that can be used for this type of exercise.

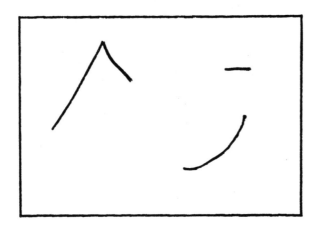

Writing Fantasy

Here are a number of "What if ..." ideas to give students inspiration as they begin writing tales of fantasy. You may choose to use only one topic at a time, letting students discuss the possibilities suggested by the idea. A warming-up period of this type leads to more enthusiastic and creative writing.

1. What if eating lemons made people sour?
2. What if you had a tiny dog the size of your finger?
3. What if you had a pet monkey that was invisible?
4. What if you were the teacher of this class?
5. What if a rich man told you he would give you any two things you could name?

6. What if your aunt sent you ten dollars to spend any way you wished?
7. What if you were a stowaway on a ship?
8. What if cats could talk?

A Writing Center

Create a Writing Center in your classroom where supplies and resources can be kept.

Use furniture you already have. A heavy cardboard box can provide the cubicle, or place a table below a bulletin board where ideas can be presented. A circular table can be used with supplies in the middle. Encourage students to suggest ideas for developing the center.

WRITING POETRY

Even young children enjoy writing poetry. Beginning with unrhymed free verse and moving to experiments with varied poetry forms, students of all ages can write effective poems.

We recommend that you introduce poetry orally through voice choir experiences: humorous poetry, narratives, poetry that can be sung. Writing poetry is also exciting when students discover that they can produce satisfying cinquains, diamantes, and limericks.

Begin with Unrhymed Poems

Free verse is a very successful kind of poetry for students at all levels. You can begin in a variety of ways.

• Introduce similes by asking students if they can complete these expressions:

as cold as _____
as busy as _____
as quiet as _____

Chances are, they will supply: ice, a bee, a mouse, respectively. Explain that these comparisons are called *similes,* a form of expression that we use often. Ask them if they know additional examples, and write them on the chalkboard:

as slow as molasses
as big as an elephant
as hungry as a bear

These similes are good descriptions, but they have been used so often that they are no longer fresh and interesting. Challenge them to think of new ways of describing one of the qualities listed. For example, have students complete the phrase "as slow as _____ ." As students suggest endings, write the ideas on the board in the form of a poem.

As slow as —
    a turtle crossing the road,
    a child just learning to type.
    honey dripping from a spoon.

After students have composed this poem collectively, ask them to follow the same pattern as they explore ideas about another quality: quiet, soft, hard, busy, small.

• Focus on the senses by taking students on an observation walk. Prepare a duplicated chart on which they can take notes while outdoors.

Night
Dark, gloomy,
Sneaking, slipping, threatening,
Violence, crime, business, activities,
Striding, shopping, visiting,
Light, safe,
Day!

• A third poetry pattern that students can write successfully is the Japanese *haiku* (hi´ koo). The form consists of three unrhymed lines that fall into a syllabic pattern:

Five syllables
Seven syllables
Five syllables

These subtle little poems most often present a scene from nature, but with the ingenuity of the young writer, can encompass any subject matter. The fact that there are no rhymes removes a certain artificiality that appears at times in children's efforts to follow rhyme schemes.Here are samples of haiku that can be discussed with your students before they begin to write original samples.

Soft Lights

Candlelight flickers—
Soft shadows hide wrinkled age;
Sorrow is shaded.

Patterns

Look up to the blue!
Silken leaves pattern the sky
Fingering sheer air.

Have students use colored paper to fold 4" × 6" paper fans. Their haiku can then be printed on 2" × 3" white paper that is attached to the fan. Scatter the original fans over a bulletin board with the simple caption: HAIKU. For variety, hang the fans mobile-fashion from the branch of a tree, or distribute fans to classroom visitors during Open House.

EXPOSITORY WRITING

Expository writing is often factual writing that reports, but it can also state opinions in writing that attempt to persuade the reader to take a specific point of view. The basic element of expository writing is the formally developed paragraph. Longer reports incorporate the same basic paragraph in various combinations. Notetaking and library research are skills associated with expository writing.

Paragraphing

Talk about paragraphs with students and be sure they understand the difference in our use of this term when we mean to indent the first word in a sentence or a group of sentences. Have them observe printed dialogue, noting that each time a new speaker begins talking we indent, but the speaker does not always say a group of sentences that could be called a paragraph.

Expository Paragraph Formula

Teach the students the formula for writing a basic paragraph.

Paragraph = 1 Topic Sentence + 3 Supporting Sentences + 1 Concluding Sentence

P = 1 TS + 3 SS + 1 CS

Example:

I like cats. They are very clean. They are independent. They love to be petted. Cats are good pets.

Writing Paragraphs

Introduce the expository paragraph by beginning with ideas. Ask each student, for example, to write five "I believe" statements. After thinking about these ideas, ask the student to select one to use as the topic sentence for a paragraph. Following the formula, the student writes three reasons for the belief and composes a concluding sentence. The result is a strong statement of opinion.

Book Reports

To have students think more clearly about a book you have just read aloud, ask them to write a paragraph beginning.

I think_____is_____.
(title)   (adjective)

Provide a choice of adjectives: well written, entertaining, humorous, intriguing (anything but "good"), and have the students complete the paragraph by substantiating their beliefs. Compare the paragraphs by having samples read aloud. Then have students follow the same procedure with a book they have read independently.

The Five-Paragraph Essay

The formal essay or "theme" is directly related to the basic expository paragraph. Show students exactly how they are related:

Basic Paragraph	Essay
TS	P 1: Introductory Paragraph
SS 1	P 2: Expands SS 1
SS 2	P 3: Expands SS 2
SS 3	P 4: Expands SS 3
CS	P 5: Expands CS

EDITING AND EVALUATION

The teacher should not be a copy editor for students. They will learn more effectively if they are actively involved in editing their own work. Students can begin with self-editing, then work in pairs, and finally in small groups.

• Students should learn the basic editing skill of reading their work aloud. Reading a sentence aloud helps them determine if it "sounds right."

Talk about the students' "ear for languge," that is, their knowledge of English grammar. It is linguistically sound for us to ask, "Does it sound right?" as we edit our work or that of others.

• Students can work in pairs to edit work that is to be published. They should begin by reading the work aloud. Have students observe that reading someone else's paper aloud enables them to be more critical because they do not supply missing words. They also see misspelled words.

Students who edit each other's work should sign their names at the bottom of the first draft to assume responsibility for the job.

• Students should learn to work with small groups, each composed of four to six students. These groups provide an audience, other than the teacher, for whom they write. Reading their work aloud in small groups, furthermore, means that all students can read to an audience in 15-20 minutes.

Teach students how to respond to the work of others in a considerate, helpful way. First experiences should be very positive— tell students they are to ignore what they do not like and make only positive comments that encourage the writer to keep writing.

Writing Folders

It is not necessary that all written work be turned in to the teacher. The successful writing program requires that the student write almost every day; some students are especially enthusiastic and continue their writing efforts at home. Each student should have an individual folder where all writing is filed.

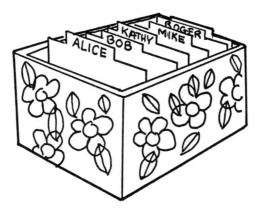

Recognizing Good Work

Read aloud stories or parts of stories that you consider particularly effective. Indicate your reason for being impressed with the writing you present in this way. At times, let the author come forward to read his or her own work.

Projected Writing

Use the overhead projector to project written work on a screen, so that the whole class can view a paper at once. New methods of preparing transparencies for this projector permit the teacher to reproduce pencil-written compositions quickly and easily for this purpose. You may want to remove the name of the writer so that no embarrassment will be felt.

The values of this type of examination of written work are that all students are viewing the same work as you suggest corrections and mark directly on the transparency. Discuss the paper, pointing out errors but emphasizing those aspects of the paper that are praiseworthy—interesting imagery, use of a new word, a well-phrased sentence, some good dialogue, or a catchy title. Working with the group in this way demonstrates to the whole class the sort of things you value in their papers. Their own thinking will be directed along these lines as they write, and as they evaluate the work of others.

Holistic Assessment

At the beginning of the year, have each student write in response to the same stimulus. Score these papers by grouping them:

1. Very weak—minimal coverage of the topic; numerous errors.
2. Average—adequate coverage of the topic; some errors.
3. Outstanding—excellent coverage of the topic; few errors.

This set of papers is to be kept as a comparison for evaluation. Holistic scoring can be done quickly for a whole school or a school district. A group of teachers can serve as readers for a district assessment. This is a good way of seeing how students compare to others in the same group.

Diagnostic Assessment

Occasionally, check a set of papers to note the kinds of errors individual students make. Not all students need the same information to improve their writing. You may find, however, that ten students in fifth grade need special help with the use of commas in a series. You can teach that skill to the students who need it while other students work independently.

Parent Conferences

Have students write on the same topic just before parents come in for conferences. Have students use a code number rather than their names on these papers. Then, rank the set of papers from weak to strong.

As you talk to the parent(s), you can quickly identify their child's writing and show them how the child's writing ability compares to others in the room. Parents do not always have this frame of reference in evaluating their child's work.

NOTE: Remember that children should be evaluated in two ways—they can be compared to other children, but they should also be evaluated for their own growth. Be sure to consider both ranking in the group and individual progress.

MAKING WRITING PUBLIC

Publishing their writing provides an incentive for students to edit and to improve their writing. Publishing may take the form of a display on the bulletin board, a gift, informal collections of students' writing, or a formally published writing magazine.

Reading Stories

The tape recorder provides an effective means for presenting the writing efforts of your students. Each student can read a story or poem that he or she has written to produce a tape of materials to be presented to parents who visit the classroom. Tapes of this nature are also excellent items to exchange with schools in other lands to let them become familiar with students in our country.

Writing for Parents

Prepare a collection of student writing to share with parents at the annual Open House. Include something by every student in this publication.

Student writing can be published in the form of a small literary magazine. This publication serves as an incentive for good writing and can include a variety of writings of varied lengths so that all students can contribute something. Short stories, poetry, interesting imagery, unusual words or phrases—these are some of the kinds of writing to be included.

Let students choose a name for the collection. Then distribute this publication to other classes and other schools to let them know what your school is doing. This publication is also an excellent demonstration to parents of the work being done at school.

Bulletin Board Displays

One bulletin board may be used regularly to display student writing. Use such captions as WRITE ON!, THIS IS OUR BEST, WRITE RIGHT.

Students who have written diamante poems can display them on paper cut in diamond shapes.

Haiku might be mounted on large leaves or flowers for seasonal displays.

Art Enhances Writing

Students may mount their poems and stories on paper and create a frame to make an attractive display.

In addition, student artwork can be focused on creating attractive covers for longer stories published in book form.

Writing Books

Students can write original books themselves, modeling them after library books they observe. After writing a story they would like to publish, show them how to bind the book to make it look as real as possible. Students might experiment with books of varied shapes, as suggested by the content of each book.

4. Spelling, Dictionaries and Handwriting

Spelling is related to both reading and writing. As children learn to read, they become aware of the relationship of *decoding* (figuring out what a written word means) and *encoding* (putting a spoken word into written form). Writing words reinforces the beginning reader's knowledge of phonics, too. Writing the word *fire*, for example, cements the student's awareness of the relationship between the sound /f/ and the letter symbol we often use to represent that sound.

As children attempt to write the many words they know, they soon find a need to refer to the dictionary, a fascinating book for students of all ages. We must be careful, though, to avoid teaching practices that make dictionary skill development sheer drudgery. Working with dictionaries should emphasize knowledge of spelling, but it should also aid vocabulary development.

RELATING READING AND WRITING

Phonics is commonly taught from the point of view of the reader. Instead of making phonics instruction a "one-way street," the effective teacher constantly points out the relationship between reading a word and spelling it. The two-way phonics diagram points out the interrelationship between spoken words and written words as they are processed by a learner.

As the child becomes an able reader and writer, working between oral and written language is almost automatic. The teacher's

job is to facilitate that automaticity, removing as many obstacles as possible.

Sound and Letter

Reinforce children's knowledge of how the sounds they speak are related to the letter-symbols they write and read.

While standing at the board, ask students:

Who can tell me a word that begins with the same sound as *horse?* (Write the suggestions on the board.)

      help   hall   Harry   honey   hundred

Who knows the name of this letter? (Point to the capital form and note the difference.)

Let's write the letter *h* in the air. Now write it on your paper.

Which word on the board is *hall?* Can you copy that word on your paper

Yesterday we studied *t* and wrote *tall.* Can you write *tall* today? (Have a student print the word on the board.)

Dictation

Have students "be secretaries" as sentences are dictated to them. Challenge the students to see how perfectly they can write the dictated sentence. Choose sentences that contain words the children should be able to spell. Examples are:

I saw two boys at the park.
When will you come to my house?

When you dictate, insist that the students first listen. Have them repeat the sentence together before they begin to write. Following their writing, have several students print the sentence on the board. Talk about the spellings while everyone corrects his or her own mistakes. The next day, dictate the same sentences again as students try to avoid making the same mistakes.

Phonogram Families

Prepare sheets of words that contain the same phonogram, but with different initial consonants:

more	cart	sand
tore	part	hand
wore	dart	band

Introduce the first set and have students underline the part of each word that is the same. Ask who can spell *tore* (wore, more). Then ask if anyone can spell *sore* (core). Ask the students to print these words at the bottom of the list and to underline the part of the words that matches with the other words listed.

Presenting words in pattern groups assists children in learning to spell many words. Notice, too, how phonics skills are being reinforced.

After the students know how to do this kind of activity, present the same lesson on tape for use at a Listening Center. Prepare additional worksheets using new sets of phonogram families.

Word Chains

Use this word chain activity to encourage students to use their spelling knowledge. The activity can be presented in several ways.

Have younger children complete the chain on a full page activity sheet.

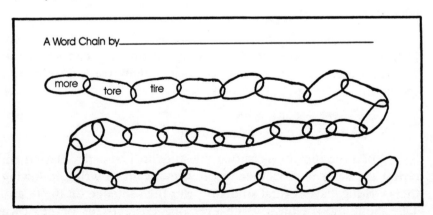

A Word Chain by_____

more   tore   tire

For variety or with older students, begin several Word Chains on the board or on long sheets of paper. Have the children work together in making the lists as long as possible.

more	sand	fine	ring	side
mare	hand	find	sing	ride
care		kind	sang	tide
___	___	___	___	___
___	___	___	___	___
___	___	___	___	___

In either case, the students are to follow certain rules:

Only one letter is changed each time.
Each time a letter is changed, a word must be formed.
If a new word cannot be made, go back and revise the list.

Personal Spelling Dictionaries

For an individualized approach to spelling, have each student make a small dictionary with one page per letter. Students can enter words during writing activities or can just decide to enter words that they would like to learn to spell.

 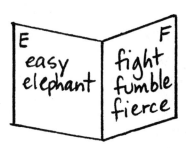

Periodically, have a CHALLENGE DAY when students can see how many of their own words they can spell. Let the students work in pairs to check each other.

Attacking "Big Words"

Teach or review the initial blends of consonants which begin so many words: *bl, br, ch, cl, cr, dr, fl, fr, gl, gr, pl, pr, sc, sh, sk, sl, sm, sn, sp, st, sw, spl, str, scr, tr.* Give students practice in hearing these beginning sounds by saying words and having them write the first two or three letters of the word. Select words that they won't necessarily know how to spell; they will delight in trying "big words" they have never heard before! If they listen carefully to the sounds heard, they can often spell the whole word correctly.

clamber	flamboyant
breeze	platitude
praise	drenched
striped	slovenly
scratch	sprightly

Common Suffixes and Prefixes

Children need to learn to spell the common suffixes and prefixes so that they will be able to spell words using them. The spelling of these syllables can be taught together with their meaning as the students list words using various prefixes or suffixes. Here are some of the more common ones:

Prefixes	*Suffixes*
in, im, un, en	ing, ed, er
pre, per, pro	ness, less, ful
ex, con, dis	ly, y, le
de, re, be	tion, ment, ish

Taking Advantage of New Words

While reading or talking to students, take advantage of new words that may be introduced. If you are using the word *catch* with a reading group, for example, point out the family of words that are spelled in the same way: *batch, hatch, latch, match, patch, snatch, scratch.* Ask students if they can name words that rhyme with *catch* as the words are written on the board. Have them observe how knowing a key word (catch) can unlock the spelling of a whole group of words.

Then print the word *watch* on the board, asking if anyone knows that word. Have students note that the spelling of this word matches that of the group, but the pronunciation is not the same.

Be alert to the possibilities for this type of teaching, which may be totally unplanned.

A Pattern Puzzle

Puzzles and riddles can focus attention on spelling in an enjoyable way. Riddle-Me-Ree is a good puzzle that makes students conscious of spelling patterns. Each line provides the clue for one letter that appears in the word:

I like YES but I don't like MAYBE;
I like IN but I don't like ON;
I like ALL but I don't like NONE;
I like VERY but I don't like MUCH;
I like WE but I don't like YOU;
I like RED but I don't like BLUE.
   Riddle-me-ree;
   What can it be?

The first letter must be S because both Y and E appear in MAYBE. The second letter must be I because N appears in both words. The third letter could be A or L while the fourth might be V, E, R, or Y. These are harder because no letters are eliminated. The fifth letter will be W or E, and the sixth will be R or D because E appears in BLUE. With these conclusions written down, students can pore over them to try different possibilities. (The answer is SILVER.)

After students work this puzzle, challenge them to construct other puzzles based on such short words as CAT, BOOK, FIVE, HAPPY. Have students exchange their puzzles to see if classmates can solve them.

CONTINUED GROWTH IN SPELLING

Spelling growth should be as individualized as possible. Having students study lists in spelling books is less useful than working with words selected from the student's own writing—words the student really needs to know how to spell—so evaluate your approach to spelling instruction to be sure students are not wasting their time. Promote growth in the ability to spell easily and accurately through the activities described in this section.

Pretesting Diagnosis

To determine just how well students spell, give a spelling test—either a commercial one, or using words selected from the textbook at the grade level of the students.

Challenge students to pass monthly hurdles of lists of commonly used words that everyone needs to know how to spell. Select 10 to 15 words from the sight words on pages 120–121, and provide a list of the words that students can study. Discuss ways of studying, and tell each student to choose the method that works best for him or her.

Before requiring students to study any word list, give a pretest. Students should not have to study words they already know how to spell.

Teaching Rhyming Skills

Help students identify words that are spelled alike by constructing rhyme lists. Compile a list of rhyming words by using the students' knowledge of phonics. For example, make a rhyme list for the common word AIR. Print the letters of the alphabet on the board. Then, with the students, go through the alphabet in order, trying the consonants to see if they form a new word when placed before AIR. Cross out the vowels because they are not useful beginning sounds. Cross out c because it stands for /k/ or /s/, and x because it has no sound of its own. Place u after q to help students remember the sound /kw/. Thus, the rhyming alphabet will look like this:

$$\text{a̶ \quad b \quad c̶ \quad d \quad e̶ \quad f \quad g \quad h \quad i̶ \quad j \quad k \quad l \quad m}$$
$$\text{n \quad o̶ \quad p \quad qu \quad r \quad s \quad t \quad u̶ \quad v \quad w \quad x̶ \quad y \quad z}$$

Rhyming with Blends and Digraphs

Continue the rhyming activity by showing students a chart on which the blends are listed. Be sure they know that in blends each of the two (or three) consonants are heard.

bl	cl	dr	fl	gl	pl	sk	sm	sp	spr
br	cr		fr	gr	pr	sl	sn	st	str

Add the digraphs and combinations of blends and digraphs: *ch, sh, th, thr, shr.*

Categorizing Spellings of Rhymes

After completing the rhyme list using the beginning consonants, blends and digraphs, have students identify the several spellings that rhyme with AIR. The list can then be regrouped according to spelling:

AIR	CARE		BEAR	WHERE
pair	bare	stare	pear	'ere
fair	dare	blare	tear	there
hair	fare	snare	swear	
lair	hare	scare	wear	*Others*
flair	mare	Clare		their
stair	pare	glare		they're
chair	rare	spare		prayer
Clair				

Ask questions about this extended spelling family to help students become aware of the information presented.

1. Which spelling of this sound is most common?
2. Which spelling is uncommon?
3. How many pairs of homonyms (words that sound alike) can you find?
4. Which words are uncommon, perhaps not known to you? (If no one can identify the meaning, have someone use the dictionary.)

Activity Sheet for Phonogram Families

Prepare activity sheets that students can work with independently at first.

Name _____   Rain, Rain, Go Away!
Date _____

See how many rhymes you can find for RAIN. If you work hard, you may find more than 20 rhyming words to list.

Now group the words you have found according to their different spellings.

RAIN	LANE	REIGN	VEIN

Which two spellings are most frequently used? _____
Which two spellings are uncommon? _____
List any sets of homonyms you can find:

_____   _____

_____   _____

_____   _____

What interesting words did you discover? _____

_____

Students should follow the procedures described earlier for compiling a rhyme list. After compiling the list, students should group the words into spelling patterns.

After the students have found as many rhyming words as possible, talk about the group of words and compile the list on the board or an overhead transparency.

RAIN		LANE		REIGN	VEIN
Cain	plain	bane	sane	deign	rein
gain	train	cane	vane	feign	skein
lain	slain	Dane	wane		sein(e)
main	Spain	Jane	crane		
vain	strain	mane	plane		
chain	sprain	pane			
brain	twain				
grain					

Discuss the words to help students become aware of the meanings as well as spellings. Students can write notes on the back of the activity sheet and keep these sheets in a spelling notebook for future reference.

Thinking About Spelling Patterns

Choose one pattern or characteristic of English spelling and begin the game like this:

Leader: I'm going to Paris and I plan to take along food, tools, and a broom. Would you like to go along?

1st Student: I'd like to take scissors. May I come?

Leader: No, I'm sorry, You can't come on this trip.

2nd Student: I'd like to take the moon along. May I come?

Leader: Yes, that's fine. You may come along. (Game continues. Clue—words containing *oo.*)

Leader: I'm going to Timbuktu. I'm going to take a blackbird, popcorn, and a jigsaw puzzle. Would you like to go along?

1st Student: I'd like to take a scarecrow. May I come?

Leader: Yes, you may come.

2nd Student: I'd like to take a robin. May I come?

Leader: No, you can't go with us this time.

3rd Student: I'd like to take a clothesline. May I come?

Leader: Yes, you may go with us. (Game continues. Clue—compound words.)

As students become familiar with this game, they will think of many other interesting ideas to feature: the initials of their own names, words associated with a theme, words that begin with the same phoneme but not the same letter, words that end with the same phoneme, and so on.

For more lesson ideas to stimulate listening and thinking skills, see *Reading Strategies: Activities to Stimulate Slow and Reluctant Readers* by Iris Tiedt ($4.50 postpaid from Contemporary Press, Box 1524, San Jose, CA 95109).

Applying Phonics Knowledge

Point out the ease with which many seemingly difficult words can be spelled when the student knows consonant and vowel sounds as well as prefixes and suffixes. Say a word carefully, pronouncing each syllable clearly. Give the students time to try spelling the word before you have someone write it on the board. Try these words:

plantation	blatantly	clutching
discontinuing	entanglement	invocation
perfection	preferment	remarkable
understandingly	belaboring	vacationing

When presenting unfamiliar words, it is a good idea to provide a synonym or brief meaning for the word, as many alert students will learn interesting words in this way.

Challenging Gifted Students

Change-abouts represent a real challenge to better students. The object is to change one word into another in as few steps as possible. Each step consists of changing one letter to make another word until the desired word is reached. Duplicate one completed example with the others only partially completed so students can finish them. Include space on the sheet for the students to make "change-abouts" of their own that they can share with others.

Heat to Cold	*More to Less*	*Green to Black*
heat	more	green
head	lore	Greek
held	lose	creek
hold	loss	creak
cold	less	croak
		crock
		clock
		block
		black

Focus on a Phoneme*

This puzzle focuses attention on the phoneme /g/ and the alternate ways of spelling that phoneme in English.

¹G	U	²E	³S	T		⁴G	A	⁵P		
H		G	T		⁶G	I	R	L		
⁷O	L	G	A			G		A		
S		⁸G	O	E	S		⁹G	O	A	L
¹⁰T	A	¹¹G				¹²G	U	M		
	¹³R	A	G	¹⁴S		E				
¹⁵G	¹⁶H	A	S	T	L	Y				
	A	P		A		¹⁷G	R	A	M	
¹⁸G	E	¹⁹T	²⁰G	L	U	E				
U		W	Y							
E		I								
²¹A	G	O								

*From *Spelling Strategies* by Iris M. Tiedt. (Contemporary Press, Box 1524, San Jose, CA 95109).

Across

1—someone staying in
   your home
4—opening
6—young woman
7—Russian girl's name
8—does go
9—score
10—game of catch
12—something to chew
13—old cloth
15—horrible
17—weight in metric system
18—obtain
20—sticky liquid
21—in the past

Down

1—an unreal being
2—in a bird's nest
3—male deer
4—jobs for a musician
5—bad disease
11—fruit
14—used ore
16—city in Holland
17—man's name
19—small stick

Codes

Using codes provides good practice with spelling because students have to know how to spell words they want to encode.

The simplest code relates numbers and letters:

1 = a	14 = n
2 = b	15 = o
3 = c	16 = p
4 = d	17 = q
5 = e	18 = r
6 = f	19 = s
7 = g	20 = t
8 = h	21 = u
9 = i	22 = v
10 = j	23 = w
11 = k	24 = x
12 = l	25 = y
13 = m	26 = z

Write messages in this code on the board, so that students have to figure them out when they enter the room, a good way of getting a group to settle down quickly.

Encourage students to invent their own codes. They might vary the number code previously listed by beginning with 1 = d or 1 = z. They can also make code wheels like this one, where a letter is represented by another letter. Thus, W would be written as B, or J would be written as O.

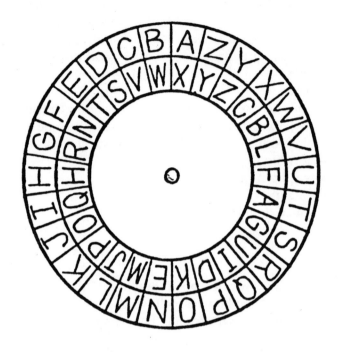

WORKING WITH DICTIONARIES

Students learn how to use the dictionary as meaningful purposes for its use arise. Students can use it to learn alphabetical order, and how to find information. The activities presented in this section will help you make dictionary study enjoyable.

Primary Alphabet Activities

Introduce the alphabet in order by displaying it as a reference for letter forms. Some children, aided by eager parents, will quickly learn to say the alphabet in order, but this is not an appropriate mastery level skill expected in kindergarten or first grade. Make a game of learning alphabetical order gradually as students appear ready to learn this skill.

• Place two sets of alphabet cards in the chalk tray. Let two students see who can arrange the letters in alphabetical order quicker. Permit others to challenge the winner to determine the ABC Champion of the classroom.

• Call out one letter of the alphabet. Then call on a child who must name the next three letters in order.

• Hold up an alphabet card. The child named must supply the letter that immediately precedes the given letter.

Alphabet Activities for Older Students

Using alphabetical order for varied purposes provides practice and develops automaticity in working with this skill. When we say *m*, for example, we want students to think of the middle of the alphabet (and also the middle of the dictionary).

• Challenge students to make a list of words based on the alphabet. Accept any words at first, then later require longer words to extend their vocabularies.

Easy Words	*More Than Six Letters*
Ant	Automobile
Brown	Bumptious
Calico	Calendar
Deep	Destructive
Each	Equality
Farm	Fantastic
Gone	Gorgeous
Help	Heavenly
Ink	Irritating
Junk	Jealousy
Kite	Knighthood
Light	Litigation
Mine	Medication
Now	Nuisance
Open	Organization
Pen	Palindrome
Quit	Quiescent
Rat	Righteous
Sun	Signature
Tame	Tantamount
Under	Understanding
Van	Versatile

Easy Words	*More Than Six Letters*
Wagon	Worthwhile
X-ray	Xylophone
Yellow	Youthful
Zoo	Zealous

• Use flashcards to present interesting words to locate in the dictionary: fluctuate, harangue, zealous, ambivalent, gargantuan, meritorious. Although the emphasis in this activity is on speed, it also exposes students to new words. Choose words that the students probably do not know, but could use. After locating and discussing several of these words, talk about methods of finding words quickly in the dictionary. Point out that you immediately turn to the end of the dictionary if the word begins with *z*, or to the front if it starts with *a.* The other letters fall in between, of course, but we have some idea of their relative position in the book. Practice trying to hit the right section for several letters as they are called out such as *b, t, b, n.* Also discuss using the guide words at the top of each page. Another skill is scanning the list, often aided by the index finger. (Why is the forefinger called the "index finger"?)

• Making puzzles often leads students to the dictionary. If the puzzle demands words that begin with specific letters, puzzle construction provides a purpose for using the dictionary. Students will enjoy composing acrostics that feature interesting words. In the acrostic, the first letter of each word used (read vertically) helps to spell a word.

Study
Children
History
Organization
Obedience
Learning

You may wish to supply a definition for each word, indicating only the number of letters in the word. If the student correctly solves the acrostic, he or she will find the secret word.

Vocabulary Development

As students use dictionaries, they become self-motivated to pore through the words. Encourage students to explore words by providing varied word activities that are fun as well as challenging.

• Students learn more through creating original crossword puzzles than they do through solving those you prepare or purchase from commercial sources. Duplicate a large 15″ × 15″ puzzle frame for student use. Show the students how to fill in words that interlock, forgetting about definitions until the puzzle is completed.

H	A	L	L	O	W	E	E	N	■	Y	I	E	L	D
O	L	D	E	S	T	■	N	E				V		
N	O	S	E	S	■	S	T	A	T	E	M	E	N	T
E	N	■	■	I			R	T				N		
Y	E		■	F			A	■				I		
■				Y			N					N		
C				■			C					G		
E							E					■		
N						■								
T														
U														
R														
Y														
■														

Student puzzles can be smaller or irregular in shape. Completed puzzles with answers can be placed in a class book of crossword puzzles. Reproduce one occasionally for the whole class, and for holidays encourage students to work with appropriate shapes, such as a pumpkin or valentine.

• An exciting game that features vocabulary development and the patterns of English word endings, Word Brackets, sends students directly to the dictionary. For this game, print a word vertically on the board. Choose a holiday word, one connected with a subject being studied, or an interesting new word that you wish to introduce. To the right, print the same word with its letters reversed in order as shown. The object is to insert letters between those given to make new words, the longer the better, for every letter inserted gives the player a point.

H	a	r	m	o	n			Y
I	n	v	e	n	t	o		R
S	o	l						O
T	e	n						T
O	a	s	i					S
R	a	b	b					I
Y	e	l	l	o	w	i	s	H

After students have played this game several times, discuss what they have learned about English spelling:

1. When words being with vowels, you can usually find something that begins with such prefixes as *a-* or *an-*, *ex-* or *en-*, *in-* or *im-*, *on-*, and *un-*.

2. Certain letters signal commonly used suffixes. For example:
   S is easy because any plural can be used.
   G means the word can end with *-ing.*
   Y means the word can end with *-ly.*
   R means the word can end with *-er.*
   H means the word can end with *-th* or *-ish.*
   C means the word can end with *-ic.*

3. Many English words end in *e;* not many end in *a.* An ending of *i* is possible with Greek plurals: radius, radii. Endings of *o* and *u* are also rare: hero, silo, gnu, impromptu.

• Introduce more mature students to the synonym dictionary (thesaurus) and try to have several copies available for their use as they write. Have students compile a class thesaurus. Each student can prepare one or more pages featuring one commonly used word with suggested synonyms, as shown:

```
BIG
        huge
        large
        enormous
        gigantic
```

● Challenge students to compile a list of Synonyms for Said on a bulletin board, and include pictures of people talking. Provide 4″ × 12″ strips of paper on which students can print their synonyms to mount on the display.

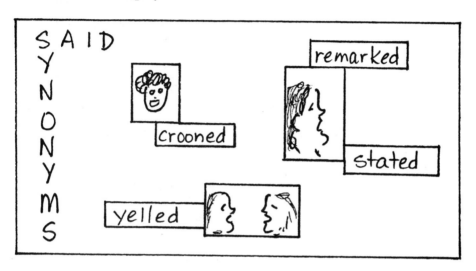

FOCUSING ON HANDWRITING

The emphasis in handwriting should be on legibility. Students usually learn manuscript printing and later work with cursive writing. Some schools are even introducing italic-style writing based on calligraphy, and students can enjoy learning to write beautifully and use calligraphy to enhance their original writing.

Introducing Manuscript

Group the letters according to their structure, presenting the simplest shapes first.

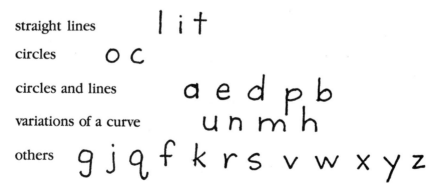

A Copy for Parents

Since many parents are not familiar with the letter forms used, send a copy of the manuscript alphabet home. Knowing what the child is learning in school will enable them to help the child at home.

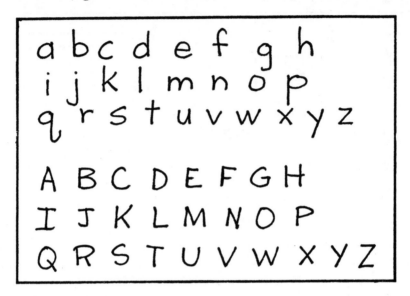

Left-Handed Writers

Never force a child to change the preferred writing hand. Parents should understand that trying to make such a change may be damaging to the child.

Discuss left-handedness with the class as a point of interest. Children who are left-handed will perform no differently than other children who write with the right hand. They simply reverse the direction of the paper on their desk.

Examining Handwriting

Handwriting is a means of communicating. Have students examine their own handwriting to see if the letters are clear enough so that other people can read them.

Suggest that students turn a page of their writing over and hold it up to the light to observe the slant.

Ask students to circle letters that they have trouble writing, and then give them help at the board to be sure they know how a difficult letter is made.

Sentences Containing All the Letters

Students enjoy practicing writing the letters of the alphabet in a novel way. Let them practice the following sentence which contains the 26 letters:

The quick brown fox jumps over the lazy dog.

The students might also write the letters together in one line:

abcdefghijklmnopqrstuvwxyz

Italic Writing

Introduce italic writing, which is not too different from manuscript writing in the lower case. The upper case letters, however, are different from the block letters of manuscript in that they are more graceful.

A A A A A B B B
C C D D E E E F
F F F G G G H H H
I J J J J K
K K K L L L M
M M M M N N N N
O O P P P P Q Q Q
R R R S S T T T T
U U U V V V V W
W W W W X X X X
Y Y Y Y Y Z Z & & &
& 1 2 3 4 5 6 7 8 9 0 ?

Students can use felt pens or crayons at first. Later, introduce calligraphy pens, which are available from art supply stores or the school's art department.

Material for Writing

Give students short quotations to write in calligraphy. Later, they will enjoy looking through books of quotations to select their own.

A picture is a poem without words.—*Horace*

A thing of beauty is a joy forever.—*John Keats*

To climb steep hills requires slow pace at first.—*Shakespeare*

For every minute you are angry you lose sixty seconds of happiness.—*Ralph Waldo Emerson*

An excellent book of quotations for this activity is *Quotes for Teaching* by Sidney Tiedt ($2.50 postpaid from Contemporary Press, Box 1524, San Jose, CA 95109).

Examples of Calligraphy

Bring in examples of calligraphy that students can imitate. This Chinese proverb on page 111, for example, is inspirational.

Poetry in Calligraphy

Let students work with calligraphy and short poems. Have them combine calligraphy and other art as shown on page 112.

If there is right in the soul,
There will be beauty in the person;
If there is beauty in the person,
There will be harmony in the home;
If there is harmony in the home,
There will be order in the nation;
If there is order in the nation,
There will be peace in the world.

Chinese Proverb

The Eagle

He clasps the crag with crooked hands;
Close to the sun in lonely lands,
Ringed with the azure world, he stands.

The wrinkled sea beneath him crawls;
He watches from his mountain walls,
And like a thunderbolt he falls.

—Alfred, Lord Tennyson

5. An Effective Reading Program

Children who are beginning to read need to learn decoding skills—the ability to identify letters and to relate them to the sounds they represent. At this time you should emphasize the concepts referred to as phonics and word analysis techniques, with the aim of helping students become independent readers, and providing them with word attack skills that will be useful when they encounter new words.

At this beginning stage, you should also emphasize comprehension and the overall goal of reading instruction: gaining meaning from the printed word. Students will learn to read more quickly if they learn to associate reading with something meaningful; thus, reading aloud, computer-assisted reading, or following a taped story all help students gain meaning as they learn to read.

In this chapter we describe activities that can be used with beginning readers as well as those who need to review basic skills. We also present exciting strategies that stimulate reading at all levels and which can be used to develop reading abilities in such fields as social studies, science, and mathematics.

GETTING READY TO READ

We need to pay special attention to a student's *readiness* to read. Unless a student has a facility with language—words, concepts, experiences—he or she will never become a good reader. It is important, therefore, to emphasize oral language activities during preschool years, nursery school activities, and primary grade programs. Oral language development is also an important consideration for older students who have difficulty reading.

Reading Aloud

Try to read aloud to your students every day. Choose humorous stories, such as *Alexander and the Terrible, Horrible, No Good, Very Bad Day* by Judith Viorst (New York: Atheneum, 1976, K-3), or a book that has chapters of continued adventures, such as *Pippi Longstocking* by Astrid Lindgren (New York: Viking Press, 1950, 4-6). Children will hurry to their seats after recess if they know that you always read to them at that time.

Reading aloud is a delightful experience for both teacher and child. This sharing brings a sense of camaraderie and pleasure into the classroom. Reading aloud, however, also teaches children *how* to read. As they listen, students are learning

- new vocabulary in the context of sentences;
- how language ought to sound—the flow and intonation as you read fluently;
- the way a skillful author tells a story, using interesting words and figures of speech;
- new sentence structures and phrases showing the grammar of English.

A story that you read aloud also provides the stimulus for speaking and writing activities. In just a few minutes, the whole class hears a piece of literature that they can talk about or write about. Following the reading of Judith Viorst's book, for example, have the class name all of the horrible things that happened to Alexander. Write their suggestions on the board: gum in his hair, no dessert, a tooth cavity—just to name a few. This is an excellent listening comprehension activity that can lead to the sharing of personal experiences orally in small groups and perhaps, later, in writing a memory story.

Choose Good Books

Parents and teachers help children learn to read as they read aloud. Naturally, we want to choose the very best books for reading. Here are some suggestions.

DePaola, Tomie. *Strega Nona.* Englewood Cliffs, New Jersey: Prentice-Hall, 1975. (PS-3)

Emberley, Barbara. *Drummer Hoff.* Englewood Cliffs, New Jersey: Prentice-Hall, 1967. (PS-1).

Hogrogian, Nonny. *One Fine Day.* New York: Macmillan, 1971. (K-3)

Keats, Ezra Jack. *The Snowy Day.* New York: Viking, 1962. (PS-1)

McCloskey, Robert. *One Morning in Maine.* New York: Viking, 1952 (K-3)

Ward, Lynd. *The Biggest Bear.* Boston: Houghton Mifflin, 1973. (K-3)

Zindel, Paul. *I Love My Mother.* New York: Harper & Row, 1973. (K-3)

Boston, Lucy. *A Stranger at Green Knowe.* New York: Harcourt Brace Jovanovich, 1979. (4-7)

Gates, Doris. *Blue Willow.* New York: Viking, 1940. (4-7)

George, Jean. *My Side of the Mountain.* New York: Dutton, 1975. (4-9)

Gipson, Fred. *Old Yeller.* New York: Harper & Row, 1964. (7-up)

Henry, Marguerite. *King of the Wind.* Skokie, Illinois: Rand McNally, 1948. (2-9)

Selden, George. *The Genie of Sutton Place.* New York: Farrar, 1973. (4-up)

Speare, Elizabeth. *The Witch of Blackbird Pond.* Boston: Houghton Mifflin, 1958. (7-up)

Yep, Laurence. *Dragonwings.* New York: Harper & Row, 1975. (7-up)

Adams, Richard. *Watership Down.* New York: Macmillan, 1975. (7-up)

Cooper, Susan. *The Grey King.* New York: Atheneum, 1975. (4-9)

L'Engle, Madeleine. *A Wrinkle in Time.* New York: Farrar, 1962. (7-up)

Neville, Emily C. *It's Like This, Cat.* New York: Harper & Row, 1963. (7-9)

Pearce, Phillippa. *Tom's Midnight Garden.* Philadelphia: Lippincott, 1959. (6-9)

Pope, Elizabeth. *The Perilous Gard.* Boston: Houghton Mifflin, 1974. (6-up)

Tolkien, J.R.R. *The Hobbit.* Boston: Houghton Mifflin, 1938. (5-up)

Dictated Experiences

Beginning readers, and those who are slow learners or who need help with language learning, will benefit from dictating sentences to the teacher or an aide. Print or type the sentences as the student dictates them so that he or she can immediately read the sentence in print. Because the student dictated the sentence, he or she will be able to read it and will begin taking the first steps in learning to associate what is *spoken* with the letters used to *write* it. The student might then draw a picture of the dictated sentence.

I have a kitten named Muffy.

Gradually, students should dictate longer and longer stories. As soon as the stories are written, they should read them. Teach the students to practice reading in pairs, too, whereby one student can be the "teacher" who listens to the reader. Then the "teacher" can ask such questions as:

Point to the word *kitten.*
Can you tell me what this word is? (Point to the word.)

Words Around the Room

Printing words on objects in the classroom supports children's efforts to read. Place large word cards on the chalkboard, window, door, desk, chair, library, bookcase, etc. Later, remove the cards from their places, and show students the cards one by one while asking who can put the card in the right place. In this way, students will become more aware of the words and will consciously read them. Add other cards to the room as they are needed, and encourage students to use these words in writing sentences.

If you have a few minutes while waiting for dismissal or in between lessons, ask questions about the words.

Who can tell me a word that begins like *library?* (look, Lucy, line)
Look at this sign. It has two words (teacher's desk). Who can point to one of the words and tell us that word?

A Reading/Listening Center

You can create a Reading/Listening Center around a tape recorder or cassette player. Plan space at a small table for several students around each machine. Show students how to use the center for tape-assisted reading.

To develop a set of recordings, you might purchase commercially prepared tapes, but you can also make your own. Each time you read a book aloud to the class, for example, turn on the recorder to make a tape. Obtain several copies of the book so students can read the book with the assistance of the recorded reading, an excellent way of supporting the student who is having difficulty reading at any level.

Talk Abouts

Provide a variety of stimuli to motivate student talk in the classroom. In addition to short books or chapters of books, use a short film, a walk around the school, an unusual object, and things to feel, smell or taste.

After students talk together about the object or experience, provide a structured beginning to stimulate writing.

I think_____.
I heard_____.

After writing several structured sentences, students can read their statements to others. Mount them on the bulletin board, too, to permit other students to read the sentences.

Acting Out

Creative drama techniques offer exciting ways of responding to common experiences or stories that have been read. Have students begin with pantomime.

- opening the cereal box, preparing the cereal, eating it
- choosing a book at the library, sitting at a table, reading
- calling the dog, putting on the leash, going for a walk

These activities build student consciousness of the elements (or details) of a story. Other students can try to guess the action pantomimed.

As students become familiar with acting out, they can use such familiar stories as "Cinderella" or "The Little Red Hen." Acting out is an excellent way of increasing and checking on comprehension of stories that have been read together.

Memorizing

Students who have never read a book may be helped to accomplish this task by literally memorizing the story. Each child chooses a book or story that he or she wants to read. The teacher, aide, or another student prepares a tape of the selected material. That individual student then studies the material, reading it aloud with the tape. Soon, the student begins reading without the tape, using memorization as well as the beginning skills of word recognition. The important thing is that the child makes a commitment, and you guarantee his or her success. After the first book, the next one should come easily!

BASIC DECODING SKILLS

Beginning readers need to be introduced to the letters of the alphabet and the combinations of these letters (graphemes) that we use to represent the sounds we speak. Students learn the intricacies of English spelling as they observe the relationship between reading and writing a word. Phonics and word analysis skills help students read new words independently.

Although basic decoding skills are essential to learning to read, do not dwell on isolated instruction and practice drills too long. Continue to stress reading for meaning through the techniques described in the preceding section as you gradually expose beginning readers to decoding information. The important goal is to move students into reading for meaning, looking at books, trying to read as much as they can by themselves. Through reading, they will reinforce the skills they have been shown, and they will acquire new ones abstracted from their reading (much as they learned to speak in early years). Older students, particularly, should be reading and learning these skills in context, rather than completing workbook or duplicated drill sheets.

Identifying Letters

Students need to learn to identify the letters of the alphabet that we use to write English words. This skill is necessary in order to talk about language, the appearance of written words, and how to write them. Introduce the letters in a variety of ways.

• Display an alphabet chart in the classroom to which students can refer when they need to. Use manuscript print for beginning writers, but later display a cursive alphabet.

• Talk about letters as you work with primary students. Print a student's name on the board each day and talk about that name.

Harold Burke

How many letters are in Harold's first name?
How many letters are in his last name?
Do you see two big, capital letters?
Who knows the name of this one? (point to "H")
Who knows the name of this one? (point to "B")

You can spell each name aloud together as you point to the letters. Sometimes you may refer to a name that you looked at before. "Do you remember another name that began with the same letter as Harold's?" (Hilda, Harriet, Henry.)

• Using blocks, letter cards, and large cardboard letter shapes are examples of activities that give children experience in finding letters they know, learning to identify new ones, and beginning to put letters together to spell words. They are good ways to help children learn this basic decoding skill.

Comparing Symbols, Letters, and Words

Prepare activities that reinforce the students' knowledge of symbols, letters and words. In each row, have the students locate the two items that are the same.

O	□	X	☆	□

H	B	T	B	A

ball	no	ball	and	fast

Learning to compare shapes, letters, and words focuses student attention on similar and different details. They will continue to use this skill as they advance in reading.

NOTE: Learning the letters in alphabetical order is a skill needed only in working with the dictionary or an index. Though it may be picked up incidentally, it should not be stressed in beginning reading.

First-Day Reading

Youngsters usually expect to read when they first come to school. Make a point, therefore, of helping them to read and give them something they can take home to read. An easy way to do this is by focusing on colors or number words, and things that can be easily identified. Prepare a sheet with four large pictures that children can color, and teach them to read the phrases.

Sight Words

Although decoding skills do help students read independently, many words should be recognized by sight. We use many common words, such as *in, and, with,* so frequently that stopping to sound them out is impractical. Applying phonics generalizations to some of them (the, of) is literally impossible, too.

Prepare flashcards for this list of common words that occur with high frequency and are not easily sounded out.

a	for	not	them
about	from	now	then
after	get	of	there

again	give	off	these
all	go	old	they
always	goes	on	think
am	good	once	this
an	got	one	those
and	had	only	to
any	has	open	too
are	have	or	try
around	he	our	under
as	her	out	up
ask	here	over	upon
at	him	pull	us
ate	his	put	very
away	how	read	walk
be	I	red	want
because	if	right	was
been	in	round	we
before	is	run	well
big	it	said	went
both	its	saw	were
but	let	say	what
by	like	see	when
can	long	shall	where
come	look	she	which
could	make	show	who
did	many	so	why
do	may	some	will
does	me	soon	with
done	much	stop	work
don't	must	take	would
down	my	tell	write
every	never	that	yes
find	new	the	you
first	no	their	your

Remember that these words are difficult to learn. Many are related in spelling (who, why, when, where), and they do not always carry meanings that might help students identify them (an, at, is, very). Therefore, do not drill, drill, drill and expect every primary youngster to read this list perfectly. Do, however, encourage students to make sentences using these words.

Do you like to swim?
Yes, I like to swim.

Where did you go on Saturday?
We went to the park.

Setting up patterns that use the words in context helps students learn to read and write these common words.

For older students who need review, you might duplicate a sheet of the words, and challenge them to see if they can read each word (even if they memorize the list at first). Then begin timing them to see how fast they can read the list correctly. Have them make a personal graph.

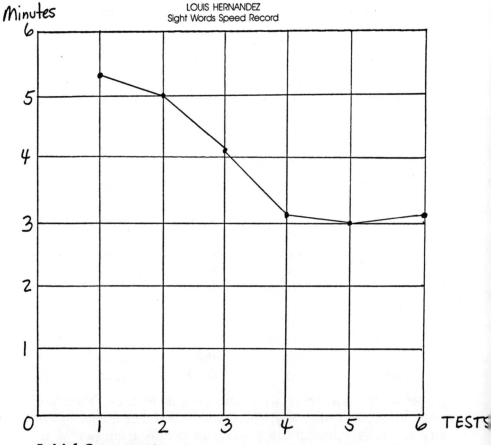

LOUIS HERNANDEZ
Sight Words Speed Record

Minutes

TESTS

Initial Consonants

The beginning consonant sounds are among the first to be learned by the young reader. Here are a number of activities that provide the much needed practice in identifying these sounds.

• "Concentrate" features consonant sounds and memory. You might begin by saying, "I am going to Paul's house and I'm going to take along a pear. What will you take, Mary?" Mary responds, "I am going to Paul's house and I'm going to take along a pear and a pencil." Each person adds one more item begining with the same sound. for young children, you may have them repeat only the last item, or, each child can simply name one new item to be taken. This activity can be used to focus attention on the blends, too, as the group visits Brenda, Trudy, Clara, or Smitty.

• Here is an old favorite that children can use for indoor recess. The leader begins, "I see something that begins with B." Children raise their hands to guess—Blackboard, Bulletin Board, Ball—until the correct word is guessed. The one who guesses the right word then stands in front of the class to be the leader, and so on.

• Let children get in line for recess or going home by sounds. "All those whose first names begin like *tangerine* may get in line." "All those whose last names begin like *lemon* may line up." (If time runs short, simply say, "All those who have a vowel in their first names may get in line." That should take care of everyone else!)

Consonant Blends

In studying the initial blends, you can use many of the same techniques that are used with the single consonants. Here are several additional ideas that have been found especially effective with the study of blends.

• Even young children are intrigued by "big words." Pronounce some words and let the students take turns in identifying the first two letters. Some examples of the words are Planet, Grasshopper, Glaring, Precious. The answers can be printed or written with each student correcting his or her answer as the correct one is given.

• Ask the class, "How many words can we name that start like *blue?*" The children will orally suggest any words which begin with the same sound—black, blouse, bloom, blossom, blood. When that sound appears to be exhausted, move to another blend. When incorrect words are suggested, repeat the sound you are using in order to help the students hear the sound correctly.

• "What Word Do I Have in Mind?" Primary children enjoy trying to "read your mind" as you give them hints about the word you want them to guess.

I grow outside. You can stand under me.
I start like the word *trouble.* What word do I have in mind?

• Divide the group into teams of five or six players for a review in the third or fourth grades. Each team is given a different blend— BL, CR, CL, GR, GL, SP, ST, TR and so on. When the leader says, "Go," the first team member walks to the board and writes a word beginning with that blend. The second player does the same thing. A player who cannot think of a word goes to the board and draws a straight line (which loses time for the team). Players continue taking turns until "time" is called.

Score by adding *one point for each letter in every correctly spelled word. Add two points only for a word which was misspelled. Deduct 2 points for each straight line drawn.* This relay can be adapted to individual participation on sheets of paper with all students using the same given blend. Exchange papers for scoring.

Word Wheels

Have students construct word wheels to help them practice spelling and reading words grouped in families. Wheels can be constructed of colored construction paper or tagboard (for greater durability). Each student cuts two circles with 8½" and 4½" diameters. A brad is inserted in the center of each circle to hold the wheels together and to permit students to turn them. To complete the wheels, have students print blends at the edge of the smaller wheel and phonograms on the outer circle. Encourage students to use phonograms that will combine with many blends.

common consonant blends	*common phonograms*
bl, br, cr, cl, dr, fl,	aim, at, arm, ail,
fr, gl, gr, pl, pr, tr	ear, est, eel, ee,
sc, sm, sn, sl, sp, st,	eam, eal, end, ip,
sw	ape, ow, ide, ade,
	ate, ice, od, ait,
	uck, ing, and, eak,
	ame, ill, ack, ace

Have students turn the wheels to see how many words they can make. They can compete to see who can find the most words on a single wheel, and also, whose wheel will produce the most words.

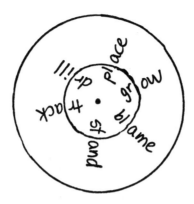

Vowel Sounds

Here is a chart we have used in teaching students the basic vowel sounds: long, short, and followed by R.

Vowel	LONG	SHORT	+R
A	ate	at	far
E	neat	net	her
I	bite	bit	sir
O	go	not	nor
U	use	fun	fur

NOTE: We recommend teaching only A, E, I, O, and U (Y has no long or short sound, but at times substitutes for the sounds of I and E). We question the advisability of calling W and X vowels, for they only influence the sound of the vowel that precedes them as is true of many other letters like R and L.

Wordlists

Have students compile lists of words they know that begin with common blends. Also include three-consonant blends, such as *spr* and *str.*

Discuss the combinations of letters that represent entirely different sounds, technically called *digraphs*. Students will benefit from compiling a list as you write the words on the board.

th	ch	ch /k/	ch /sh/	sh
the	cheat	chorus	chute	shape
there	cheer	chronic	chiffon	shoe
this	child	chemist	chauffeur	shelter

You might also add QU, a combination of letters that is pronounced /kw/, or THR, three letters that spell two sounds.

Making Words

Prepare charts for practice in using consonant beginnings with common endings. Let students take turns pronouncing the words made.

Will each one make a word?			
P	ine	B	ake
F	ay	M	all
M	at	S	and
	it		at
	ail		ore

Word Basketball

Begin this game by having students take out a social studies or science textbook. Each student should use a copy of the same book and turn to the page you specify. Then each student places a sheet of paper over the page so that only the first three letters of print show. The students try to complete a word that begins with these three letters.

The longest words give the highest score, so students should try to think of such long words as: *retiring, placate, frequently, thirteen, heroine, swishing, sprinter, earnestly, mucilage, insistently.*

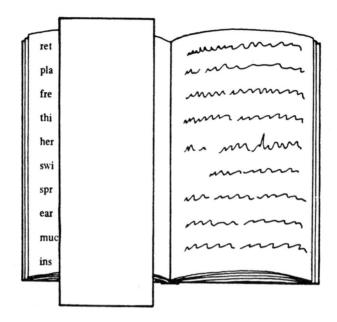

ret
pla
fre
thi
her
swi
spr
ear
muc
ins

Duplicate scoring sheets like this one and give a copy to each student. They will turn to dictionaries eagerly as they try to find long words that begin with specific letters. This activity is a great stimulus for using the dictionary and building vocabulary as students discover new words.

	Letters	Word	Strokes
1.			
2.			
3.			
4.			
5.			
6.			
7.			
8.			
9.			
10.			

EMPHASIZING COMPREHENSION IN READING

The reason we read is to gain meaning—whether from a story read for enjoyment or a science book read for information. The greatest emphasis, therefore, should be on teaching for comprehension, and the following activities help to do just that.

Comic Strip Reviews

The student who enjoys drawing will be pleased to review a book by drawing illustrations comic-strip style to tell about a particularly good incident. Displayed on the bulletin board, this type of review will attract the attention of other readers.

Bulletin Board Display

One student might like to review a book by arranging a bulletin board display. He or she could cut illustrations from magazines or draw some to use. The display might include a brief description of a thrilling part of the book, or pictures of the main characters, telling a little about each one. This type of activity encourages creativity on the part of the student.

Reporting Unusual Information

At times, a brighter student can contribute much to the general knowledge of the class by researching a topic related to a unit of study currently under investigation. Reports of this nature encourage the reading of nonfiction and the use of library research either in your school or at the public library.

Books Featuring Handicapped Children

Books can increase empathy for children who are handicapped. Such books are helpful for the handicapped as well as students who have no visible handicap. Recommend and read aloud these books to your students.

Blume, Judy. *Deenie.* Scarsdale, New York: Bradbury, 1973. (6-8)
Cleaver, Vera and Bill. *Me Too.* Philadelphia: Lippincott, 1974. (3-6)
Little, Jean. *Take Wing.* Boston: Little, Brown, 1968. (4-6)
Spence, Eleanor. *The Nothing Place.* New York: Harper & Row, 1973. (5-up)
Wrightson, Patricia. *A Racecourse for Andy.* New York: Harcourt Brace Jovanovich, 1968. (4-6).

Wolf, Bernard. *Don't Feel Sorry for Paul.* Philadelphia: Lippincott, 1974. (3-6).

Reading Across the Curriculum

Help students find fiction and nonfiction that enrich studies in other areas of the curriculum. For example, introduce students to other languages by using such phrases as:

Wunderbar! (Wonderful! German)
Adiós, amigo. (Goodbye, friend. Spanish)
Ja. Si. Oui. (Yes. German and Scandinavian, Spanish, French)
Tenga cuidado! Prenez garde! Attenzione! (Be careful! Spanish, French, Italian)

Let students share their native languages or invite parents to talk about life in other countries.

A Class Motto

Have one of your students print and decorate a motto for the class to which you can refer frequently.

The more
YOU read,
the better
YOU read!

Make sure that the time spent on reading instruction really does include time for reading material that is interesting to students—magazines, funny stories, newspapers, books about topics of interest.

Discuss the following quote by James Baldwin: "You think your pain and your heartbreak are unprecedented in the history of the world, but then you read. It was books that taught me that the things that tormented me the most were the very things that connected me with all the people who were alive, or who had ever been alive."

Uninterrupted Sustained Silent Reading

Uninterrupted Sustained Silent Reading (USSR) is a novel name for the old practice of free reading. Because it has more structure and organization, this strategy has gained support. Here is the procedure:

1. Everyone reads (the entire school personnel—the principal, teachers, janitors) to make it clear that reading really is important. It is good for students to see adults reading.

2. The choice of reading material is open—magazines, books, newspapers. Students should learn that reading has something to offer each of them. It is imperative, therefore, that a variety of reading matter is available.

3. No attempt is made to evaluate reading or to require reporting of any sort. Each person is reading for personal enjoyment and enrichment.

It is recommended, however, that some time be given to sharing interesting things that students are reading about. You might schedule a Talking Time during which students can share ideas or ask questions that others can discuss.

Treat USSR seriously. Require that students get something to read immediately, sit down and begin reading. Be sure that you read, too!

Book Reporting

Traditional ways of requiring book reports on everything students read have been proven to stifle, rather than stimulate reading. If you really feel that you need some record of a student's reading, try different approaches.

- Have each student keep a Book Log in which he or she enters the name of each book selected for reading and the author of that book. Then the date of beginning reading that book is entered. At the end of each reading session, a few sentences are recorded.

> *Island of the Blue Dolphins* by Scott O'Dell.
> Begun October 24, 1983.
>
> October 24: I am curious about why Scott O'Dell
> chose to write this story. What is going to
> happen to Karana?
>
> October 25: I admire Karana. She must have been
> very brave. I would have been scared!

- Students who complete a book can schedule a time to tell others in a group about the book. If several students have read the same book, they may discuss the book together with other interested students listening or asking questions. Schedule several Book Talk groups at one time. Everyone in the room should sign up to attend one of the groups, but limit the number of how many can go to any group as space dictates.

Responding to Books

Stimulate student creativity by having the students respond in an original way to a book they have read. These productions can be shared with the group on a designated Book Day. Brainstorm various ways of sharing:

> clay modeling—create a character
> poster—advertise the book
> scroll theater—paint scenes from the story
> flannel board figures—tell the story
> dress a doll—present the main character
> diorama—depict a scene on a small stage

Arrange a small prize for the most creative way of sharing, or the most unusual presentation to stimulate student interest.

Sharing Magazines

Students enjoy reading and sharing magazines. Order subscriptions for several different ones if you have funds, and encourage students to bring in copies of ones they receive. Many adult magazines such as *Sunset, Reader's Digest, National Geographic,* and *The Saturday Evening Post* include articles of interest to older students. Check *The Writer's Market* for additional addresses and descriptions of such publications as these:

Child Life. 1100 Waterway Boulevard, Indianapolis, IN 46206

Children's Playmate. 1100 Waterway Boulevard, Indianapolis, IN 46206

Cricket. Box 100, La Salle, IL 61301

Highlights for Children. 803 Church Street, Honesdale, PA 18431

Jack and Jill. 1100 Waterway Boulevard, Indianapolis, IN 46206

Nursery Days. 201 8th Avenue South, Nashville, TN 37202

A Background of Stories

A student's background of stories adds to his or her interest in reading, and is important for general cultural background. Play records of stories that children should get to know. An example is the recording of Kipling's *Mowgli* and *Just So Stories* read by Basil Rathbone (Caedmon TC 1038).

You might want to send for catalogs from the following companies that handle records of this sort:

Folkways/Scholastic Records, 50 W. 44 Street, New York, NY 10036

Educational Record Sales, 153 Chambers Street, New York, NY 10107

Understanding Others

Purchase books for the school library that add to students' understanding of others. Choose some of these books to read aloud.

Steptoe, John. *Stevie.* New York: Harper & Row, 1969. (PS-3)

Turkel, Brinton. *The Adventures of Obadiah.* New York: Viking, 1972. (K-3)

Yashima, Taro. *Crow Boy.* New York: Viking, 1955. (K-3)

Zindel, Paul. *I Love My Mother.* New York: Harper & Row, 1975. (K-3)

Zolotow, Charlotte. *A Father Like That.* New York: Harper & Row, 1971. (PS-3)

Zolotow, Charlotte. *The Quarreling Book.* New York: Harper & Row, 1963. (K-3)

Krumgold, Joseph. *And Now Miguel.* New York: Crowell, 1953. (6-up)
Little, Jean. *Kate.* New York: Harper & Row, 1971. (5-7)
Neville, Emily C. *Berries Goodman.* New York: Harper & Row, 1965. (5-9)
Wojciechowska, Maia. *Shadow of a Bull.* New York: Atheneum, 1964. (5-up)

Getting to Know Authors

The able reader should begin noting the author of each book he or she is reading. They can learn to use *Current Biography* to find information as well as the *Reader's Guide to Periodical Literature.* Each student may select one author to investigate, developing an information booklet about this person. The booklet might include a brief biographical sketch, illustrations, any appropriate magazine or newspaper clippings, résumés of books by this author, and so on. Library research should be used to locate as much information as possible.

Suggested authors for this type of study include:

Susan Cooper	Lloyd Alexander
Robert Lawson	Madeleine L'Engle
Mary Norton	Kenneth Grahame
A. A. Milne	Dr. Seuss (Theodor Geisel)
Norma Klein	Vera and Bill Cleaver
Emily Neville	Scott O'Dell
Nina Bawden	Elane Konigsburg
Paula Fox	Zilpha Keatley Snyder
Marilyn Sachs	Sharon Bell Mathis
Ursula LeGuin	Judy Blume

Cutting a Title

Have students write the title of their book on the fold of a piece of paper. They then widen each letter and make sure each letter has a connection on the fold. The students may need to practice writing the title several times in order to get the spacing right. Choosing short titles makes the job easier, too. After cutting out the title, students can select attractive contrasting construction paper on which to mount the title. These designs can be used as covers for books about their reading.

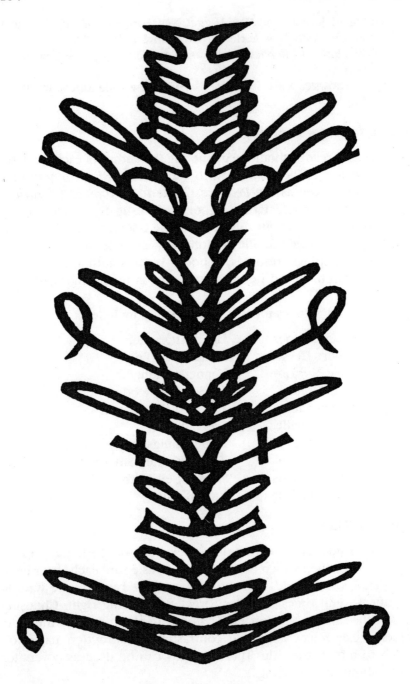

A Book Fair

Have your students take charge of planning a book fair. The whole school may participate in this fair, which should include displays of books for sale by at least one commercial book dealer. Usually dealers will give the school a percentage of the sales made (which can be used to buy more books for the school library).

In addition to the sale of books, have students plan activities that feature books. They might, for example, invite each classroom to present a lifesize walk-through display on books.

6. Mathematics

Since mathematics is part of our daily lives, even the youngest students should learn to use these concepts early. Like science, math instruction should focus on more than just facts and figures as we involve students in thinking and working with numbers creatively.

BEGINNING MATHEMATICAL CONCEPTS

Children begin working with numbers early in life, knowing many mathematical concepts before entering school. Your job is to build on what they already know.

Math Awareness

Help students become aware of the many ways we are involved with mathematics as we go about our daily activities.

• Brainstorm a list of the many ways we use math every day.

The date—day, month, how many days until ...
Telling time—grandfather clock, digital watch
Giving ages—months, years
Measuring—height, weight, recipes
Buying food and items—prices, tax
Reading maps—distances, miles above sea level

• Create a class collage of numbers including as many different kinds of math uses as possible. Bring in newspapers and magazines for a clipping and pasting session.

• Number associations challenge students to list things they associate with each number. (There may be multiple suggestions.)

  2 (twins, pair of shoes, age of younger sister)
  11 (student's age, TV channel, 5 + 6, Storytime)
  49 (7 × 7, uncle's age, 46 + 3)
 1492 (discovery of America, an address)
  144 (12 × 12, a gross, someone's weight)

• Think of a geometric shape, such as a triangle. In how many ways does this shape appear in your life? Also try cone, cylinder.

| gable of roof | letters V, W, M, N, A |
| triangle (instrument) | number 4 |

Numbers in Our Language

Talk about prefixes in English words that have numerical meanings. Compile a list and display it on a bulletin board.

1 unicycle	2 biplane	4 quadricycle
1 uniform	2 carbon dioxide	4 quadrangle
1 unicorn	(CO_2)	4 quarter
1 unipod	2 binoculars	5 quintuplets
1 monoplane	3 triangle	6 hexagon
1 monogram	3 triplets	6 sextuplets
1 monorail	3 tripod	7 September
1 monocle	3 trisect	7 septuplets
1 monochord	3 triplane	8 octopus
1 monologue	3 trioxide	8 October
1 carbon monoxide	(O_3)	8 octagon
(CO)	3 trio	9 November
2 bifocals	3 tricycle	9 nonagon
2 bisect	3 tricolor	10 decimal
2 bicycle	3 trivet	10 December

Then have your students make posters that depict the words suggested.

The Numbers in My Life

Have students make individual lists of the numbers that are important in their lives.

birthdate
telephone number
street address
zip code
number of family members
height
weight

Discuss the numbers that adults have to know, too, such as their social security numbers.

Math-Related Words

We do not always realize that we are dealing with mathematical ideas when we make comparisons, for example:

small, smaller, smallest
big, bigger, biggest
many, more, most
few, less, least

Plan classroom experiences that will make such comparisons real. Students can compare their heights by measuring each other and preparing a large graph to show who is tallest and how the others compare in height.

Beginning Work with Numerals

As children learn to write, they practice writing numerals as well as letters. Make writing practice meaningful to children by associating the concept with the figure.

- Have each student make a Number Book that contains a page for each numeral from 1 to 10. On each page, mount clippings from newspapers and magazines illustrating that number concept. Included can be the figure itself, as well as pictures that illustrate this number such as: 2 dogs, 3 ducks, or 4 horses. Older students can collect numerical figures used in various ways—prices, sizes, quantities—with problems constructed using the information collected.
- Play "What's My Name?" with young students who are learning to recognize numerals. Write on the chalkboard (or on large cards) a figure like 7, asking, "What's My name?" The students can answer in unison or you can call on individuals.
- Give each child a paper with numerals in squares to play "Can You Find Me?" As you call out, "My name is 7; can you find me?" each child must cover the 7 with a square of construction paper. To introduce the numerals, you can show a card or write the figure on the board as you speak the words, so children begin to associate the name with the shape of the figure. This activity can be used with progressively advanced numbers.
- Knock on your desk (or a drum) while the children count the number of beats. Have one child select the card that tells how many beats there were. (Use this technique and have the children write the figure also.)

Recognizing Numerals

Students will know many of the numeral shapes before they enter school, but some may confuse 6 and 9, for example. So provide practice in recognizing numbers just as you do letters of the alphabet.

- Use pages from old calendars to create "Calingo," a game featuring numbers up to 31. As in Bingo, call out numbers randomly as children cover the numbers called. They can try to cover three in a row, diagonally or straight (vertically or horizontally). Children can serve as Callers.

• Display cards on the chalktray. As you call out a number, two children race to see who can pick up the correct card first.

• Simple designs can be drawn on a sheet of paper on which coloring instructions tell children how to create a picture.

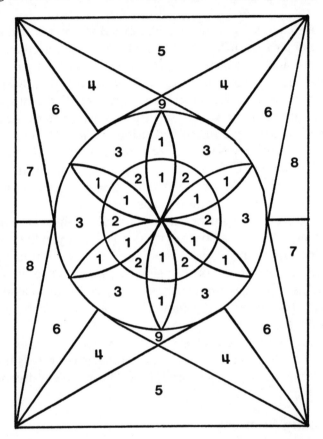

Color Key:

1—purple
2—yellow
3—orange
4—green
5—blue
6—red
7—pink
8—brown
9—black

Help students learn the color words by including a piece of colored construction paper by each word, or by coloring in a small square beside each word.

• Display numerals around the classroom. They can be used in conjunction with words for both number and word orientation, for example: 1 desk (taped on your desk), 5 windows (taped on the window area), or 2 doors (taped on a cupboard). Talk about the meanings of the figures and words on these cards so that students become familiar with them. Refer to the cards during school and point out other number concepts, such as on the calendar, illustrated around the room.

Writing Numbers

Children need practice in writing the different numerals from 1 to 10. Stress legibility just as you do in any handwriting. Have students observe that different forms of some numerals are used, for example, **4** and **4** .

• Have students write simple patterned sentences that combine practice in writing numbers in meaningful context. Using sentences also provides reading and spelling reinforcement.

I see 2 books. (show 2 books)
We have 3 chairs. (point to 3 chairs)

Ask students to make sentences about things in the classroom. Print a sentence on the board, saying, "Now, can you write Leslie's sentence?"

• For students who have difficulty in forming the numbers, provide large wooden or cardboard letters they can feel or trace. They might also trace numbers you write on the chalkboard or posterboard.

• Have students make a calendar for each month. As they fill in the numbers for the dates, they will practice all of the numbers several times.

Number Concepts

Students need to know what the number 5 represents and how that concept compares with the one represented by 3. You will need to demonstrate and then involve students in handling items they can count repeatedly. Have a Number Center where they can work with tasks that reinforce this knowledge.

• Prepare a poster of the numerals with illustrations that show how many items each figure represents. Children can refer to this chart when needed.

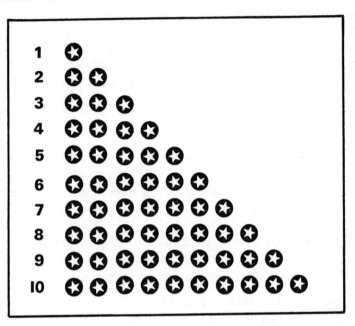

• Mount a different number on each section of an egg carton. Have students count buttons or other small items to put in the appropriate section. Children can check each other to see if the numbers are correct.

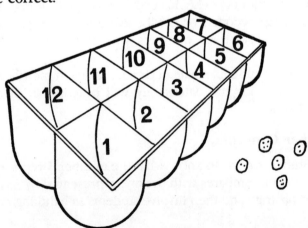

The Sequence of Numbers

Children need to learn the numbers in order, beginning with one to ten and moving to higher sequences. The same activities can be adapted to learning the sequence of numbers at any level, but here we focus on working with the beginning levels of one through ten.

- Give each student a number tag. Then have the class line up for lunch or recess by number, turning their tags toward you so you can quickly check the correctness of their order.
- Use a box full of small objects (nuts, pebbles, beans) to encourage counting. Have one child count to 25 while another gathers as many of the objects as possible, moving them one by one from the box to the table. See which child can gather the most items.
- Mount numerals on flower shapes (airplanes, animals) that students can use on the flannel board as they practice putting them in the correct sequence.

More Work with Numbers

Many activities will support the student's ability and ease with numbers. Present several of these learning experiences each week so that students can then work independently.

- Have the class or a group of children act as Counters while children jump the rope, hop, or bounce a ball. Record the scores on the board to introduce a variety of written numbers.
- Have students estimate (write estimates on the board) the number of items in a group and then count them to discover the exact amount. Use beans, macaroni, nuts, or bottle caps in a jar. For a real treat, use paper-wrapped candy (enough for the class) and have the Counter pass a piece to each student.
- Play a circle game with each child holding a number card. One person walks around the circle and tags a person on the back. The tagged person must count out his or her number, perhaps 5, then chase the Tagger. The object is to catch the Tagger before he or she gets all around the circle.

Share a Number Poem

Display this anonymous poem and discuss the ideas presented. You might have the students read it aloud.

How many seconds in a minute?
Sixty, and no more in it.

How many minutes in an hour?
Sixty for sun and shower.

How many hours in a day?
Twenty-four for work and play.

How many days in a week?
Seven, both to hear and speak.

How many weeks in a month?
Four, as the swift moon runn'th.

How many months in a year?
Twelve, the almanac makes clear.

How many years in an age?
One hundred, says the sage.

How many ages in time?
No one knows the rhyme.

THE MATH CENTER

Designate a special place in the classroom as the Math Center, where students can work to develop mathematics skills. The Math Center provides for individual needs in studying arithmetic facts and computational skills, and is an effective individualized method of working with mathematics instruction. The student who needs additional practice with the multiplication facts, for example, will find varied ways of helping him- or herself, while the gifted student can work on more appropriate challenges.

Number Language

Talk about math as a universal language that everyone can read. Note, however, the different words we use for numbers.

English	*ten*
French	dix
Italian	dieci
Spanish	diez
Portuguese	dez
Romanian	zece
German	zehn
Dutch	tien

Swedish	tio
Danish	ti
Norwegian	ti

Addition and Subtraction Facts

• Addition Wheels can be prepared on circles of posterboard. Print numbers around the circle as shown here.

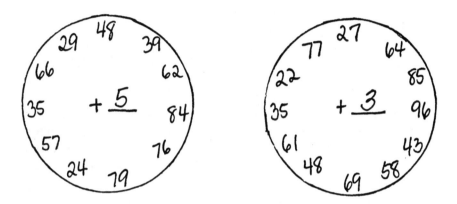

Students add a given number to those on the circle, writing their answers on a slip of paper. Write the answers for adding specific numbers (7, 8, 9) on the back of the circle so students can check themselves immediately.

• An enormous problem fascinates students as they fill the page with figures. Present one problem a day at the Center.

```
   987654321            123456789
   876543219             12345678
   765432198              1234567
   654321987               123456
   543219876                12345
   432198765                 1234
   321987654                  123
   219876543                   12
 + 198765432          +          1
```

• "Dizzy Quiz" consists of a series of questions you ask to which the answer is always a number. The numbers are added to find the total score at the end of the quiz. Sample questions are:

1. How many letters are in your first name?

2. How many brothers (sisters) do you have?

3. How many pencils are on your desk?

4. How old are you?

5. How many lines are on your paper?

6. How many stripes are on the United States flag?

7. Give yourself ten points if you are wearing something red.

Multiplication and Division Facts

Show students that multiplying and dividing are reverse processes, so that knowing the facts in one process teaches the facts in the other.

• Give students a number (45). Ask what two numbers they associate with it (9 and 5). Continue naming other Magic Numbers (56, 81, 35, 24). Point out that certain numbers may be associated with more than one set of numbers, for example, 36 (6 and 6; 4 and 9).

Then prepare sets of cards that students can use to improve their skills. Make cards for 2, 3, 4, 5, 6, 7, 8, 9, 10, 12, 14, 15, 16, 18, 20, 21, 24, 25, 27, 28, 30, 32, 35, 36, 40, 42, 45, 48, 49, 54, 56, 63, 64, 72, and 81, and print related facts on the back of each card. Students can practice multiplication and division by working with either side of the card.

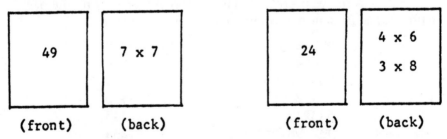

(front)   (back)   (front)   (back)

• Challenge students to see if they can "Beat the Clock" by multiplying the numbers around a clock in one minute. If the Leader calls, "It's five o'clock," students multiply by five and write the answer outside the clock face.

Prepare pages of clock faces that students can use individually or in small groups.

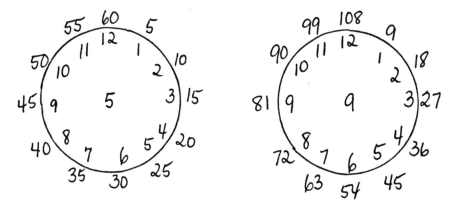

• Have students count off by eights or fours or nines as they get in line: 8, 16, 24, 32, 40, 48, 56, 64, 72. The next student begins again with eight, or you may assign a new number, such as six.

• The Wheel of Nine is constructed like the example shown here. It can be used by several students who are studying the multiplication or division facts involving *nine* (other numbers may also be used). A Leader uses a long rubber-tipped pointer to indicate a figure (7) that the players must multiply by nine and complete to indicate the correct answer (63). For division, the Leader would point to the outside figures (72) that the players must divide by nine and try to indicate the correct answer (8). Other circles can be constructed for facts that present difficulty such as 6, 7, and 8. Circles can also be made for addition and subtraction.

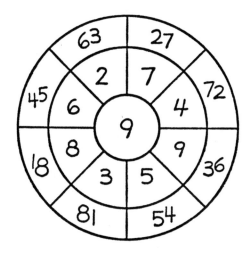

Prepare multiplication and division wheels on large sheets of paper that can be folded for storage. Students can lay the wheels on a reading table or mount them on a bulletin board to use for review practice.

• "Tee Square" is a good game that is used relay fashion. The first player in each team draws a "T" on the board. The Leader then calls off five numbers which are written by each player on the left side of the T. The Leader then calls, "Times 3" or "Plus 6" which the players must write at the top of the T before immediately writing the correct answers on the right side of the T.

× 3			+ 6	
5	15		6	12
7	21		2	8
4	12		9	15
3	9		5	11
9	27		8	14

• Write the numbers 1, 2, 3, 4, 5, 6, 7, 8, 9, 0 on the board, the four signs +, −, ×, and ÷, and an = sign. Without talking, point to number, sign, number, and then the = sign. Each student must write the answer without any repetition of the problem. A checker for each row can quickly count the number of right answers for his or her row, recording the score on the board.

• Ask your students, "Which number does *not* belong in the group? Why?" Here are some examples.

$\frac{3}{7}$ $\boxed{\frac{4}{6}}$ $\frac{2}{5}$ $\frac{4}{9}$ (can be reduced)

236   279   837 $\boxed{21}$ (not in hundreds)

$\boxed{2}$ 9   7   5   21   13   25   (not odd)

Timer Tasks

Have one or two kitchen timers or three-minute egg timers at the Math Center to challenge students.

• Set the timer for 30 seconds (or any appropriate time) as you ask students to write, for example, the multiples of 6. Or make a cassette of instructions:

"Here is a series of numbers. Write each one on your paper. 82, 94, 27, 38, 45. When I say 'begin,' multiply each number by 7. Then when you hear the bell, stop your work. Ready? Begin. (several seconds of silence; then bell sound) Here are the correct answers. 574, 658, 189, 266, 315. How did you do?"

• Give a copy of this activity to each student, who is challenged to multiply each number by a given number. Have the students write their answers below the figures given as they go up and down the "mountain." Be sure to set the timer for one minute.

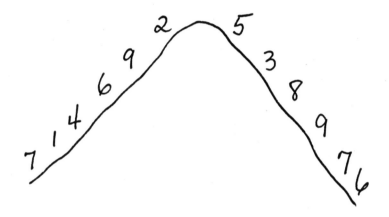

Listening and Math

Use the cassette player to present math activities that stimulate listening abilities as well as reinforcing knowledge of arithmetic facts. Prepare tapes and worksheets for students, with answer keys in THE ANSWER BOOK kept at the Center so students can check their work immediately. If they make more than two errors (or any suitable number) on an exercise, they must repeat it until they get a better score.

• Prepare a number of questions featuring whatever facts students are working on.

Addition: "I have 6. Write the number that will make it 11."
(child writes 5)

Subtraction: "I have 12. Write the number that will make it 3."
(child writes 9)

Multiplication: "I have 6. Write the number that will make it
42." (child writes 7)

Division: "I have 63. Write the number that will make it 7."
(child writes 9)

Students can also play this game using number cards.

• Children love mental math, so prepare a number of sets of
these directions that they can follow at the tape recorder or cassette.
Give the answer on the tape.

Take 9. Add 6. Divide by 3. Multiply by 5. What is your
answer? (25)

Take 2. Multiply by 6. Subtract 4. Multiply by 5. Add 8.
Divide by 6. What is your answer? (8)

PUZZLES AND INTRIGUE

Working with math should be more than computation if students are to become truly excited about working as mathematicians.
Challenge your students with puzzles; stimulate their knowledge of
words with new vocabulary from mathematics; encourage their
reading about the lives and work of men and women who have
devoted themselves to creating new ways of thinking. Your enthusiasm for mathematics will be contagious.

Food for Thought

Display several quotations around the classroom. Here is one by
Bertrand Russell.

"Mathematics possesses not only truth, but supreme beauty."

Challenges

Test your students' thinking skills with these challenges.

• How much dirt is there in a hole 3½ feet by 4½ feet wide and
24 inches deep? (There is no dirt in a *hole*, only air.)
• Multiply 999 × 9 × 0. What's the answer? (How many
students multiplied 999 × 9? The answer to the problem is 0.)

• Which is heavier—a pound of candy or a pound of printer's lead? (a pound is a pound is a pound.)

• Mr. Hale, an insurance salesman, drove 450 miles one day while visiting his clients. He drove 50 miles an hour for 3½ hours and 40 miles an hour for 1¼ hours. How many miles did Mr. Hale drive in all? (450—the number given at the start of the problem.)

• A butcher is 33 years old, 6 feet 2 inchs tall, wears a 16½ shirt and a size 12 shoe. What does he weigh? (Meat.)

Interesting Patterns with Numbers

Students will be intrigued by playing with numbers that have interesting properties.

• Have students multiply 37037037037 by multiples of 3 to discover what happens.

• The diameter of the universe in miles is 10^{26}. How is that number written? (100,000,000,000,000,000,000,000,000)

• Numerical reversals are interesting to students because when the sign is changed, the answer reverses. Duplicate these samples on a sheet of paper and ask whether anyone can discover any others.

$$9 + 9 = 18 \qquad 9 \times 9 = 81$$
$$24 + 3 = 27 \qquad 24 \times 3 = 72$$
$$47 + 2 = 49 \qquad 47 \times 2 = 94$$

• How does this progression work out? Why?

$$1 \times 9 + 1 = 10$$
$$12 \times 9 + 2 = 110$$
$$123 \times 9 + 3 = ?$$
$$1234 \times 9 + 4 = ?$$

A Math Board

Frame a section of the bulletin board where you display a challenge or information related to math. Include an envelope in which students can deposit their solutions. At the end of each week, discuss the problem presented and the solutions students turned in.

• Can you complete this multiplication table?

$$123456789 \times 9 = 1,111,111,101$$
$$123456789 \times 18 = ?$$

$$123456789 \times 27 = ?$$
$$123456789 \times 36 = ?$$
$$123456789 \times 45 = ?$$
$$123456789 \times 54 = ?$$
$$123456789 \times 63 = ?$$
$$123456789 \times 72 = ?$$
$$123456789 \times 81 = ?$$

• Take any three-digit number with no repetition of numbers and no zero. Reverse the order of these digits subtracting the smaller from the larger. Then add the difference to itself in reverse. The answer is always 1089.

$$\begin{array}{r} 976 \\ -679 \\ \hline 297 \end{array} \qquad \begin{array}{r} 297 \\ +792 \\ \hline 1089 \end{array}$$

• Select a number from 1 to 9.   6
   Multiply this number by 9.   54
   Multiply that number × 12345679 (omit 8)   666666666
Have several people try this, to note the effects with other numbers.

• Can you solve these problems Roman style?

$$\begin{array}{r} MCXLVI \\ - \quad XXV \\ \hline \end{array} \qquad \begin{array}{r} MMDCLXIX \\ + \quad CMXXV \\ \hline \end{array}$$

• Magic Squares provide practice in using facts, but the form of the problem is so different that students scarcely realize that they are really drilling on number facts. Here are samples of varieties that students can construct.

6	1	8		8	?	6		1	?	2
7	5	3		?	5	?		3½	3½	?
2	9	4		4	?	2		3	?	?

• Tricky Triangles are fun, but they require a little thought. See how many students can solve this problem before you give the solution. The object is to fill in the numbers from 1 to 9 so that the sides of the triangle add up to 17. See if students can invent other triangles.

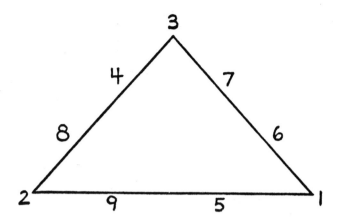

Five-Minute Math

Often, a math activity makes good use of the few minutes that remain while waiting for the lunch bell or recess. The activity can be used, also, by students who finish cleaning up after an art activity.

- Play "Buzz," the familiar parlor game that is usually based on the number 7. Players count in turn 1, 2, 3, 4, 5, 6, BUZZ. For every multiple of Seven (7, 14, 21, and so on) or every number containing a seven (17, 27, 71, 72, and so on) the player must substitute BUZZ or drop out of the game. Use other numbers for variation and practice.
- Count in sequence in addition rather than multiplication. Begin counting by 4s from the number 5 (5, 9, 13, 17 ...). For practice in using subtraction, reverse the process; count by 6, for example, from 81 (81, 75, 69, 63, 57 ...). This "Martian Math" game requires concentration!
- "Shopping" is a game that begins like this:

"I went to the store and bought chocolate for 15 cents." The next child adds an item—"I went to the store and bought chocolate for 15 cents and an apple for 5 cents. I had spent 20 cents." The third child adds another item—"I went to the store and bought chocolate for 15 cents, an apple for 5 cents, and a box of cookies for 20 cents. I had spent 40 cents."

- Progressive addition (or subtraction or multiplication or varied processes) is done individually on sheets of paper. A Leader directs the group: "Take 47; add 168; add 469; add 719. What's your answer?" As time permits, have another problem given.

Real-Life Math

Give students activities that simulate real situations in which they need to use math skills.

• Students can write problems using the figures given in a catalog or newspaper advertisement. A sheet of problems is attached to the front of each catalog. These problems can then be worked in turn by various members of the class.

Turn to page 34. Mary wants to buy three blouses (# G345). How much will the blouses cost? How much will they weigh?

• Try to obtain duplicate copies of a grocery ad for your class. Then all students can work with the same information as they write problems that are exchanged.

Write a shopping list on the board for which each student is to compute the total.

Give the students a sum of money ($20) to spend. They can list the items purchased as they try to spend the exact sum of money.

• Study the advertisements for a sale. Figure out the prices quoted at discounted rates—15%, 20%, 33%. Include the federal tax on luxury items and any local sales tax.

• Play "Cash Register." Give the class the costs of a number of items for practice in column addition. Who can be first to ring up the total?

• Triple this recipe for cookies.

2½ cups flour
½ cup milk
¾ cup butter
1½ teaspoon vanilla
1⅓ cups sugar
½ cup nuts
¼ teaspoon nutmeg

- Figuring interest at the current rate, if you deposited $1000 in the bank today, what would your account be worth when you graduate from high school?

Writing Math Stories

Students who have difficulty learning how to solve word problems will find it easier after they have written original stories of their own. Introduce these ideas for students to use as models.

- Write three numerals on the chalkboard—3, 7, 2. Ask the class to tell you a story about these three figures. Students might say, for example:

> Three children went walking. Four other children joined them, so there were 7 children walking. Five children stopped to play which left only 2 walking.
>
> I had 3 cents. Mother gave me 4 pennies for helping her, so I had 7 cents. I bought a candy bar for a nickel, which left me only 2 cents.

- Provide a story on the board or on a duplicated sheet in which all figures are omitted. Let the students supply them and find the answers to the questions, as in this story.

> Nick wants to buy a_____.
> The_____costs_____, but Nick has only_____.
> How much more money does Nick need?_____

- Oral number stories are good ways to introduce the use of all arithmetical processes. Read the problems aloud and have students decide what process must be used. They can orally identify the key words that assist them in deciding which process to be used— "difference," "how much more," "altogether," and so on. If students have repeated difficulty with "story problems," this method is a good one for examining the problem together.

Math Words

Introduce students to new words that have been coined for math concepts. They can also become familiar with number prefixes and the meaning of other words related to math concepts.

• What is a *googol?* This word was given to the number 1 followed by 100 zeroes, a number so large that it has few practical applications, even in astronomy. The word, coined by 9-year-old Milton Sirotta, was published in *Mathematics and the Imagination* by Edward Kasner, Milton's uncle. All the words ever spoken would not amount to one googol. A googolplex is even larger—1 followed by a googol of zeroes. Incomprehensible!

• After presenting activities that introduce geometric concepts, prepare a sheet of words used in this field. Have students write the definitions of these words, and add others as they are encountered.

circle	radius
concentric	polygon
triangle	angle
square	pentagon
hexagon	octagon
inscribe	circumscribe
rectangle	hypotenuse

• Introduce your students to these two helpful mnemonic devices.

"A *rat in* the *house might eat* the *ice* cream" is a humorous help in spelling ARITHMETIC.

Which is Up and Which is Down—NUMERATOR or DE-NOMINATOR? Numerator contains U for Up. Denominator begins with D for Down.

Math and Women

Studies show that girls perform well in mathematics in the elementary grades. Because of social pressures and lack of encouragement, however, many female students do not select advanced math courses in high school or college. Few women, therefore, choose math-related careers. We need to overcome this kind of sex discrimination in the early years.

• Feature women mathematicians or scientists. Ask your library media specialist to suggest books about women who are presented in books for children. One interesting source is *Math Equals: Biographies of Women Mathematicians + Related Activities* by Teri Perl (Reading, Massachusetts: Addison Wesley, 1978).

• Ask students to investigate the achievements of these women in math:

Hypatia	Emilie du Chatelet
Lida Barrett	Joan Birman
Maria Agnesi	Sophie Germain
Lenore Blum	Evelyn Boorman
Mary Somerville	Ada Lovelace
Leila Bram	Jane Day
Sonya Kovalevskaya	Grace Young
Judith Elkins	Mary Gray
Emmy Noether	Adelaide Harmon
Judy Green	Grace Hopper
Mary Wheeler	Sylvia Wiegand
Linda Keen	Nancy Kopell
Vivienne Mayes	Tilla Milnor
Alice Schafer	Martha Smith
Judith Roitman	Linda Rothschild
Jean Taylor	Karen Uhlenbeck

Mystifying Your Friends

Elementary school students will think you can read their minds when you demonstrate these mystifying processes.

• The answer for this activity is always 22!

Take a number from one to nine.	8
Write the same number beside it.	88
Double this number	176
Divide by your original number.	176 divided by 8
The result is always 22. Why?	Result: 22

• You will always know when this student was born with this activity.

Write the number of your birth month.	10 (October)
Multiply by 2.	20
Add 5.	25
Multiply by 50.	1250
Add your age.	1261 (11)
Subtract 250.	1011

First number in the answer (10) is
the month of your birth; others are
your age (11).

Challenging Gifted Students

Provide instructions for independent challenges for bright students. After they learn how to work with the process independently, they can instruct other small groups of interested students.

• Casting out nines is a way of checking column addition which is often new to students in elementary school. Attention is focused on multiples of nine as well as addition.

6489	0
7349	5
2381	5
2515	4
18734	5

1. Add the numbers across in each figure (6489 adds to 27). Discard any whole nines, writing the remainder to the right (27 contains exactly 3 whole nines so the remainder is 0). Repeat this process for each figure including the addition answer.

2. Add the remainders which are above the addition line and cast out nines (5).

3. If the latter number coincides with the remainder obtained from the addition answer, the answer can be assumed correct.

• Here is an easy way to multiply by eleven.

$$\begin{array}{ccc} 34 & 49 & 325 \\ \times\ 11 & \times\ 11 & \times\ 11 \\ \hline 3\ 7\ 4 & 5\ 3\ 9 & 3\ 5\ 7\ 5 \end{array}$$

$$3+4 \qquad 4+9 \qquad 3+2 \quad 2+5$$

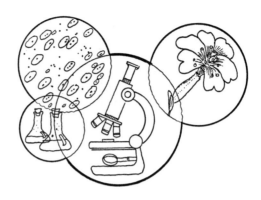

7. Science as a Way of Knowing

As we teach science in the elementary school, we should emphasize discovery through creative thinking, accurate observation, questioning logic—processes that engage students in active learning.

STIMULATING THINKING

In all aspects of the elementary school curriculum, thinking should receive greater emphasis than it presently does. The ideas presented in this section will strengthen the thinking process in other subject areas as well as in science.

Brainstorming

A basic way of attacking problem solving in any area of study is brainstorming. Usually, this activity begins in a group situation but it can also be done individually. Introduce the process to students by following these steps.

1. Define the problem. Write it on the board. *Example:* How can we make our schoolgrounds more attractive?

2. Invite suggestions from students. Make it clear that even the wildest ideas are acceptable. Record every suggestion on the board. *Examples:* Plant flowers around the flagpole. Build a gazebo near the back entrance. Pull the weeds near the baseball diamond.

3. Evaluate the long list of ideas. Place a "1" before those ideas that could be done immediately and require no money. Place a "2" before ideas that seem feasible but require funds, permission, further thought.

4. Erase those that have not been given a number. Make a copy of List 1 and List 2. Discuss the action that should be taken next.

As you work with brainstorming, make sure that all students have a chance to participate. You may begin by going around the group asking for one suggestion from each person.

Critical Thinking

Discuss the importance of taking information students read or hear with the proverbial "grain of salt." Challenge students to think more critically.

• Have students write short essays about what would happen if they accepted everything they read or heard as the TRUTH. They would follow the commands of every advertiser, accept the advice of everyone they met, and believe every superstition.

• Encourage students to question "facts" presented by other students and the teacher. Insist on facts, not just generalizations. Ask the questions, "Where is your data?" or "Can you prove that statement?" Develop the habit of "looking it up" in reliable reference books. Make students constantly aware of the usefulness of such books as encyclopedias, almanacs, atlases, and dictionaries to substantiate their arguments.

• Investigate propaganda devices—begging the question, glittering generalities, colored words, and so on. Alert students to watch for examples of these devices in advertising. Have them try to write "slanted" material as they attempt to "sell" an idea or product.

Categorizing and Classifying

Provide a duplicated list of 50 to 100 miscellaneous words. Let students work in small groups as they consider ways of grouping the words. Have them compare the different ways selected.

Play games that are based on categories. "Animal, Bird or Fish" requires students to identify the names of various animals. The

Leader points to one person and names, for example, "Wildebeest," then begins counting from 1 to 10. The person must call out "Animal" before the number 10 is said.

Lively Discussions

Introduce topics of general concern that students can discuss.

Living on the Moon
Providing Food for Interspace Travel
The Replacement of Manpower by Automation
Increased Longevity
Living Peacefully with Other Nations

List on the board the many aspects of the problem to be considered. In discussing automation, for example, students might begin with a general discussion of the meaning of automation, how it affects individuals, where it occurs, how it affects society in general. They can also list possible solutions to the problems involved. Students may find that they need to read in order to discuss this problem more intelligently. Some students may investigate articles and report their findings to the class.

A Class Motto

Display this quote by John Dewey:

"Every great advance in science has issued from a new
audacity of imagination."

An Exercise in Logic

Present these statements on the chalkboard. Have a student read them aloud as the others think about what is said.

1. All mosquitoes are insects.

2. All insects are mosquitoes.

3. Some insects are mosquitoes.

4. Some insects are not mosquitoes.

Ask these questions as students record their answers on a strip of paper. Discuss the question in turn.

Which pair of statements may both be False, but cannot both be True? (2 is false and 4 may be, but both cannot be true)

Which statements are True? (1, 3, 4)

Which pair of statements might both be True, but cannot both be False? (3 and 4 can be true, but both cannot be false)

Educated Guesses

Provide activities that teach children to use the information available to them as they work with problem solving. Help them identify clues, limitations, and so on that enable them to make "educated guesses."

Present a sealed box containing an unknown object (something a little unusual). What is in the box?

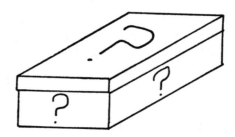

Pass it around the room allowing the students to shake it, weigh it, and so on. Record any guesses on the board. Then erase any guesses that are too heavy, too big, could not make the appropriate noise, etc. After the box is opened, discuss those answers that might have been correct.

Limited Information

Provide students with copies of "The Blind Men and the Elephant" by John C. Saxe. Read the poem aloud and then discuss each stanza as students read the words spoken by each man.

The Blind Men and the Elephant

There were six men of Indostan
To learning much inclined,
Who went to see the elephant
(Though all of them were blind),

That each by observation
Might satisfy his mind.

The first approached the elephant,
And, happening to fall
Against his broad and sturdy side,
At once began to bawl,
"God bless me! but the elephant
Is very like a wall!"

The second, feeling of the tusk,
Cried: "Ho! what have we here
So very round and smooth and sharp?
To me 'tis mighty clear
This wonder of an elephant
Is very like a spear!"

The third approached the animal,
And, happening to take
The squirming trunk within his hands,
Thus boldly up and spake:
"I see," quoth he, "the elephant
Is very like a snake!"

The fourth reached out his eager hand,
And felt about the knee;
"What most this wondrous beast is like
Is mighty plain," quoth he;
"'Tis clear enough the elephant
Is very like a tree!"

The fifth, who chanced to touch the ear
Said: "E'en the blindest man
Can tell what this resembles most
Deny the fact who can,
This marvel of an elephant
is very like a fan!"

The sixth no sooner had begun
About the beast to grope,
Than, seizing on the swinging tail
That fell within his scope,
"I see," quoth he, "the elephant
Is very like a rope!"

And so these men of Indostan
Disputed loud and long,
Each in his own opinion
Exceeding stiff and strong,

Though each was partly in the right,
And all were in the wrong!

So, oft in theologic wars
The disputants, I ween,
Rail on in utter ignorance
Of what each other mean,
And prate about an elephant
Not one of them has seen!

Discuss the last two stanzas, helping students with words that may be new to them. *Ween* is an old word meaning "imagine" or "suppose"; *prate* means to "talk foolishly" or "babble." Ask students if they can think of modern-day happenings in which statements could be made based on partial information—partly right, but entirely wrong!

Memory Training

Provide activities that help students remember items or sequences. Arrange on a tray a collection of 30 or more small articles—pin, nail, thumbtack, string, eraser, pencil, rock, card, book, rubber band, paper clip, flower, chalk, marble, etc. Place the tray on a table around which the students can form a circle to look carefully at the items included. After a period of three minutes, remove the tray from sight and ask each child to list every item he or she can remember. When all have completed their lists, compare the number of items listed. Then compare the lists with the contents of the tray. You may want to repeat this activity.

Asking Questions

Discuss the importance of knowing how to ask the right questions. Encourage students to develop a questioning attitude. Maintain a Question Box in which any student can place a question. Once a week, have a discussion period during which any questions in the Box are removed and presented for class discussion and possible solution. Discuss the ways of finding the required answers—books, letters to resource people, telephone calls to local experts, a reference librarian. Encourage students in their efforts to discover the answers through experimentation in school or at home.

Levels of Questioning

Demonstrate the different levels of questioning as students discuss a book they have just read. Ask students to move from questions that are answered by *facts given* to questions that delve *beneath the surface,* as in these examples based on *Cinderella.*

FACT: Who helped Cinderella go to the ball?

INFERENCE: Why didn't Cinderella's stepsisters like her?

JUDGMENT: Did the story end satisfactorily?

IMAGINATION: How do you think the prince felt when he found the glass slipper that Cinderella dropped?

"Scientific" Poetry

Poetry may introduce many ideas related to science, so display some as part of science bulletin boards to enhance the information presented.

A Riddle

First it was a pretty flower, dressed in
pink and white,
Then it was a tiny ball, almost hid
from sight.
Round and green and large it grew—
then it turned to red.
It will make a splendid pie for your
Thanksgiving spread.

(an apple)

The Rainbow

Boats sail on the rivers,
And ships sail on the seas;
But clouds that sail across the sky
Are prettier far than these.
There are bridges on the rivers,
As pretty as you please;
But the bow that bridges heaven,
And overtops the trees,
And builds a road from earth to sky,
Is prettier far than these.

Christina Rossetti

THE SCIENCE CENTER

Have students help you create a Science Center for the classroom. Develop this Center together gradually as you acquire equipment. Students can suggest and make activities for the Center like those described here.

A Simple Beginning

Create the Science Center by using equipment and furniture that you have on hand. A simple Center is made by placing a reading table below an existing bulletin board.

Science Materials

Have students brainstorm the kinds of materials that would be handy to have at the Center. They may suggest such items as magnets, differents kinds of metal objects, scales, books about science and plants, etc.

As you make a list, you may want to discuss the different studies that are included in the broad term of "science": chemistry, biology, botany, electronics.

Try to obtain kits that contain a basic collection of materials that would be useful. Often, science materials are sitting on storage shelves unused.

Useful Books

Borrow books from the public library to supplement those you may have in the classroom or in the school media center.

Berger, Melvin. *Oceanography Lab.* New York: John Day, 1973. (2-4)

Brown, Joseph E. *Wonders of the Kelp Forest.* New York: Dodd, 1974. (3-7)

Carson, Rachel. *The Sea Around Us,* rev. ed. New York: Oxford University Press, 1961. (5-up)

Dowden, Anne Ophelia. *The Blossom on the Bough: A Book of Trees.* New York: Crowell, 1975. (5-up)

Hirsch, S. Carl. *Meter Means Measure: The Story of the Metric System.* New York: Viking, 1973. (7-up)

Hoke, Helen, and Valerie Pitt. *Whales.* New York: Watts, 1973. (4-up)

Mason, Herbert. *The Fantastic World of Ants.* New York: McKay, 1974. (5-9)

Trost, Lucille W. *The Amazing World of American Birds.* New York: Putnam, 1975. (6-up)

A Unit of Study

To provide focus for the Science Center, you may want to develop a unit of study in which all students can participate. The focus might be on North American birds, whales, how television works—the topics are endless. Whatever topic is discussed, let the students

- select appropriate books,
- collect needed equipment and materials,
- outline the study,
- plan activities and procedures to be followed,
- divide into search teams,
- publish results.

Feature books related to the class study. If, for example, the class is studying birds, mount bird pictures on a nearby bulletin board and display books about birds. Let students use pictures to learn to identify the birds, particularly those common in your area. Suggest related writing activities that may be done voluntarily—poetry about birds, puzzles that describe birds, nature stories involving birds.

Magazines

Students will pore over science magazines that are placed at the Center. Be sure to keep the publications current and up to date, and remember that your better students can handle adult reading material.

Analog: Science Fiction and Science Fact. 350 Madison Avenue, New York, New York 10017.

Asimov's SF Adventure Magazine. Box 13116, Philadelphia, Pennsylvania 19101.

Boy's Life. Boy Scouts of America, National Headquarters, North-Brunswick, New Jersey 08902.

Elementary Electronics. 380 Lexington Avenue, New York, New York 10017.

Family Health. 149 Fifth Avenue, New York, New York 10010.

Mechanix Illustrated. 1515 Broadway, New York, New York 10036.

National Wildlife. 225 E. Michigan Avenue, Milwaukee, Wisconsin 53202.

Natural History. 79th Street and Central Park West, New York, New York 10024.

Ranger Rick's Nature Magazine. 1412 16th Street N.W., Washington, D.C. 20036.

Science Digest. 224 West 57th Street, New York, New York 10019.

Science News. 1719 N Street N.W., Washington, D.C. 20036.

Games

Duplicate games that stimulate interest in science. Have copies of these activities in a box where students can easily get to them.

• Challenge students to complete an alphabetical list of science subjects.

ANIMALS	FLOWERS
anteater	aster
baboon	black-eyed Susan
cougar	calendula

• Use a word related to science to name the theme for words in specified categories. The answers must begin with the same letter as that in the theme word.

	SCIENTISTS	INVENTIONS
C	Curie	cotton gin
H	Halley	
E		
M		
I		
S		
T		
R		
Y		

The word at the left can be any science term: BIOLOGY, WEATHER, NUTRITION, HEALTH, ASTRONOMY.

• Stimulate interest in constructing crossword puzzles that incorporate science information as a theme.

OUR SUN—A STAR (by Julie Johnson)

ACROSS

1. Without our sun, all life would perish and the air would _____ .

5. Solar eclipses occur when the_____passes between the earth and the sun.

6. The Norsemen named their _____ god Balder, the shining one.

7. Without the power of the sun, _____ would not grow.

10. Located in the Milky Way, our _____, are one hundred billion stars, one of which is our sun.

11. Babylonians thought the sun, Shamash, gave wisdom and was _____ of evil.

13. Our sun is large enough to fit over a _____ earths inside.

16. In 1500 B.C. on Salisbury Plain, England, a sun temple called _____ was erected.

17. The Greek's sun god _____ represented music and poetry.

18. In _____ times, the sun played an important part in the lives of people as a symbol of many things.

DOWN

1. The sun is composed of gases and is like a huge nuclear _____ .

2. Not only does the sun _____ moisture from the sea to give us rain; it also gives us day and night and our seasons.

3. It takes the sun 25 days to _____ once on its axis.

4. The ancient Egyptians worshipped the sun as a deity called _____ .

6. Dark spots or_____ measuring up to 90,000 miles long can be seen on the surface of the sun.

8. Gaseous prominences or _____ _____ can erupt from the sun's surface to a height of about 140,000 miles.

9. Looking directly in the sun can result in the damage of your _____ .

12. Diameter of the sun is about 864,000 _____ .

14. Quetzalcoatl, the Aztec's sun god, was worshipped as a _____ in green feathers and was the bearer of widsom and peace.

15. The outermost layer around the sun that looks like a halo is called the _____ .

Student-Invented Games

Have students invent games that use science information. Inventing the games themselves requires students to research needed information, and stimulates their thinking as they plan and organize the games. Show students basic card game formats such as "Old Maid" or "Fish" which they can adapt. Board games such as "Uncle Wiggly" also offer useful models.

• Following the "Old Maid" model, students need to develop pairs of cards, such as INVENTOR/INVENTION or BIRD/STATE. A funny odd card is needed to produce a set of 52 cards + 1. The object is to find pairs that can be laid down, thus getting rid of the cards. No one wants to hold the odd card when the game ends.

• Following the "Fish" model, students prepare a set of cards in sets of four that are related.

Mammals
Reptiles
Fish
Crustaceans

Cards should include the name, some factual information, and a picture of the item.

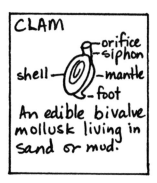

• Students can incorporate scientific questions and answers in board games. Create a background for the trail that players follow.

Cards are drawn to direct the play. Sometimes, students are directed to move backwards; at other times, a card may give students a bonus move forward of several spaces. Cards should be on heavy posterboard for durability. Make the boards on posterboard, too, and tape two sections together with vinyl tape so the board can be folded for easy storage.

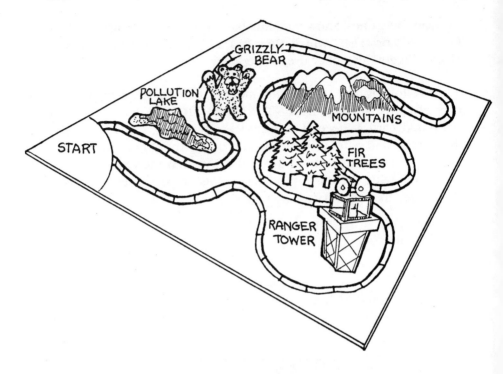

CHALLENGING SCIENCE ACTIVITIES

Because the study of science covers so many broad areas, it offers something of interest to every student. Teaching science effectively means engaging the interest of each student and having them involved in hands-on activities that lead to learning. In addition to the Science Center approach, you might try these classroom science experiences.

An Annual Science Fair

Initiate a science fair in your school or for the whole district. This popular fair will probably become an annual event!

Announce the fair several months in advance so that students who wish to enter will have ample time to plan their entries and to complete any experiments. As part of the announcement, you can explain the purpose of the fair to the parents, list any regulations regarding participation, and suggest suitable types of entries. Areas that students can explore independently for this activity include plant growth; collections of rocks, leaves, shells, seeds; electricity; magnetism; nutrition; and so on.

Each student who wishes to enter the fair should complete (before a stated deadline) a simple form stating the type of exhibit or experiment he or she plans to make; filing this form gives the school some idea of the number of participants to expect, and it also provides impetus to the students to get started on the projects.

The fair should be held on Saturday so parents can attend, as there is usually much interest on the part of families. Each student participating should be present to demonstrate or explain the exhibit as those attending the Science Fair view it. Judges can be selected to award ribbons or certificates (every entry should receive some mark of recognition). If prizes are to be awarded, books in the science area might be considered.

Stamps Featuring Science

Encourage students to collect stamps that feature science-related topics: plants, animals, inventors.

The official birds and flowers of the fifty states have been featured on lovely commemorative stamps. Try to have samples of these for your students.

Students might try to design their own science-related stamps, similar to those issued by the Postal Service.

Gifted Students

Stimulate your more able students to investigate science areas that intrigue them.

- Have the student teach a science lesson to the class—setting up an experiment to demonsrate to the students. He or she can explain the processes involved and answer any questions.
- The student can investigate the biography of a well-known scientist. He or she can collect clippings about the person to be studied and read books and articles to prepare a booklet that the class can use as reference material in the Science Center. The booklet can include illustrations, a time line of the scientist's life, a chart explaining the discoveries of this person. There are many possibilities as subjects for this study, including Henri Becquerel, Marie Curie, Hans Geiger, Harold Urey, Albert Einstein.
- The student might make a sundial for the school. Before beginning the construction, the student should read about sundials to explore the possibilities of the project.
- The student might experiment with natural vegetable dyes to determine what colors can be obtained by the use of leaves, roots, bark, and so on. He or she can compare the results of any local plant materials such as elderberry bushes, onions, carrots, beets, pokeberry bushes. As the student experiments, he or she can save a sample of muslin dyed with different types of juices to be mounted on pages in a report.
- Another student who is interested in astronomy might develop a helpful set of 35 mm slides showing the different constellations. Holes are pricked in used film to simulate the stars. Each constellation is studied, the slide is prepared and labeled, and a card is prepared containing the story of the constellation to accompany each slide.

Young Scientists' Club

An intriguing after-school activity is a club for students who are especially interested in pursuing this area of study. Have students brainstorm creative names for their club—Experimenters, Catalyzers, The Investigators, Young Scientists. Activities might include:

- fieldtrips to local industries
- guest speakers, including parents with special expertise
- films on science topics
- nature hikes to identify trees, wildflowers, birds
- stream and river studies
- fund-raising to buy new science books for the library
- sharing of articles in science magazines
- experiments planned by the instructor, parent, or student
- preparation for the Science Fair

Class Collections

Begin a collection of science materials from nature. A shell collection might begin with a field trip to the beach, or the sharing of a student's own collection. These collections can include pictures as well as actual items.

Have students talk periodically about the class collection. When someone brings in an interesting addition, such as a bird's nest, for the Science Center, take time to examine the way the bird assembled the nest, discuss what type of bird might have made the nest, and so on. Such collections can stimulate many reading and writing activities.

Scientific Research

Introduce Students to the procedures followed by any scientific researcher. Then have them conduct small research studies following these methods.

Selection and Identification of the Problem: A one-sentence statement of what you plan to study.

Hypothesis: Your guess of the results of your study.

Collection of Data: Getting the information or facts to prove or disprove your hypothesis. What method will be used?

Analysis of Data: Deciding what you have collected and what it means.

Findings: Statement of the results of the study. Was the hypothesis right or wrong?

Implications: What was the importance of this study?

Topics that are suitable for the young researcher are many and varied. Here are some suggestions.

Speed of cars passing the school.
The most commonly planted trees in the neighborhood.
Are boys absent more than girls?
Favorite television programs.
The germination periods of various seeds.
Favorite colors, foods, school subjects.
Opinion polls; interviews.

Relating Art and Science

Students learn scientific facts as they work with many different art projects.

• Buy blueprint paper. Cut it into squares (in a darkened room) and store the paper in a heavy manila folder until you use it. Arrange flowers, leaves, designs, string, and so on in a pleasing arrangement on a piece of paper. After the arrangement is planned, transfer it (in darkened room) to the blueprint paper. Then expose the arrangement to the sun for approximately 5 minutes. Wash the paper twice in clear water, then dry it flat under a weight before framing.

• Study the mixture of colors by shining light through combinations of cellophane. Discuss the rainbow spectrum with the use of a prism to produce this spectrum. How does the mixing of paint differ from the mixing of *light* colors?

• Focus on the identification of leaves as they are gathered in the fall. Press the brightly colored leaves until thoroughly dry; then mount each leaf on black construction paper that is cut out, leaving a black edge to frame each leaf. Scatter these leaves over a bulletin board or arrange them on a paper tree shape.

• At Christmas time arrange a display of evergreen boughs to decorate the room, while at the same time assisting students in learning to identify the varieties of evergreens—pines, firs, hemlock, and others typical in your locale.

• Make mobiles with each mobile featuring varied types of animals—Mammals, Fish, Birds, Extinct Animals, Insects, Reptiles, Animals from South America, Animals in Our State, Farm Animals, Animals That Give us Food, and so on. Each student can use a combination of materials—figures clipped from magazines and mounted on stiff paper, animals drawn on stiff paper, small light-weight animals of papier-mâché, items associated with the animals on the mobile (foods they eat, their native habitat, etc.), and other decorative additions of colored paper, plastic, or metal.

Science Vocabulary

Students will be interested in learning new terms that appear in the newspaper or in scientific journals. Encourage them to share new words they encounter.

Science Fiction

Students enjoy reading science fiction. Provide time for talking about the scientific knowledge that such writers as Jules Verne had, and the fact that they were often able to predict inventions or events that now have actually occurred.

Science fiction extends trends that are present in society today, with the author presenting a "What If?" situation. Suggest that students check the library card catalog for books by these authors:

Alan Nourse	John Christopher
Andre Norton	Robert Heinlein
Arthur C. Clarke	Ray Bradbury
Jay Williams	Peter Dickinson

Truth Is Stranger Than Fiction

Nonfiction about science can be as fascinating as fiction, so introduce students to new science books that come out each year.

Try to subscribe to science magazines for your class. If individual students subscribe, they may be willing to share issues after they have read them.

Introduce students to Isaac Asimov, a biochemist who has written hundreds of books ranging from excellent science fiction, to textbooks on science, to books about the origins of words. They will enjoy his book *Words of Science and the History Behind Them* (New York: New American Library, 1969).

Exploring Astrology

Since the very earliest times, men have been trying to read the wisdom of the stars. They noticed the way the position of the stars changed and related this to happenings on earth, such as the growth of crops. This kind of study is called astrology.

Astro is a Greek Word that means "star," and *logy* means "study." Other words that are based on these same roots are:

aster	psychology
asteroid	biology
astronomy	physiology
astronomical	

Today, with our interest in space travel, we have become more interested in how, for example, the position of the sun might affect the amount of radiation coming from the sun. Scientists have found that some of the early ideas about the effects of the sun, moon, and planets on the earth have real scientific bases. An interesting book for young readers, *Astrology, Wisdom of the Stars,* was written by Larry Kettelkamp (New York: Morrow, 1973. 5-9).

According to traditional astrology, each person is born under a sign that influences that person's development.

Virgo	August 23—September 22
Libra	September 23—October 22
Scorpio	October 23—November 21
Sagittarius	November 22—December 21
Capricorn	December 22—January 19
Aquarius	January 20—February 18
Pisces	February 19—March 20
Aries	March 21—April 19
Taurus	April 20—May 20
Gemini	May 21—June 20
Cancer	June 21—July 22
Leo	July 23—August 22

The sign for most of the month of September, for example, is Virgo. People born under this sign are supposed to be pure in mind and body, love learning, take good care of themselves; they are supposedly practical and orderly and interested in beauty and art.

Copy the Virgo sign and the constellation to mount on the bulletin board. Find the other signs and constellations and display these as well.

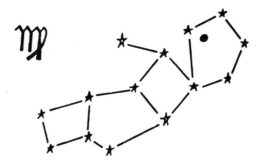

Science Displays

Have students work in teams to prepare displays related to science.

• CURRENT NEWS can introduce students to the topic of electricity. Use a length of electrical wire to form the letters of the caption and to guide the eye around the bulletin board. On a table below the board, have students display electrical magnets or any other electrical connections they have learned to make.

• WHO HAS SEEN THE WIND? makes a good caption for a display featuring the effects of the wind—movements of trees, water, storms. Have students copy several poems such as Robert Louis Stevenson's "The Wind" and Christina Rossetti's poem which begins, "Who has seen the wind?" This topic offers students an opportunity to write original poetry and stories that illustrate wind effects.

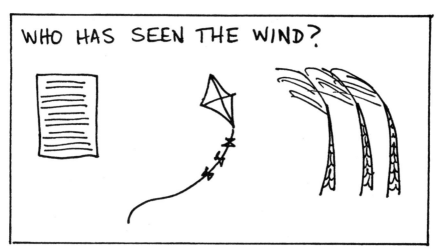

• ANIMAL, VEGETABLE, MINERAL is a caption that can accompany a group of pictures clipped from magazines—various animals, plants, and rocks, plus items more difficult to identify such as a table, book, hammer, pencil, box, glass, and so on. Provide cut-out paper letters (A, V, M) that students can pin on each picture as they try to correctly identify the item.

• PILOT TO NAVIGATOR focuses student attention on material about flying. Display pictures illustrating the principles of flight or a collection of pictures of different types of aircraft. Below the bulletin board feature books about this topic.

8. "Come Alive" Social Studies

The study of our society and people as they interact through space and time should be exciting to students. How students react to social studies is directly related to how we present lessons and the extent to which students are involved in active exploration.

Emphasize the study of events that are close to students in time and place. Then move to happenings that are more distant in space (foreign countries) and time (history). Remember, too, that the social studies can encompass a wide variety of information and areas of study; in addition to history and geography, introduce topics related to sociology, psychology, dialectology, multicultural teaching, and anthropology. Bring in studies of both language and literature to enrich the learning process. Studying concepts related to people around the world, people of the past and the future, provides rich material for engaging students in learning.

The strategies described in this chapter can be adapted for varied subject matter. The activities, too, will suggest many other ideas for oral language, reading, and writing.

WHAT'S HAPPENING AROUND US?

Focus on current events as students read the newspaper and news magazines and listen to television and radio coverage of what is happening locally and around the world. Social studies activities will promote the development of such language arts skills as listening, speaking, writing, and reading.

Vocabulary and the News

Each week discuss words mounted on a display called WORDS IN THE NEWS. Encourage students to mount words, phrases, and sentences from the newspaper, or notes of language from television reports. Talk about the meanings of words used in context as well as the events to which the words are related.

Speaking About Current Events

Current happenings provide interesting things to talk about. Help students become involved in decision making that concerns them directly, whether it be a local or national problem. As they develop their knowledge of social studies the students also become better speakers.

• Invite foreign students to visit your class to talk about their countries. If there is a college or university nearby there are usually foreign students who can be contacted through the Student Personnel Office. Churches and other local organizations can often supply names of students or adults in the community who might speak to your class.

• Hold "Man on the Street" interviews asking the people who are interviewed some question of current interest. Interview students in your own room or conduct interviews in the school hall or lunchroom if this is practical.

• Two teams of students can prepare arguments for both sides of a current issue. Issues of more immediate interest to young students can also be used to allow youngsters to air their opinions and to develop the habit of forming an opinion. Here are two suggested topics that are suitable for this type of presentation:

All children should go to school six days a week.
Students should begin to learn a foreign language in first grade.

• The preparation of a news broadcast emphasizes the importance of studying current affairs. A news broadcast can be planned for your classroom each Friday with students alternating roles so that all participate. This newscast can also be presented to other classes; you may arrange to exchange broadcasts with another room. Use the school address system to broadcast a schoolwide presentation of the news once a week, including school news along with state, national, and world coverage.

Writing to Clarify Current Issues

Students can write statements of their own opinions of current issues. They can also use writing as a means of obtaining additional information.

- Discuss the events that might occur if a person who lived one hundred years ago were to walk into our world today. What, for example, would Thomas Jefferson think of our government? What things would appear odd, amazing, wonderful, or distasteful to him?

Let each student choose a figure in history about whom to write a story. Have the student write his or her story pretending to be the person who is suddenly transported to the present time and describe the events that happen.

- Sometimes we take for granted words and their meanings. Do we really know what words like CITIZENSHIP and FREEDOM mean? Have students take time to think about these important words as they write essays on the following topics:

Citizenship is...
Freedom is...
Democracy is...
The United States is...
Liberty is...

- Students who become interested in certain aspects of the news should be encouraged to write letters requesting information or commending the actions of some person in the news. If, for example, a student has been studying the work of the Supreme Court, he or she might write to one of the justices regarding a decision made on a case.

Encourage students to write to members of the Congress. These representatives of the people are glad to supply information about current affairs—new bills being considered, their opinions regarding certain issues, government-printed pamphlets that are highly informative, and so on. They will certainly respond in some manner to letters of inquiry.

Who Is in the News?

Have students explore a country or people who are currently in the news. They can prepare a bulletin board to display pictures and information.

EXPLORING THE PHILIPPINES

Land Area: approximately 115,600 square miles (about the size of Nevada)

Made up of 7,100 or more islands spread over 500,000 square miles of the Pacific Ocean.

Population: 47 million (70% under 30 years of age; 83% Roman Catholic)

Languages: Tagalog, Cebuano, Ilocano, Hiligaynon, Bikol, and Waray

---

Provocative Quotes

Display quotations related to current events. A committee of students can search for appropriate quotations.

"I would rather be right than President."—*Henry Clay*

"To gain the supreme victory, it is necessary, for one thing, that by and through their natural differentiation men and women unequivocally affirm their brotherhood."—*Simone de Beauvoir*

"Ask not what your country can do for you; ask what you can do for your country."—*John F. Kennedy*

"I know of no way of judging the future but by the past."
—*Patrick Henry*

"I regret that I have but one life to lose for my country."
—*Nathan Hale*

A good source of quotations to use in the classroom is *Quotes for Teaching* by Sidney Tiedt (Contemporary Press, Box 1524, San Jose, California 95109).

What Happened on This Date?

Display a monthly calendar that features significant events on a timeline.

Have students take turns presenting information about the events listed, and encourage them to devise creative ways of sharing research on these topics with other members of the class.

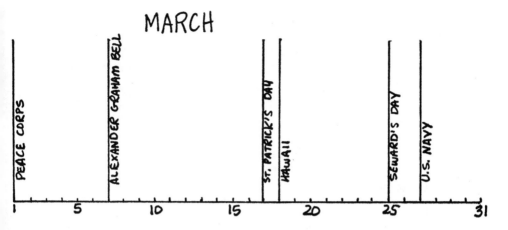

LEARNING ABOUT OUR HISTORY

We try to make history "come alive" for young people, so the following activities involve students in a hands-on approach to studying the past.

Making History

Discuss with students the fact that history is being made as we live. Ask students to write an imaginary history that includes them. Choose a date twenty years in the future, when they will be adults. They will need to decide what kind of career they would like, where they will live, and what kinds of events will be happening in the country and in the world.

Into Another Time

Students will also gain much insight as they imagine themselves living in another period of history. Suggest topics like these:

I was aboard the Santa Maria.
I was the daughter of Martha Washington's best friend.
I lived next door to Paul Revere.

Dramatization can take all forms—skits, tableaux, pantomimes, dialogues. Students will learn much by preparing the presentation of an event through any dramatic technique. Two students could, for example, play the roles of General Grant and General Lee as Lee surrenders. Original dialogue based on their reading about this event can be written.

Tableaux might be arranged around a central topic such as EXPLORING THE NEW WORLD, with each tableau featuring one explorer posing before an appropriate background. Frames for tableaux can be cut from large cardboard packing boxes supported by two poles or boards nailed to the sides. Students walk behind this frame to present the scene they have prepared. Other members of the class may guess which explorer is being portrayed.

The History Of...

Students learn much about the study of history by writing short histories about topics that interest them. Some students might be intrigued by the history of various sports—football, baseball, rugby, cricket—or the history of fashions. Other subjects of more general interest include libraries, printing, your school, a building in your town, or an event of local significance. A student might write the history of the city as seen through the eyes of a landmark—an old tree, a river, or a road.

Dear George

Have students assume the character of a person in history, such as George Washington, Abigail Adams, or more contemporary figures such as Ronald Reagan or Maurice Sendak. Students can write letters to other persons in the room making appropriate comments or asking questions about events in which that person was involved, such as Dr. Seuss writing to William Shakespeare.

Modeling History

A sand table (or large shallow boxes of sand) can be used to portray historical events—the bombing of Pearl Harbor or Custer's last stand. Students become engrossed in depicting battle scenes after library research determines the people present and something of the topography involved. Illustrations in books often supply good information for this type of activity.

Papier-mâché can also be used to build scenes on stiff cardboard or plywood bases. Buildings can be constructed of cardboard as can other structures that are needed to complete a particular historic scene. Groups of students can work as teams, or individuals can work on smaller projects.

Lifelines

Have students construct a lifeline after reading the biography of an important historical figure: Sacageawea, Queen Elizabeth II, Ralph Bunche, Abraham Lincoln. This lifeline may cover a short period in the person's life so as to record events in more detail, or it can outline the person's life from birth to death noting significant events.

Calendar Dates

Referring to the Teacher's Calendars in Chapter 1, have students take turns preparing a two-minute daily feature on a person or event. Presentations might include:

- teaching a song related to an event or person
- presenting a puzzle based on the person's name
- a series of pictures illustrating events
- interesting anecdotes about the person

Vocabulary Study and History

Many interesting words have developed in connection with historical events and figures. Several you might want to discuss with the class are noted below.

Yankee—Used in the 18th century to denote the Dutch in America; corruption of *Jan*, the Dutch name for John.

Bunk or Bunkum—Derived from the name of a Congressman's county, Buncombe, in North Carolina. He made a speech that was pointless and wordy, the origin of the word *bunk*, meaning foolish, untrue chatter.

Have each student prepare a page illustrating the interesting origin of a word to be included in a class book called WORDS IN HISTORY. Other words associated with history that students can investigate are:

ballot	assassin	emancipation
pilgrim	radical	sabotage
propaganda	filibuster	civilization

There are numerous books on the origin of words for use by you and your students.

Funk, Wilfred. *Word Origins and Their Romantic Stories.* New York: Funk and Wagner.

Morris, William and Mary. *Dictionary of Word and Phrase Origins.* New York: Harper & Row, 1977. (7-up)

Famous Date Bulletin Board

A famous date in history provides an eye-catching caption. Cut the figures from newspaper or from the cover of a magazine. Preparing a display for the year 1849, for example, will send students to history books for information about the gold rush days of California.

The I-Search Paper

History offers stimulating topics to research as students try to locate information about something they would really like to investigate further. Ask students to write three to five questions for which they would like to find answers.

What do we know about Amelia Earhart?
Why were the Aztecs so smart?
What was the state of Ohio like before settlers arrived?

Then introduce the I-Search paper. Follow the outline given here and make reproducible copies for students. Because students are searching for something they want to discover individually, they will be less likely to copy paragraphs from an encyclopedia. Insist that they use at least five different sources of information including books, people, letters, and telephone calls.

THE I-SEARCH PAPER

You are going to investigate something that you would really like to know about. First, you need to decide what you want to know, so complete these lines:

I would like to know _____.
I would like to know _____.
I would like to know _____.

Now choose one of these three subjects to investigate. Think about how you can find information. Then begin searching for information and write notes about what you find.

Go to the library and look for:

> The Reader's Guide
> Almanacs
> Atlases
> Encyclopedias
> Books about your subject

Talk to people by using:

> Yellow pages of the phone book
> Interviews with family and friends
> Visits to businesses

Write to:

> The state capital
> The U.S. government
> City officials

Then your report is ready to be written. Include these four parts:

Part I: *Statement of the Problem*—What did you decide to investigate?

Part II: *Procedures*—Describe how you went about your search.

Part III: *Findings*—What did you find out? You may outline the information or prepare graphs. Use any method to present your information.

Part IV: *Conclusions*—What will you do now? Tell how you will use the information you discovered.

Present your I-Search paper to the class. Share the information you discovered and show the group any objects or material you may have obtained. Be prepared to answer any questions from the group.

History Games

Challenge students to use their knowledge of history by playing and constructing games. In this way, students review information in an enjoyable, nonthreatening manner.

• For "Who Am I?" each student has a name pinned on his or her back. Use names from the area or period of history that you are currently studying. Bill, for example, comes to the front of the room, and turns so that all can read "his name," and then asks questions that require YES or NO answers. Bill tries to identify his personality through these questions as quickly as possible. The number of questions that may be asked by each student is limited so that all may have a chance to participate.

• "ABC's of History" is a paper-and-pencil activity that encourages students to use reference books. Each student is to list in alphabetical order WOMEN IN HISTORY, PLACES IN AMERICAN HISTORY, or some other category. Listing MEN IN HISTORY, for example, a student might begin:

A—Adams
B—Benjamin Franklin
C—Cabot

Each student tries to find as many as possible (one name per letter) within a given time. Letters may be skipped and filled in out of order.

Involving Gifted Students

Remember to provide special challenges for gifted students. Help them to broaden their knowledge through enrichment activities that can be shared with the other students.

• An AMERICAN HEROES CALENDAR can be developed by one student or a team of students with each one taking certain months of the year. Listed on this calendar are the birthdates of people involved in literature and science, presidents, industrial leaders, explorers, patriots, etc.

• THE LITERARY HISTORY OF OUR STATE can be the title of a report in booklet form that discusses the writings of authors who have lived in your state or whose stories were set in that locale. Brief biographical sketches and lists of books written by each author can be included.

• Poetry can be written by the able student to stimulate interest in historic events and people. Permit freedom of form and length with stress placed on the ideas expressed.

• Essays provide a means for expression of ideas by the able student. Supply a variety of provocative topics—such as "What If?" topics—to stimulate his or her imagination.

WHAT IF—we had not purchased Alaska?
WHAT IF—the South had won the Civil War?
WHAT IF—the United States had participated in the League of
          Nations?

• Have the student learn a song, such as Johnny Schmoker, to teach the class.

Johnny Schmoker

Pennsylvania Dutch Folk Song

John-ny   Schmo-ker,   John-ny   Schmo-ker

np
Can   you   sing?---   Can you   play?---
Kannst   sing- en?   Kannst du   spiel- en?

I   can   play up-   on   my   drum----------
Ich kann   speil- en   auf   mein   trom- mel.

Rub-a- dub-a- dub, this   is   my   drum--------
Rub-a-dub-a- dub, das   ist   mein   trom- mel.

Assessing Student Knowledge

Finding out what students know about a subject serves two purposes: (1) it guides your teaching of a unit, and (2) it evaluates what a student has learned after studying a subject for a period of time. Think of assessment as part of the learning process, not just as a means for "grading" students.

• When a unit of study has been completed, *have students compose questions which are submitted to you as possible test items.* Students can learn to construct multiple choice questions, matching questions, true and false items, and straight recall questions. Select at least one item from each person's page of questions with no large number coming from any one paper. Constructing the questions serves as an excellent review, exposes students to a variety of test items, and assists you in preparing a good test. You can add a few test items yourself to cover any areas not covered by student-constructed items.

• Short quizzes (perhaps 10 true/false items read aloud) on material can serve to assist students' learning of information. Give the answers immediately, with each student noting the information he or she did not know. These scores are not recorded, but serve only to point up areas that need further study.

• Clustering around a topic is an innovative way of seeing what students know, and it stimulates interest in finding out more about topics listed. Present this technique to the whole group as you write on the chalkboard. Later, students can cluster independently as they need to.

AROUND THE WORLD

Students enjoy working with maps and globes as they locate places they have heard of, and atlases and other reference books add to the interest of finding information about places around the world. The activities described in this section will stimulate students to develop geography skills as they work with longitude and latitude and other geographic concepts.

An Area Study

Have students begin a study of their state or the area they live in. Individuals can sign up to work on committees that will investigate such topics as:

the history of the area
people who live in the area today
ways of earning a living
mapping the region
the animals that can be found locally
trees and plants that are characteristic of the area

Students can interview older people who live near the school, a fascinating way to find out what happened in the "good old days." Students can record the interviews and then write an interesting paper about the facts they collected.

Beginning Map Skills

Even the primary grades need maps of variety in the classroom if students are to take full advantage of opportunities to learn geographic information. The globe is a good type of map for teaching young students that the world is round as they search for locations and become accustomed to the shapes and sizes of land areas.

Running the Compass

Make a large circle on the playground with four directions marked off, to play a game called, "Run the Compass." Have the children count by fours and stand at the center of the circle. As the Leader calls out a number and a direction, "Threes, West," all the children having the number Three must run to the West. The Leader tries to catch any who are not safely at that point of the compass. Later, add the intermediate points—Southeast, Southwest, Northeast, Northwest—so that there are eight positions.

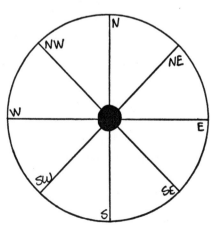

To change positions, children must always run through the center.

Life-Size Maps

Especially effective in the primary grades are maps that the children can actually experience, maps they can construct. Even kindergarteners can lay out a city street (perhaps the street corner near your school) using blocks and cardboard cartons to simulate buildings and houses. Other landmarks can be noted also, such as large trees (a big circle of green construction paper laid flat on the floor or attached to the end of a dowel), stop signs, traffic lights, and so on.

Before developing the map, have the class take a walk around the area to be mapped. After the map is begun in the classroom, walk around the area again to note any corrections to be made. Use this type of street map to teach safety practices, to present concepts of directions, and to encourage role playing and creative dramatics.

Older students can construct similar maps on a smaller scale using large sheets of cardboard or plywood as a base. Buildings and other landmarks can be constructed with small boxes and construction paper, surrounded by small vehicles, people, animals, and other things.

Making Outline Maps

The opaque projector will assist you in preparing large, inexpensive outline maps of the United States (with or without state boundaries), North America, and the world. Any small map in a textbook can be enlarged with this projector directed toward a large sheet of mural paper or tagboard. Outline the map quickly with a pencil when the projector is turned on. Then turn off the projector while you complete the outlining of the map with a felt pen. Students can add washes of thin blue tempera paint to indicate water; other features can be added according to your needs. Print names of countries with the felt pen as you identify them with the class. Maps can be drawn on the chalkboard for temporary use.

To assist students in drawing freehand maps, have them first draw light lines to divide the paper into fourths, eighths, or sixteenths. By dividing the map to be reproduced into the same number of areas, students can more closely place each land mass in the correct location.

Games to Reinforce Map Skills

Provide outline maps of the United States or the world that students can use as they devise games. Challenge their creativity by asking who can make up an interesting game that uses map skills and information. Here is one example.

• "To the Rescue!" provides an opportunity for students to practice the location of latitude and longitude on maps. Beside a map (of any area) on which both latitude and longitude lines are marked, mount airplane shapes cut from colored construction paper. On each airplane print the latitude and longitude where that plane has been reported "down" because of engine trouble.

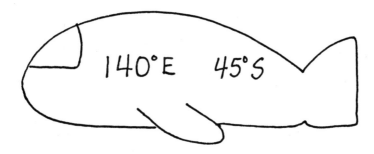

The problem is to locate each plane's position so that the crew can be "rescued." Let students take turns moving each plane to its correct position on the map. For added practice, students can remove the planes and locate them again. You may also print positions on both sides of each plane to double the number of times the plane can be located.

• "City, Country, Continent" is an excellent game for reviewing various place names. As the Leader points to a person, that student tries to answer before the Leader counts to ten.. "Anchorage—1,2,3,4,5,6,7,8,9,10!" The student must call, "City!" before the count of ten. Other classifications can be substituted in this game according to the information studied.

• "Chain Reaction" is a game that continues around the circle until someone makes a mistake. This last letter of a given place name provides the key to the next name to be added. In a Chain Reaction of Cities, for example, the Leader might name Boston, which ends with an N. The next player must name a city beginning with N, for instance, New York. The next player must now name a city beginning with K, Kansas City, and so on—Yorkville, Edinburg, Georgetown, Nashville, Erie.

Locational Skills

Prepare a sheet or two of place names with which students should be familiar.

the fifty states
large cities in your state
capitals of the world

Keep these sheets near a globe or map so that students can practice finding these places in their spare time or when you assign them to this work center.

You can also feature unusual place names during the year just as a matter of interest. During December, for example, ask the class how Christmas Island got its name. Post this question on a bulletin board and add the answer when a student finds it. (Christmas Island was discovered by Captain Cook on December 25, 1777.) Encourage students to contribute similar names for investigation.

Relays

Geography relays are interesting and can involve many students. One student serves as the Leader and calls out names of locations— Peru, Kenya, Sweden, New Zealand—while team members take turns indicating the correct location. A Scorekeeper keeps score on the chalkboard for all teams. As one team correctly locates the given place, the Scorekeeper adds one point to that team's score. When a team member fails to locate the place within the time limit (60 seconds, timed by the Scorekeeper), the next team up may be given the same place to locate.

Acrostic Puzzle

The first letter of each word to be identified in this acrostic puzzle helps to spell the key word, which is the theme or subject of the activity. The number of letters are indicated for each word and the definition is given at the right.

S _ _ _ _   The people of this land (Swiss)
W _ _ _ _ _ _   An important product (Watches)
I _ _ _ _ _   Neighbor to the South (Italy)
T _ _ _ _ _ _ _   Biggest industry (Tourism)
Z _ _ _ _ _ _   Large city (Zurich)
E _ _ _ _ _ _   Continent located on (Europe)
R _ _ _ _ _   Inland waterway (Rhine)
L _ _ _ _ _ _   _____ of Nations met here
                               (League)
A _ _ _ _   Mountains (Alps)
N _ _ _ _ _ _ _   Position during WWII (Neutral)
D _ _ _ _ _   Ski center (Davos)

Stimulating Library Research

Provide a purpose for searching for information. Students will then see research as a "treasure hunt."

• Students can gain much information in an interesting way as they prepare travel posters or brochures tempting the tourist to visit a certain country, city, or area. Students can pretend to be advertising agents for the locality selected as they explore various means for advertising the desirable aspects of a visit to Canada, New Mexico or Hawaii. They can send for sample advertising material by writing to the Chamber of Commerce for several cities.

• A good type of independent activity is the collection of pictures and information about topics related to social studies activities. Students who have time will especially enjoy compiling booklets of information about worthwhile topics as they explore them in depth. Topics that may be used include:

Animals That Help Us
Children in Other Lands
Transportation Today and Yesterday
Winter Ways
Living in the Desert
Houses Around the World
Life in the Jungle

Challenging Crossword Puzzles

Crossword puzzles can review a study or challenge students to locate information in a variety of sources.

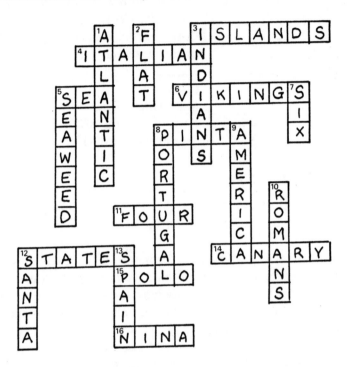

CHRISTOPHER COLUMBUS AND HIS VOYAGES

by Julie Johnson

ACROSS

3. Columbus discovered the Bahama _____.
4. He was an _____ navigator born in 1451, who died in 1506.
5. Many sailors had believed the waters of the Atlantic were filled with dangerous giant _____ serpents.
6. It is believed that _____ sailed

DOWN

1. Sailing across the _____, he sailed through dangerous waters called the Sargasso Sea.
2. At one time, many people believed the Earth to be

_____.

3. When Columbus finally sighted land and people, he thought he was in India and named the people _____.

across the Atlantic to Greenland and North America before Columbus did.
8. One of Columbus' ships.
11. Columbus had much knowledge of navigation and geography which enabled him to make _____ important voyages.
12. The Sargasso Sea is so huge that most of the United _____ can be placed inside.
14. It was on the _____ Islands that Columbus had hoped to replace the damaged Pinta.
15. He read in a book about the Italian discoverer Marco _____, who had inspired him to take a sea voyage to reach the Indies.
16. He commanded three little ships, one of which was the _____.

5. The Sargasso Sea has calm waters and is completely covered with thick _____.
7. It took almost _____ years for Queen Isabella of Spain to change her mind in favor of his voyage.
8. Columbus had asked for help from _____, but the country refused.
9. On several other voyages, he sailed the Caribbean Sea and along the coasts of Central and South _____.
10. The _____ had called the Atlantic *Mare Tenebrosum*, meaning the Sea of Darkness.
12. The _____ Maria was Columbus' flagship.
13. In 1492, Columbus set sail on his first voyage with the aid of this country.

UNDERSTANDING OURSELVES AND OTHERS

Activities in the social studies should include an emphasis on self-esteem as well as on the understanding of others. Multicultural teaching begins with activities that focus on self-acceptance and move toward the studies of the many cultures that make up the complex American society.

Name Acrostics

Help students in a new class get acquainted by having them make name acrostics. Each student prints both first and last name vertically, and then chooses adjectives that begin with the letters of the names. Encourage students to select extravagantly wonderful words as they "brag" about themselves, as David Brown did.

The acrostic strip is then decorated and displayed. In this way, students see each other's names and learn new vocabulary at the same time.

DAUNTLESS
ADVENTUROUS
VORACIOUS
IRREPRESSIBLE
DRAMATIC

BRAVE
RUTHLESS
OMNIPOTENT
WITTY
NEIGHBOR

Reading Aloud

Select books that present problems and feelings that students share to read aloud to your class. As you read, students are hearing book language, the kind of language they are expected to read and to write. They are also learning new words and concepts.

Neville, Emily. *Berries Goodman.* New York: Harper and Row, 1965, (5-9)
Yashima, Taro. *Crow Boy.* New York: Viking, 1955. (K-3)
Zindel, Paul. *I Love My Mother.* New York: Harper and Row, 1975. (K-3)

A "Me" Collage

Have students plan a collage that tells as much as possible about themselves. Let students pore over magazines as they select pictures and words that relate to their lives. Talk about the kinds of things they might include: a baby picture, cloth from a favorite piece of clothing that has been outgrown, a small toy. When the collage is completed, students can frame it with yarn or contrasting construction paper, or it can be cut into a circle or oval.

Promoting Self-Esteem

You can help students develop self-esteem by using teaching strategies that make them feel good about themselves.

1. Let children know that you like them.

2. Make sure that students can succeed in doing what you ask of them.

3. Provide positive reinforcement—displays of all children's work, a pat on the back, an A for what the child achieved.

4. Help children know that you value individual differences.

Sharing Feelings

Provide open-ended topics about which students can write. As they share their writing, they feel good about themselves and others. Use such topics as:

I am afraid when...
I feel happy when...
Sometimes I think...

Language in Your School

Have students make a survey of the many languages spoken by children in the school. Almost every classroom includes students who speak languages other than English. Then, plan to recognize the presence of these languages and cultures in various ways.

• Have an assembly with representative music, art, and literature that features the school's varied population.
• Have a bilingual student participate in the morning announcements, including a message in a language other than English.

Ethnic Foods

Have students try the many foods that different groups contribute to our society. Here is one for fry bread.

Fill the electric skillet half full of oil. Turn on high to heat. Measure into a bowl 4 cups flour, 3 teaspoons baking powder, and 1 teaspoon salt. Gradually add 1½ cups water as you stir. Knead the dough until it does not stick to your hands. Add a little more flour as needed. Divide the dough into small balls. Then flatten them until thin and make a hole in the center like a doughnut. Slide into hot oil. Fry on each side until light brown. Remove and drain on layer of paper towels. Eat while warm.

Chinese Brush Painting

Combine art with reading and the study of the Chinese culture. Try your hand at the beautiful figures used in classic Chinese writing.

Use 9" x 12" white art paper, a brush, and black tempera paint to create the words shown here.

man   beautiful   country

Talking About Names

Talk about the many different kinds of names represented in your classroom. You might read *Tikki Tikki Tembo* by Arlene Mosel (New York: Holt, Rinehart and Winston, 1968. K-2), a story beautifully illustrated by Blair Lent, that explains why most Chinese people have short names.

Make a chart of students' first names. Are any the same? Are there variations of the same name? Students might be interested in knowing the many ways of saying a name, for example, John.

John (English)   Sean (Irish)
Ivan (Russian)   Shane (Irish)
Jannis (Greek)   Ian (Scotch)
Jean (French)   Juan (Spanish)

Evan (Welsh)   Iban (Basque)
Hans (German)   Giovanni (Italian)
Johannes (German)   Jan (Dutch)
Johan (Norwegian)   Yohanna (Arabic)

Roleplay

Playing reverse roles helps students understand the thinking of other people—siblings, parents, teachers. Set up a situation in which, for example, parents are conversing. Two sets of parents might be having dinner together. Ask your students what the parents might discuss; then have students take turns playing the parent roles. After the roleplaying experience, ask students to discuss or write about their feelings.

Calligraphy

Collect interesting quotations that students can discuss and then have some of your more able students experiment with calligraphy as a way of displaying the words of well-known people or proverbs from different cultures.

A journey of a thousand miles begins with one step.

LAO-TZE

A Family Tree

Have students prepare a gift for their family as they explore genealogy.

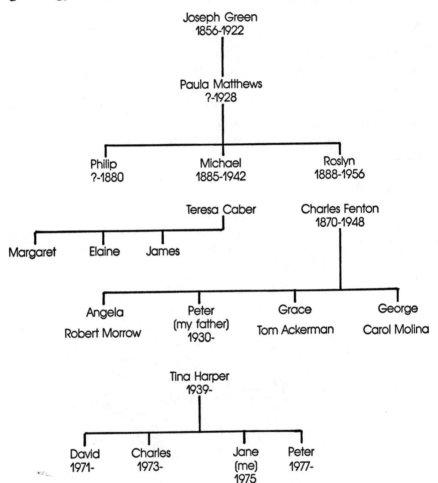

9. Learning With Music

Music is universally enjoyed as a way of expressing feelings and communicating with others. Music can enhance studies across the curriculum as students listen to the music of other cultures and try their dances; make music as they sing and use simple instruments; and respond to music in a wide variety of ways as an integral part of the classroom.

In this chapter we explore different ways of engaging students in music—singing, dancing, composing, and responding to music. Our aim is to assist students in enjoying music through listening, and to provide opportunities for students to make music themselves. We also want to help students to respond to music that they hear and to explore music offered as enrichment experiences in other subject areas.

ENJOYING MUSIC TOGETHER

In order for students to enjoy music, we need to make music available. There are many ways of including music in the elementary school curriculum.

A Music Center

Encourage children to explore music by developing a Music Center. At certain times, they can experiment with any instruments there—piano, xylophone, flutes, autoharp, rhythm instruments. Feature books and articles about music and musicians, pictures of lesser-known instruments, songbooks, and sheet music. A record player and radio can also be included. Let students contribute their own ideas to this Music Center, too.

Repertoire of Songs

Singing in the classroom develops a good feeling of camaraderie. Begin with songs that students already know and then add new ones to develop a repertoire of songs that your students can enjoy together. Depending on the ages of the students, include the following kinds of songs:

- Nursery rhymes ("Jack and Jill," "Little Bo Peep")
- Folk songs ("Go Tell Aunt Rhody," "The Erie Canal")
- Patriotic songs ("The Star-Spangled Banner," "America, the Beautiful")
- Old favorites ("I've Been Working on the Railroad," "Jingle Bells")
- Rounds ("Row, Row, Row Your Boat," "Tell Me Why")
- Popular songs (ask students which songs they like)

Teaching New Songs

When you are teaching the class a new song, the words and music must be repeated a number of times before the children can really sing the song. To avoid monotony and boredom, vary the ways in which the song is repeated.

Only the boys or only the girls sing the song.
Half the class sings at one time.
All students with blue eyes (or brown hair) sing.
The class echoes your singing of each line.
Say the words together.
Hum the tune while thinking the words.
Small groups come to the front of the room to sing.
Each row sings a line.

Use these techniques also for singing songs with many repetitious verses.

Musical Games

To promote the students' interest in music and the people who write music, use musical games that require students to know something about musicians, composers, and to be able to recognize the melodies of well-known compositions.

• "Who Can Name It?" features familiar melodies that have been introduced to the class. Each child has half a sheet of paper on which to write the title of the selection played, and the composer, if possible. After five to ten selections have been played (in part only), provide the correct answers so each student can score his or her paper. You may keep score by rows (allowing one point per selection correctly named and one point for the correct composer and adding the scores of all in the row) for added interest. Use the tape recorder to record parts of many selections to which the children have been introduced, so this game can be played easily.

• "Who Is It?" requires pictures of composers (from magazines or newspapers) that are mounted on the bulletin board. At first, place the name of the composer and several of his or her best-known works beneath each picture. Discuss these people and their music with the class, perhaps playing parts of some of the works named. Another day, move the names and the titles of selections around so that the children can try to identify the pictured composer by matching the names and titles correctly. Also, try removing the names and titles completely, and have the children try to identify the composers and their works through total recall.

• "Name the Tune" is a game that children of all ages enjoy. Whistle or hum a tune that is known by the class, such as "Ten Little Indians." See how quickly students can identify the song by melody alone. Use this technique for introducing a new song or one known by only a few people

Singing Matched Songs

An unusual type of singing that gives practice in two-part work is that of having the two halves of the class sing two different songs at the same time. Just any two songs will not work for this activity, for the songs must be matched in time and key. Here are several pairs of songs you can use.

"Skip to My Lou" and "Ten Little Indians"
"A Spanish Cavalier" and "Solomon Levi"
"There's a Long, Long Trail" and "Keep the Home Fires Burning"

Counter Melodies

Students can compose simple counter melodies to accompany familiar songs. Remember that the new melody must be in the same key and tempo as the song with which it is to be used. A simple example makes use of the song "Twinkle, Twinkle, Little Star."

The counter melody is another way of introducing two-part singing. Other songs that lend themselves to this type of singing are "Jingle Bells" and "Are You Sleeping?"

Rounds

An excellent way to begin part singing is through the use of the round. There are many familiar ones that can be used to introduce children to this type of singing.

"Are You Sleeping?" ("Frère Jacques")
"Three Blind Mice"
"Row, Row, Row Your Boat"

Other rounds that are less well known and, for that reason, perhaps more interesting, include:

"White Coral Bells"
"We Thank Thee"
"Oh, How Lovely Is the Evening"

In order to sing rounds successfully, students must be very much aware of the *time in which the round is written* (in most cases 4/4) and the *tempo being used* by the group. As the leader, you can set the tempo by conducting, insisting that all students pay attention to your hand as you indicate the time.

Students should also learn to *hear the other parts,* so that

White Coral Bells

OLD TUNE

1 White co ral bells up on a slen der stalk;
3 Oh don't you wish that you might hear them ring?

2 Li lies of the val ley deck my gar den walk.
4 That will hap - pen on - ly when the fair - ies sing.

although each group sings different words and tune, all are aware of the completion of each phrase. Before beginning to sing any round, state the number of times each group will repeat the whole song (three times is usually enough).

After-School Singers

Encourage volunteers to sign up for an all-school chorus that meets once each week after school in a classroom or in the multipurpose room. The chorus provides an opportunity for students who are especially interested in singing to learn a wider variety of music and to further their enjoyment of music with others who are also interested.

The sponsor of this group does not have to be a music major, but he or she will need skill in conducting and, above all, in handling a large group. The chief requisite, however, is enthusiasm. An accompanist will also be needed, preferably a student or perhaps a parent. Although many songs can be taught by rote, a set of inexpensive songbooks should be purchased for this group (at least one for every two students).

Stress should be placed on enjoyment of music and singing, but at each meeting a few minutes can be spent on the skills of reading music, correct breathing, and singing as a group. This group might perform several times during the year to add stimulus to their interest.

Monthly Songfests

Encourage students to sing by having monthly music assemblies. To build up the repertoire of the student group, notify teachers ahead of time about the songs that will be sung. The assembly may be attended by the whole school, or, according to the size of the group, two assemblies may be held with younger students attending one while upper grades attend the other. The division of the assemblies also allows for the selection of songs more appropriate to interests and abilities.

Include some seasonal songs, old favorites, folk tunes, popular songs, rounds, and perhaps feature one student performer playing the piano or another instrument. A first assembly might include:

"America, the Beautiful"
"I've Been Working on the Railroad"
"Are You Sleeping?" or "Row, Row, Row Your Boat" (rounds)
"Polly Wolly Doodle"
Song prepared by one class (sung standing in place)
"The Marine's Hymn"
Individual student performance (on stage)
"Waltzing Matilda" or "Swing Low, Sweet Chariot"
"The Caisson Song" (classes can hum this tune as they file out)

Music on Display

Interest in music can be furthered by the use of the bulletin board. Here are two ideas you might suggest to students who can readily produce an attractive display.

• Use heavy black yarn to form a music staff. On the staff, place notes for the music of a short song or just the first line of a longer song with the caption WHAT SONG IS THIS? For variety, make the notes in a different shape—stars, pumpkins, leaves, bells, snowflakes, hearts, shamrocks, or flowers—according to the season or the song being displayed.

• MUSIC IN THE NEWS is the caption for a display of clippings (interspersed with cut paper notes) about music and musicians. Encourage students to bring this type of material to school if they see music news in magazines or newspapers. Several pieces of sheet music for the background would also add to the effectiveness of this display.

Playing Music

Instruments in the classroom—piano, xylophone, tonettes— will assist students in learning to read music. They will also provide motivation for the learning of musical notation.

• Colors or numbers help young students learn to play simple songs on these instruments. You may want to make several tagboard charts for songs that can be propped on the chalk tray while students play the songs. In the music for "Mary Had a Little Lamb," notice that the numbers (or colors) are placed on notes in their correct positions so students will be more ready to play when the number system is dropped. (9-3)

Mary Had a Little Lamb

OLD TUNE

• The Rhythm Band, the Kitchen Orchestra, the Silent Band or other variations add fun and interest to a program. Play a recording of a march while this band marches from the stage through the audience and back to the stage.

• Ballads can be dramatized. Try such familiar songs as "Go Tell Aunt Rhody," "Reuben, Reuben," or "Lord Randall." Students can write modern ballads that tell a story of present-day events.

Musical Instruments

The making of musical instruments can lead to a Rhythm Band or provide an interesting way of exploring the folk music of a foreign country being studied in social studies. Each student can construct one type of instrument so that all participate. Here are suggestions for inexpensive types of instruments that students can make.

• DRUMS can be made simply by removing both ends from a two-pound (or larger) coffee can. Cover both open ends with circles of inner tube rubber or linen coated heavily with shellac that can be laced with twine or cord to hold the drumheads securely in place. Drumsticks can be short pieces of doweling. The ends of some drumsticks can be padded with cloth for a different effect.

• RATTLES or MARACAS can be fashioned from gourds, if available. They can also be made from boxes or jars in which beans are placed. Toilet tissue tubes can also be made into attractive rattles by covering each end with heavy wrapping paper after adding beans or pebbles.

• STICKS are the easiest type of rhythm instrument to make. Use pieces of doweling or broomstick that are painted with bright enamel to provide simple instruments for all. Each child can use two sticks that are struck against each other, or one stick can be struck against a block of wood.

• BELLS can be sewn on wide bands of cloth or elastic to be used as Jingle Bells. Large single bells can be struck with a stick. Small bells can be attached to painted sticks.

• HUMMERS provide for the addition of a melody in a band. Tubes from paper supplies or combs covered with waxed paper allow the child to produce an interesting effect by humming directly against the paper.

• TRIANGLES can be made from a suspended piece of pipe, metal rod, or a large spike. The suspended metal is struck by another piece of metal, a silver knife, or a small hammer.

RESPONDING TO MUSIC

Students responding to music provides the necessary interaction that must occur if learning is to take place. Students can respond by clapping the rhythms of music they hear, or by repeating musical patterns. They can move to music as they dance, exercise, or interpret the melodies they hear.

Repeating Musical Patterns

Use music in the classroom to stimulate listening skills. Students must respond appropriately.

• Musical roll call can require the student to echo the tune used by you to call his or her name. Or a standard response can be taught for all to use. Here is an example.

Musical Roll Call

Now I'm call-ing Bob - by Jones, Where, oh, where is he?
(Ann Thomp-son) (she?)

Tea-cher are you call-ing me? Here I am you see.

• Musical directions can be directed toward one person or a row of students. When children are familiar with a Direction Song, they can take turns leading the group.

Direction Song

Bil - ly, Bil - ly. Lis-ten now to me.
(A - ann, A - ann.)
(Row 1, Row 1.)

Can you stand on one leg? Try it now to see.
Can you turn your-self about?
Can you count from one to ten?
Can you touch your neigh-bor's desk?

Directed Listening

If students are directed to listen for a specific purpose, listening will be more effective. Suggest that students listen and respond to music in a variety of ways.

• Encourage children to clap the rhythm or beat of recorded music. They will soon note the differences in time and learn to identify the time correctly.

• Students can listen for themes that are repeated several times. Play the melody of the theme or sing it before playing the record, if possible. Have students raise their hands each time this theme is heard.

• "Peter and the Wolf" is an excellent record to use as students listen for the instruments. Play the record often so students gradually learn to identify the flute, the piccolo, and so on.

• Listen to types of music representative of one country. Learn something of the history of this nation and its people and discuss ways in which the music may portray the customs, feelings, and ideals of this group of people.

• Compare music played by a band with that of an orchestra. How do the instruments, the tempo, the types of music vary? What instruments appear in both band and orchestra?

• Use recorded music to stimulate creative writing. Play "The Moldau," for example, asking students what they hear or imagine as they listen. Have each one write a story about this music. Other good selections for this purpose are "Danse Macabre" and "Firebird Suite."

Listening to Recorded Music

Even young students should be exposed to a variety of melodies—compositions by famous composers, folk tunes, popular music. Here are some recommended selections for use with young people.

Nutcracker Suite, Tchaikovsky
Peter and the Wolf, Prokofiev
Swan Lake, Tchaikovsky
Nocturnes and Waltzes, Chopin
Waltzes, Strauss
Hansel and Gretel, Humperdinck
Amahl and the Night Visitors, Menotti
The Moldau, Smetana
Jeux d'Enfants, Bizet
The Sorcerer's Apprentice, Dukas
Young Person's Guide to the Orchestra, Britten
Danse Macabre, Saint-Saëns
What Is Jazz? Bernstein
Through Children's Eyes, Limelighters

Identifying Rhythms

Have students identify rhythms they hear in real life—the clock ticking, rain on the roof, water dripping. Students can respond to the rhythms of recorded music by clapping, snapping their fingers, or tapping their fingers on their desks.

• Invite students to invent a rhythm on a tambourine. Begin by tapping out simple 1,2,3 or 1,2,3,4, rhythms. Then show students how to vary the rhythm by tapping two times to one beat (1,2, and 3,4,; 1,2 and 3,4; etc.).

• To emphasize various types of rhythm patterns, play a pattern on the piano or tap one on the desk. Let the students immediately reproduce the pattern. Introduce patterns that will occur in a record to be played; then have the children raise their hands or tap the rhythm when they notice it.

• Clap the rhythm of a familiar song, such as "Mary Had a Little Lamb," to see whether anyone can guess the name of the song. Have others try presenting a song in this way.

• Children can interpret many rhythms with a variety of movements even while remaining seated. Have them try these—tapping, stretching, bending, nodding, beating, patting, swaying, clapping, crossing arms or flexing fingers.

Repeating Patterns

Introduce simple patterns on the piano or xylophone. See if students can sing them back to you or play the same pattern that you did.

• Prepare a cassette of recorded patterns that students can work with independently at the Music Center. Repeat the same pattern several times and include directions: "Turn off the tape now and try to match my pattern. When you think you have it right, turn on the recorder, and we will play it together."

Sample Patterns

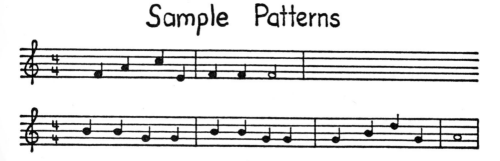

• Play a simple sequence of notes on the piano (or other musical instrument). Tell the class the first note played and see if they can reproduce the notes played on a blank musical scale as they listen for the intervals between the notes.

• Sing a melody pattern and have the class repeat the pattern as an echo. Patterns can be simple at first and become progressively more complex.

Movement Exploration

Encourage students to walk around the room in time to music. They will soon find themselves walking or skipping as the music moves more quickly. Let students try various movements in time to the music—swaying, hopping, turning, swinging arms. When someone discovers an especially suitable movement, draw this movement to the attention of the others who may like to try it, too.

Many types of animals can be portrayed when the music suggests the movements of an animal.

> Elephant—swaying two arms held together as student bends forward.
> Camel—walking on hands and feet without bending knees.
> Rabbit or Kangaroo—hopping or leaping
> Horse—galloping.
> Duck—waddling slowly.

Adding Actions to Songs

Many songs engage students in varied actions. These songs provide a nice change of pace after students have been sitting quietly for a time. Invite students to join you in such songs as:

> "Did You Ever See a Lassie?"
> "Three Blind Mice"
> "Eency, Weency Spider"
> "John Brown's Baby"

Singing Exercises

Students will enjoy experimenting with singing exercises occasionally. They will be more aware of how the vocal system works as they try some of these ideas.

• To encourage students to sing with open throats rather than with the throat constricted, direct the class to yawn and then sing *ah, oh, ee* on each note as they slowly move up the scale from C to C. Singing the syllables, *loo, ah* as indicated here is also helpful.

Singing Exercise

(Slowly)   Loo ah loo ah loo;   Loo ah loo ah loo...(Continue)

• Stress can be placed on correct enunciation of words so that the audience can understand by having only half the class sing while the others listen critically. The tape recorder can also be used to permit the whole class to hear themselves as others hear them.

• Ask a singer (perhaps a parent of a class member) to visit your class to demonstrate correct breathing. Have the students try the recommended techniques so they can later continue them.

Student Conductors

An interesting way to teach the varying rhythms of music is to show students how to conduct songs written in varied musical times. Three-four time is one of the easier times to conduct, so you may want to begin with it. *With your back to the class,* demonstrate the movement that is made by the hand; have the entire class try conducting together as they count *1, 2, 3; 1, 2, 3;* etc.

Play a record of a waltz to provide an opportunity for the entire class to practice this type of conducting. Teach the class a song in ¾ time so that individuals may take turns serving as conductors. Suggested conducting patterns are shown for 2/4, 3/4, 4/4, and 6/8 time.

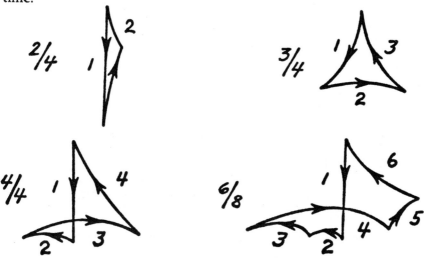

MUSIC ACROSS THE CURRICULUM

Music enriches studies across the entire elementary school curriculum. Consider ways of relating music to social studies (songs from different cultures) and language arts (poetry set to music). Ask students how reading and music are alike or how science is related to music. Such approaches add to their understanding of varied aspects of music—vocal, instrumental, dance—as well as enhancing the learning of language skills and concepts from other areas of the school program.

The Science of Music

Show students how science and mathematics are related to music as they investigate pitch, how the vocal chords work, and timing.

• Obtain one or more tuning forks (or invite a tuner to speak to the class and demonstrate the process of tuning) to show students differences in pitch. Compare the pitch of the tuning fork with the pitch of the piano or another instrument.

• Compare the length and size of strings and the size of the instruments themselves with the tones produced. The string family, for example, illustrates this idea—bass, cello, viola, violin. Compare also the flute and piccolo.

• Relate the writing of music to the study of fractions as students observe that in 6/8 time there are six beats to a measure with the eighth note receiving one beat. Care must be taken to make it clear in this case that the eighth note represents 1 part out of 6 in

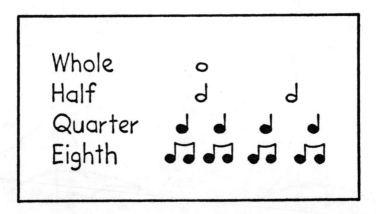

the measure (not 1 part out of 8). Have students make charts to illustrate various times and to compare the relative values of notes. Use the flannel board to compare these values. Begin with 4/4 time for a clear explanation.

• To emphasize the cutting off of consonant sounds, have the students sing the sounds of N, M, or V. Demonstrate and have them try cutting this sound sharply by suddenly pressing the nostrils closed.

Music and Language Skills

Music is a kind of language that people the world over can share. Usually, we sing words to songs so that students listen to the words or read them. Students also learn how to "read" music.

• How are poetry and music related? Ask students what ideas are used in both poetry and music. Make a list on the board:

beat	lyrics
rhythm	stanza
lines	composing
verses	refrain
chorus	read

• Teach young students the alphabet by using the familiar tune of "Twinkle, Twinkle." "The Alphabet Song" shows the phrasing for the letters.

● Develop a Music Dictionary for the class to use as a reference tool during the year. Have students prepare pages for the book defining terms, showing examples and meanings for musical symbols, describing the biographies of great musicians, and so forth.

New Words for Old Songs

Students can write songs to fit the melodies they know. Here is a song written for "The Battle Hymn of the Republic."

Setting Favorite Poems to Music

Encourage gifted students to select short poems that they especially like. They can experiment with melodies for the words using the piano, xylophone, or melody bells. As they learn to read music, they can also learn to write it and to write the song they compose.

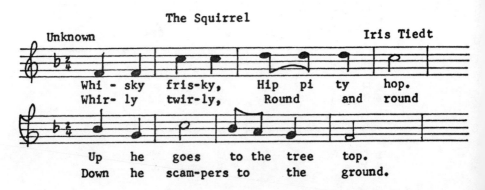

Social Studies and Music

"Alaska's Flag" can be sung to commemorate the early settlement of Alaska, the gold rush, and the vote to make this vast territory the 49th state.

Multicultural Music

Music can provide the basis for an effective program to be produced by the entire school or by one or two classes.

- "Music of Many Lands" can be the theme of an effective program with each participating room selecting one country to portray through music. The class can do a dance or two and sing songs, or prepare a brief musical skit to demonstrate customs of that country. At Christmas, this theme can feature national customs for celebrating the holiday and some of each nation's typical carols.
- *The Nutcracker Suite* can be interpreted by students as a form of creative dramatics using the recorded music as a background. *Peter*

and the Wolf is another selection that can be interpreted very effectively by primary children who portray the various characters of the story with a minimum of props as the record is played offstage.

• *Hansel and Gretel* represents an excellent story with several songs and dances that can be portrayed through the means of puppetry. Other folk tales, nursery stories, and fairy tales can also be presented through puppet shows with a background of recorded music. Children in the class can compose short songs appropriate to the story portrayed.

• More able students can center research around such topics as musicians, music of a state or nation, festivals (Las Posadas—Mexico; Hanukkah—Jewish; Chinese New Year), and periods of history.

Music and History

As you study periods of history, have students explore the music that was popular at that time to further their understanding and interest in the study. Most teachers are familiar with the minuet and Virginia Reel, which were associated with colonial times, but other periods, too, offer excellent songs for singing and dancing that the students can learn.

> Revolutionary War: "Yankee Doodle"
> War of 1812: "The Star-Spangled Banner"
> Civil War: "Battle Hymn of the Republic," "When Johnny Comes Marching Home"
> World War I: "Hinky Dinky Parlee Voo," "Goodbye Sweetheart, Goodbye," "Tramp, Tramp, Tramp!" "Over There," "You're a Grand Old Flag"
> World War II: "God Bless America," "Don't Sit Under the Apple Tree with Anyone Else But Me," "Apple Blossom Time," "We'll Meet Again," "White Cliffs of Dover"

Illustrated Folk Songs

A number of folk songs from America's history have been prepared as children's books. Students will enjoy singing and following along with the words and illustrations in these books.

> *The Fox Went Out on a Chilly Night* by Peter Spier. Garden City, New York: Doubleday. (1-3)
> *Frog Went A-Courtin'* by John Langstaff; illustrations by Feodor Rojankovsky. New York: Harcourt Brace Jovanovich, 1955. (K-3)

Go Tell Aunt Rhody by Aliki. New York: Macmillan, 1974 (PS-2)

Old MacDonald Had a Farm, illustrations by Robert Quackenbush. Philadelphia: Lippincott.

One Wide River to Cross, adapted by Barbara Emberley; illustrations by Ed Emberley. Englewood Cliffs, New Jersey: Prentice-Hall, 1966.

10. Art in the Classroom

Art activities add zest to any classroom. Students enjoy the chance to create something satisfying, so introduce them to different media and experiences.

Art also enhances instruction across the curriculum as students paint murals, make notepaper for letterwriting, and construct dioramas for sharing books. Be sure that the art activities do meet specific objectives for art instruction as well as instruction in another area of the curriculum when you correlate subjects around a theme.

Most of the activities presented in this chapter can be adapted to different grade levels.

BEGINNING EXPERIMENTS IN ART

As we introduce art activities to children, it is important that we select processes that produce satisfying results. We want to build positive attitudes toward art and the feeling in each child that he or she *can* create something beautiful.

Presenting a Lesson

To make sure that each child will succeed, remember that a good lesson includes three parts:

> introduction (warm-up)
> performance (the art activity)
> follow-up (sharing, appreciation)

The introduction might be a film, a story, a picture, or a sample of the finished product. The purpose of this part of the lesson is to motivate the students, to make them begin thinking about ideas they can use, and to provide a sense of direction. The warm-up assures that students will know what they are going to do when you tell them to begin.

The activity itself needs to be well organized, with the steps outlined on the board if the process is complicated, Materials should be prepared in advance and passed to students or laid in an accessible place. Be sure, too, that students know what to do when they complete the activity.

Sharing the artistic efforts is perhaps the most important part of an activity, for therein lies the satisfaction. Work can be displayed for all to admire, or may simply be held up so others can see it before the student goes home. Showing what children have done is stimulating to others, who will discover other ideas that may be incorporated in their next art work.

Crayons

When you introduce the use of crayons for art, have students experiment to see what effects they can produce with a crayon, such as soft shading, strong outlining, or little dots of color.

• Scribble drawing always proves successful. Have students draw an open, loose scribble with a black crayon, touching all sides of a 9″ x 12″ sheet of paper. This initial scribble is then colored with bright contrasting colors for a bold, attractive effect. Sometimes a figure or design emerges in the scribble, so the student can color the spaces to bring it out more clearly.

Have students demonstrate different kinds of lines they can draw.

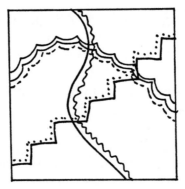

Then have each student select three different kinds of lines to use in dividing a sheet of paper. Each line must touch two sides of the page.

The students then build a design based on the lines drawn. Have the students use different colors to achieve contrasts.

• In resist painting, crayons are used to present a design or picture. After the picture is completed, a very watery tempera paint is washed over the entire sheet of paper. The waxy crayon resists the watercolor, which covers all areas that are not colored with crayon. You might suggest the following combinations:

black paint over a bright design
pale blue paint over an outdoor scene
light pink over a floral design
pale yellow over a dark design

Water-Soluble Paints

Use watercolors or washable tempera in the elementary classroom to avoid catastrophes! Water-soluble paints are also less expensive than oil-based paints.

What to Do with Colors

Teach students some basic techniques of working with colors as they begin using this *medium* (plural: *media*). They might try a series of experiments.

1. Select one color. Add a little white to the color. Then add more white. Each time white is added, make a color sample to record the change in color.

2. Try mixing colors. Begin with blue, and make a color sample. Then add a little bit of yellow. Mix, and make a color sample. Add more yellow, and mix. Make a color sample. (Do the same with red and yellow or blue and red.)

Have the students summarize their observations about working with paints:

1. Adding white to a color makes it become paler and paler.
2. Adding yellow to blue produces shades of green.

Texture in Painting

Have students experiment with adding different materials to tempera, such as coffee grounds, finely cracked nutshells, varnish or shellac, wheat paste, and soap flakes or detergent.

Dripping Paint

Students can achieve very exciting designs by dropping paint generously on wet paper so that it runs freely. Tilting the page in different ways causes the paint to mix in unexpected ways.

When designs are completed, lay them flat on newspaper to dry overnight. The designs can then be folded to form book covers or framed for attractive displays.

Applying Paint

We usually think of paint brushes for applying paint, but students might be able to suggest other ways of applying paint.

eye droppers
squeeze bottles
cotton swabs
spray guns
sticks
cotton balls
shoe polish applicators

Have students try different kinds of applicators to see the different effects that can be achieved.

Making Prints

Making different kinds of prints is intriguing. Even the youngest students can work at making prints with gadgets, while older students can advance to woodblocks and linoleum block printing. Variety can be achieved by using many kinds of printing materials and also by changing the type of cloth or paper on which prints are made.

Look at materials around you to assess their posibilities for making prints. Alert students to exploring with what they can find.

cork (mounted on wood)
potato (cut in patterns)
gadgets (glasses, lids, silverware, bottle opener)
rubber tubing or inner tube (mounted on wood)
sponge (cut in shapes)
styrofoam (carved in patterns)

First Printing Experiences

Have a number of objects handy with which students can experiment as they print for the first time. Use only a few colors so that students focus more on developing patterns with one color or seeing how pressure on the printer affects the appearance of the print.

Use thick tempera spread in foil piepans or waxed paper plates. Spread a double layer of newspaper over student desks or work tables to protect the area. You might have only six students printing at one time in order to control the amount of material needed and to decrease the movement of students while using paint and water.

Fingerprint Figures

A delightful kind of printing uses the students' own fingers as printers. Show them some of the possibilities for using the ball of different-sized fingers and the thumb as well as fingertips. Students can form charming animals and insects by adding lines with felt-tipped pens. These prints might be used to decorate notepaper or greeting cards.

Colored Chalks

Older students will have fun with colored chalk used in a variety of ways. Attractive designs and pictures can be drawn on 9" x 12" or 12" x 18" sheets of white paper. Use a large sponge to wet the paper liberally before using chalk for an especially striking effect. Wetting the paper also eliminates chalk dust.

Spray chalk pictures with a fixative (hairspray or a mixture of powered milk and water) to avoid smearing. The chalk drawing can then be used to decorate the classroom.

NOTE: White chalk used on varied colors of construction paper provides interesting seasonal variations. For Halloween, use white chalk on black paper to create a night scene bathed in moonlight. Use white chalk on blue paper for a snowy day featuring a snowman.

Fingerpainting

The whole hand is used in fingerpainting in a satisfying experience that involves movement and the feel of "squishy" paint between the fingers.

• To emphasize the feeling and movement of this painting experience, have each student work on his or her own desk first. Although no finished product remains because the paint is applied directly onto the desk, this approach is a valuable introduction to the use of fingerpaint. Have large sponges and detergent in warm water handy so students can wash their desks when the lesson is over. Students enjoy the scrubbing almost as much as the painting!

• For a longer-lasting product, use fingerpaint paper, which has a slick, water-resistant finish. Students can experiment with designs in one color, or choose two colors that blend to create a third (blue and yellow; red and blue; yellow and red).

To make inexpensive fingerpaint, you need:

3 cups laundry starch dissolved in one cup cold water
2 quarts boiling water
3 cups soap flakes or detergent
½ cup glycerine
powered or liquid tempera colors

Add the starch slowly to the hot water, stirring until the mixture clears. Cool. Add coloring (divide mixture for different colors). Add soap flakes or detergent (to assist in washability). Pour into jars with tight lids.

Uses for Student Art

To add to students' sense of achievement, plan varied uses for their art beyond that of taking it home to share with parents. Let students suggest ideas for making gifts or using art to decorate the classroom.

• Have students cut large letters from the sheets on which they have experimented to make bulletin board letters. If you plan a large display, each student might cut one letter for the caption from a 9" x 12" sheet of paper.

• Large fingerpaintings make excellent paper for covering older library books that could use a fresh look. Show students how to fold the paper around the book, how to miter corners as they fold the paper inside the cover, and how to apply a layer of paper to cover up the rough edges.

• Plan a bulletin board display that is like a quilt pattern. Let students plan a design by following a real pattern in a book or making up their own on graph paper. The students cut their designs (like cloth) and fasten them in place on a large sheet to create a "quilt."

ART THROUGH THE SCHOOL YEAR

Art experiences can result in decorative additions to the classroom, with each month suggesting themes for students to enjoy as they experiment with varied media. Here are ideas for the school year that feature holidays and seasons as a stimulus for exciting art experiences.

September

The first month of the school year is especially important as children begin to work in a new classroom. Enjoyable art activities will help make these first weeks more meaningful to students.

• Have students bring in mirrors to share as they look at themselves to begin drawing their own portraits, an excellent exercise in developing self-esteem, too.

Teach students a few basic facts about the proportions of a head and the placement of features. Students can begin by drawing a large oval.

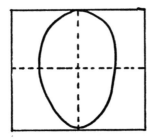

Frame the self-portraits and display them on the bulletin board so that students can get acquainted with each other. You might have students introduce themselves before hanging their portraits in the gallery.

• "What Did You Do This Summer?" is a common topic for a theme or picture, but children have written this same composition so many times that it is far from inspiring. Try some varied approaches to this topic.

Let each child contribute to a class collage depicting the activities of the summer. The collage can include ideas about boating, swimming, camping, sunbathing, traveling, places visited, and so on. Collages can also be done individuallly on a smaller scale.

Make a Crazy Quilt Mural with each child drawing a picture of *The Funniest Thing That Happened to Me.* The 9″ x 12″ sheets of drawing paper are placed side by side to fill a large bulletin board. Use bright rickrack to cover the "seams."

Write a story or poem with an accompanying illustration done in crayon covered by a wash of thin tempera. Use topics about summer activities like these:

A-Fishin' We Will Go
What Would You Have Done?
I Was the Winner
Just Imagine How I Felt

October

This month offers several themes—autumn colors, Halloween, Columbus Day, football. Plan with students the kinds of art activities that might add to learning and also make the room attractive.

• What can you do with a lovely leaf? Brainstorm ideas with students. Arrange brightly colored leaves between two layers of waxed paper. Press (between newspapers) with a warm iron to cause the sheets of waxed paper to adhere to the leaves and to each other. The leaves may then be cut out (leaving a wide margin of waxed paper) and hung mobile-fashion from the ceiling or a tree branch. These translucent leaves can also be taped to the glass windows where the light will enhance their beauty.

Glue (classroom paste will not hold) bright leaves on black construction paper. Cut around each leaf leaving a narrow strip of black showing around the leaf. Scatter these leaves on a bulletin board or use them to decorate the cover of a booklet about leaves.

Have each student prepare a page featuring the leaves of one tree including the seed pods, if possible. Several leaves of varied size are arranged attractively on the page, which is then sprayed or splattered with ink for a page of a class book on TREES WE KNOW. Each page might include information on the back about the growing habits of the tree identified. This same acitvity can be done for local plants other than trees, including interesting seeds and pods.

• Have students list all the words they associate with Halloween. Compile a class list on the board or a chart to help students spell these "scary" words:

witch	vampire
ghost	pumpkin
goblins	jack-o'-lantern

Torn paper ghosts are easily made by students of all ages. No scissors are allowed as bit by bit the ghost or goblin is shaped. Any size or shape is satisfactory; no two will be alike. Hang these goblins from the ceiling where they will dangle, fluttering with any movement of air, or mount them on windows and bulletin boards. Black cats and witches can also be made by this method.

Use orange crayon for pumpkins and white crayon or chalk for ghostly figures against black silhouettes of trees. When the crayon work is completed, wash the picture with thin black tempera.

Paint alternate stripes of white, orange, and black paint across a piece of 12″ x 18″ paper. Turn the paper so the colors drip into one another. When dry, this sheet can be used as a folder to contain stories or poetry about Halloween. It can also serve as a background for cut paper figures of various symbols of this holiday.

November

The last of the fall months reminds us of Thanksgiving and the harvesting of corn and wheat, orange and brown colors and the rusty reds of ripening apples, cooler weather, and the first frost.

• Have students cluster ideas around the word "harvest." They can write paragraphs about the meaning of harvest to display with the art ideas described here.

Use crayons to color shapes of fruit on a sheet of drawing paper. Talk about the varying shades of an apple or pear. After students have waxed (with crayon) each fruit heavily, they can use a thin tempera wash to create a lovely crayon resist.

Papier-mâché fruits can be made over crumpled newspaper centers. When thoroughly dry, students can paint the fruit realistically. Two members of the class can construct a papier-mâché cornucopia over a frame of chicken wire or stiff paper. The fruit can then be arranged spilling from the cornucopia.

Combine drama with art as children make simple Thanksgiving costumes—Pilgrim hats, brown sashes of crepe paper, Indian jewelry. Begin by having students list all the things for which they give thanks. The students might then construct a large collage entitled WE ARE THANKFUL, depicting the many things.

A scroll written on brown wrapping paper can also list the things for which the class is thankful. Have each student make an individual list with a small group of students making the class scroll—a compilation of all the lists. Decorations illustrating the ideas expressed can be added along the margin of the scroll. For the ends of the scroll, use dowel rods or rolled covers of a large magazine.

• Make turkeys out of varied materials. Use potatoes or apples and attach paper feathers and a head with toothpicks.

Paper plates folded in half can form the body for a handsome bird. Attach feathers at one end; cut duplicate heads from construction paper which are attached to both sides of the folded plate. Pipe cleaners make good feet.

Paper bags of varied sizes can be stuffed with paper to form plump turkey bodies. Add feathers and head cut from construction paper. Feet can be cut from corrugated cardboard.

December

The first month of winter suggests art related to the holidays of Christmas and Hanukkah, the first snow, holiday gifts, and vacation time.

• Children can make holiday greeting cards or gift cards. Cut 4½" x 12" construction paper to make folded cards of 4½" x 6". Students can use crayons or cut paper to decorate the front, and print original poems inside as a greeting.

Gift tags can be made by cutting 2″ x 6″ strips of construction paper and folding them into 2″ x 3″ cards.

Have students frame designs or pictures they have created. They might also illustrate or decorate a poem or a short story they wrote to share with parents as a special holiday present.

• Everyone enjoys adding decoration to an attractive evergreen. If a traditional tree is not available, have students create one with green paper branches attached to a large bulletin board, or use a large, dry branch to form a free-standing tree in a large can of sand or gravel.

Decorate small items such as pine cones, bottle caps, pieces of tile, and so on by dabbing spots of glue over their surface on which glitter can be sprinkled. Enamel can also be sprayed in a variety of colors to transform simple objects.

Let each child drip spots of bright tempera on a 9″ x 12″ sheet of drawing paper. The mixing colors produce lovely effects. When dry, this sheet is cut spirally beginning at one corner and continuing until the center is reached. The long strip of curved paper is wound loosely through the tree branches.

Crayon shavings pressed between waxed paper produce lovely paper for ornaments. Cut black or red paper into any irregular shapes or use the traditional shapes of bells, trees, stars, and holly leaves. Cut the center from each shape, which will act as a frame. Glue this frame to the waxed paper, which is then trimmed. (Two identical frames can be used together to hide the edges.) The tree lights will shine through the translucent paper with the crayon showing brightly.

Make an evergreen frame for a listing of "Merry Christmas Around the World."

Merry Christmas around the World

Joyeux Noel—France, Belgium, Switzerland
Kala Hrystoughena—Greece
Glaedelig Jul—Norway
Froeliche Weihnachten—Germany, Austria
Stretan Bozic—Yugoslavia
Buon Natale—Italy
Feliz Navidad—Spain, Mexico
God Jul—Sweden
Merry Christenmass—Scotland
Um Feliz Natal—Portugal
Nodlaig Mhaith Dhuit—Ireland
Boldog Karacsony Unnep—Hungary
Wesolych Swiat—Poland
Kung ho shen tan—Chinese
Vrolyk Kerstmis—Holland
S Rozhdestvom Christovom—Russia

January

The first month of the new year brings thoughts of calendars and New Year's resolutions. It is also wintry month of snow, skiing, and other winter sports.

• Talk about calendars and how our calendar came to be the way it is—the names of the months, the use of approximately thirty days for each of the twelve months, and the fact that other cultures have different calendars.

Create a classroom calendar on a large bulletin board on which you can feature student birthdays and information related to current events or history. Decorate the calendar with student art.

• Winter sports can be depicted in crayon with each child showing one sport—sledding, skating, skiing, hockey, iceboating, fishing through ice, making a snowman, snow sculpture. Wash the picture with thin blue tempera. Add touches of "snow" with cotton, dabs of white tempera, or imitation snow in a spray can.

• Snowflakes can be cut so that they have eight points, an easy fold for primary children. To obtain the more authentic six-pointed snowflake, first fold the paper into fourths; then fold the square into thirds, being careful to direct all folding toward the folded center.

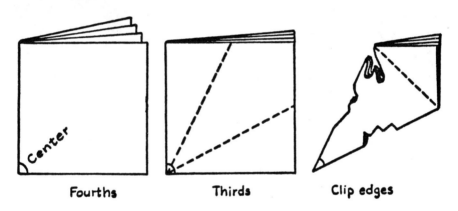

| Fourths | Thirds | Clip edges |

Use snowflakes to decorate the classroom by scattering them along the windows. Using varied sizes of paper will provide a range of very small to huge flakes. Students will also enjoy arranging their prettiest snowflakes on dark blue paper to create a lovely winter design. Snowflakes can be used to decorate greeting cards or notepaper.

February

February is known for the birthdays of many famous people—George Washington, Abraham Lincoln, Benjamin Franklin, Thomas Edison, and others. It is also the month to celebrate Black History Week and Valentine's Day.

• Challenge students to see what they can do with heart shapes. Show them how to cut hearts by folding the paper in half and cutting along the line. Then, invite the students to be creative. The results will be varied and interesting. Display openwork hearts on the windows where the light can shine through them.

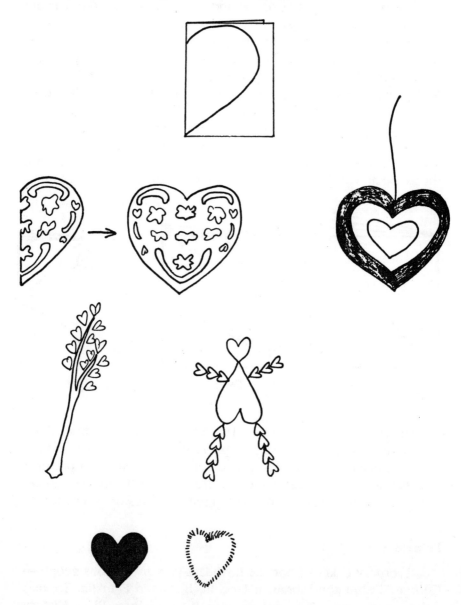

March

The first of the spring months, March is associated with wind and rain. We think of kites and the early daffodils, the signs of grass and crocus peeking through the last of the snow. St. Patrick's Day suggests shamrocks and lucky charms!

• Have students explore the uses of stenciling as they achieve interesting effects with the shamrock. Show them how to use the heart shape to create a shamrock.

Then they can create stencils that enable them to repeat the pattern in varied ways. Show students how to use both the inside of the stencil and the outside edge of the cut pattern.

• Introduce William Wordsworth's poem "Daffodils" to the class. Then show the students pictures of this lovely spring flower. Discuss the shape of the flower and draw a stylized pattern on the board. The students can creat such patterns for use with stencils or block prints.

DAFFODIL

• Students can use any of the preceding motifs to decorate thin paper for kites. Students will need lightweight sticks or firm cardboard to create cross supports, cloth for a tail, and, of course, string. Challenge students to create a kite that really flies!

April

April showers bring May flowers, spring bulbs, Easter bonnets, and sunny days. Many schools have spring vacations at this time.

• Have students make an egg tree. Let the students begin "blowing eggs" early, so that a number of whole shells are available (about two per student). The tree consists of a bare branch, big or small, which is held upright in a can of gravel. From the small branches decorated eggshells are suspended. The eggshells may be dyed with food coloring, or for an unusually lovely effect, dip the shells in enamel which has been dropped in small pans of water. The latter produces a beautiful marbleized effect.

• Young children will enjoy making large Easter eggs. On an 18″ x 24″ sheet of paper, each child crayons flower shapes, colorful lines,

or geometric designs. Then the sheet is *washed* with a thin pastel tempera—pink, blue, yellow, green. When the sheet has dried, the child cuts the paper in an egg shape. These large eggs can be displayed around the room.

• To make small Easter rabbits, use white paper candy bags stuffed with crumpled newspaper to form bodies for the rabbits. White construction paper ears (lined with pink) are attached to the head as are pipe cleaner whiskers. Use a large puff of cotton as a tail. Attach two strings to each rabbit to use them as puppets in creative dramatic activities.

May

May Day and Mother's Day suggest flowers and gifts, two ideas that may be combined.

• Have students list all the flowers they can think of as you write them on the board. Show students pictures of flowers to help extend their awareness of flower colors and shapes.

• Discuss flower shapes with the class. Have them invent flowers by experimenting with crayons to produce colorful flowerlike shapes using varied lines and colors. Add stems and interesting leaves to the flowers to achieve an overall floral design. When the students have completed the flowers, paint a yellow or pale green wash over the entire sheet, and use as a booklet cover or frame in black.

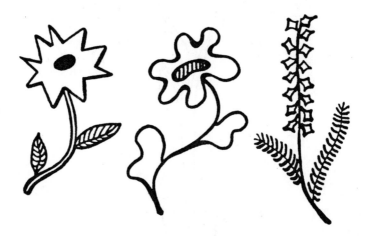

• Stitchery is another means of utilizing flower shapes as these designs are worked on burlap or other heavy cloth. Cut some flowers from bright cloth which is stitched to the backing. Other shapes can be developed with yarn and various threads. As a modern art form, stitchery produces attractive wall hangings and pictures that can be framed.

June

Nothing competes with the thought of summer during these last few weeks of school. Children might plan a gift for Father's Day or make something they could use themselves during the vacation months.

• Students can weave paper to create an attractive table mat or a wall hanging for someone they would like to remember. Use 12″ x 18″ pieces of construction paper. Direct students to cut lines across the paper as shown. From a second sheet of paper, they cut strips to "weave" into the "loom."

" Loom"

• Have students select a number of their own poems or favorites they would like to have in a small poetry anthology, a treasury of remembrances from the school year. Students can create a lovely cover by moving string through tempera between a folded sheet as described here:

> Dip the cord in liquid tempera. Lay the wet string on the right side of a 12″ x 18″ sheet of drawing paper. Fold the left side of the paper over the string. Holding the folded papers firmly (students may work in teams of two), withdraw the string, moving it back and forth as you pull from various angles. After the string has been removed, unfold the paper. A string dipped in a different color may then be used in the same manner.

ART ACROSS THE CURRICULUM

Art activities enhance studies in other areas of the curriculum. Collages and murals help students explore topics they are studying. Creating attractive covers for books, and illustrating their writing adds to the enjoyment of composing poetry and prose. Making dioramas and costumes adds interest to sharing books they are reading.

As art is used to enrich varied studies, it is important that the art processes and products remain worthwhile in themselves. Students can learn concepts about art and other media, and they can improve their skills as they create a mural that depicts, for example, the exploration of the West. We can help students become aware of art as part of the history or culture they are studying, and to consider the artistic aspects of mathematics and science.

SOCIAL STUDIES

In a humanities approach to studying history, art is an essential thread. Show students representative art from the colonial period in the United States, for instance, or point out the work of Native Americans as part of their cultures. Give students opportunities to explore varied media as they express their ideas through art activities.

Collage

A most fascinating activity that is highly versatile in the classroom is the collage, an abstract design that is often composed around a central theme. The design is developed by placing a variety of materials cut in different shapes and sizes on a backing (construction paper, cardboard, wood). These materials are arranged and rearranged as the student experiments with texture, color, balance, contrast, and interest. When he or she is satisfied with the arrangement, the elements of the collage are glued in place.

Words can be clipped from magazines and newspapers to be arranged in a collage. The collage can be simply a collection of words that are interesting to the collector, or the collection may be focused on a specific theme or study—Adjectives, French or Spanish words, Geographical Words, Words of Science, Number Words, Words of the West, and so on. The collages developed will include cut-out words trimmed in a variety of shapes as well as other pictures and materials that are appropriate to the theme of the words collected.

A collage on the theme AROUND THE WORLD WITH WORDS would include clipped words like: Rome, Africa, Singapore, London, Alaska, and so on (depending on the discoveries made) used in combination with portions of a pictured globe, maps, flags, means of transportation, newspapers (especially in foreign languages), a pair of chopsticks, and any other appropriate items.

Students can prepare a fascinating collage of clippings, pictures, symbols of events, portions of maps, colored paper scraps (for contrast), and materials suggesting geographic areas in the news. As a class project, this collage can be arranged on large mural paper with all students contributing time and material.

Individual collages can center around the activities of one person or position as well as a specific theme. Reading would provide background knowledge about the person or theme to suggest which symbolic items to include.

Calligraphy

Students can experiment with calligraphy to produce attractive posters for display. This proverb would be appropriate following a study of Native Americans.

Masks for Roleplay

Masks can be used for "acting out" activities as students roleplay situations. Students can "be" specific characters in history who are discussing events of their times.

• Large balloons can be used to form lightweight masks. Grease the balloon, adding strips of tape or newspaper dipped in wheat paste. After three or four layers of the paper have been applied and permitted to dry thoroughly, cut the sphere in half to make two masks. Features can be developed by adding papier-mache. The masks can then be painted, and yarn hair added.

• Large paper bags make effective masks for young students. Their heads and shoulders disappear into the bag as they speak through the openings cut for eyes, nose, and mouth.

• Paper plates provide the basis for easily constructed masks that are held in front of the face as the student speaks. Yarn hair can be sewn directly to the plate and features can be applied with crayons or paint. Three-dimensional effects are achieved by adding cut paper noses, eyelashes, hair, and ears.

Other Mask Uses

Masks can also be decoratively displayed in a classroom that is studying, for example, the Eskimo cultures. The classic film, "The Loon's Necklace" can be shown to motivate interest in mask forms and to provide excellent examples of a variety of masks. Here are suggestions for developing masks as art forms.

• Cut masks from black construction paper. Working with folded paper will produce a symmetrical design. Cuts can be made to form the eyes, markings on the face, and so on, which will show up clearly when the mask is mounted on white paper. Older students can use razor blades for making fine cuts in the facial area of the mask.

• Use white crayon or wax to cover a sheet of white drawing paper. Cover the resistant medium with thick black tempera which is etched (scraped away) to form a mask similar to the cut paper mask.

Develop a mask using bold, bright colors in crayon. Paint the mask and the area around it with black tempera; the entire background need not be covered, as the contrasting white is effective around the black paint.

Murals

Murals are particularly effective with broad social studies topics. Remember that planning is an important part of creating a good mural. Murals can be developed around such topics as:

The History of Our State
Clothing Through the Ages
Life in 1776
How Children Live in France
The Development of Transportation in the U.S.

• Divide the mural paper into squares, with each student assigned one square to complete. One or two students can sketch the drawing which is to be produced in mural dimensions; this drawing is also divided into squares so that each student can see what portion of the drawing will be represented in his or her square.

• After sketching a picture consisting of large simple shapes, have students paint each shape with thin glue on which are laid pieces of torn paper. Use varied shades of one color. Add interesting materials which may produce a three-dimensional effect or contrasts in texture such as curled strips of paper, straw, wood chips, dried leaves and stems, and so on.

• After a mural has been completed in crayon, apply a wash of an appropriate color to fill in the background.

• Stitch a mural on burlap with each child contributing time to various figures being developed. Use a combination of appliquéd cloth cut in various shapes and stitching done with yarn, string, and other threads.

Indian Art

Bring in books and pictures showing the art of various Indian tribes; books by Paul Goble are especially attractive. Have students investigate the symbols used for writing by these early Americans, and have them make a chart.

Indian Symbols

Bird   Deer Track   Bear Track   Friendship

Protection   Rattlesnake Jaw   Sun Rays   Rain

Medicine Man's Eye   Lightning   Days and Nights

Big Mountain   Man

The Color Wheel

Teach students different words for colors. Ask students who speak other languages to prepare a wheel like this to introduce classmates to their native language.

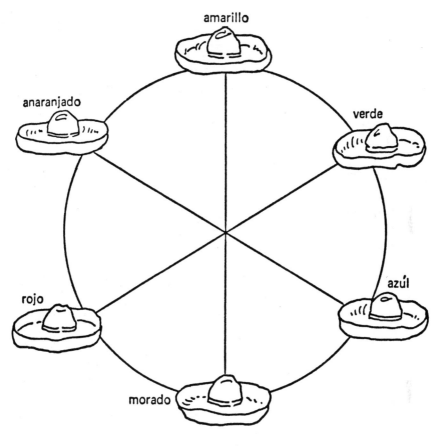

Los Colóres

SPANISH COLORS:

morado-purple   anaranjado-orange
azul—blue   rojo—red
verde-green   negro—black
amarillo—yellow   blanco—white

SCIENCE

Share examples of art related to science—exploration with light and color, beautiful pictures of plants and animals, enlargements of cells or crystals seen through the microscope. Point out to students the beauty of science—the symmetry of markings on a kitten, the pattern of the seeds in an apple, the coloring on a tropical fish.

Encourage students to use artful ways of working with ideas from science.

• A special cover lends status to a science report; yet these covers require little more time than do less imaginative covers. Try these previously discussed techniques for book covers:

Painting strips of color
Dropping colors which mix
Drawing string between folded paper
Tempera on wet paper
Crayon resists
Paint spraying
Prints with varied print blocks
Enamel drippings for glossy attractive designs

• Students who are interested in science fiction might map a world they imagine or one described in a book they have read. Students may choose to make a board game on which the map provides the background over which the players roam as they follow given directions. As students construct an imaginary world, they should think of the people and their ways of living, the climate and terrain of the land, the means of transportation, and the plants and animals that live there.

• Have students make Blotto Bugs. These bugs come in multi-colors, shapes, and sizes. Each student is given a large sheet of drawing paper. On the right half of the sheet are scattered a number of drops of paint (one color or several). The left half of the sheet is then folded over the right while the student presses the folded sheets gently to blot the paint. When the paper is unfolded (done immediately, before drying), a Blotto Bug will have been formed. Additional paint can be applied for a second folding, if desired. Feelers, antennae, eyes, and so on, can be added.

• Students of all ages will enjoy making potato print ladybugs. The prints can be used to decorate a strip along the wall or frame a display. First, have students cut the potato in half.

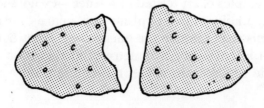

Then, cut holes (spots) and a groove (stripe).

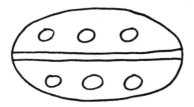

Use red tempera to print these red ladybugs on white paper. When dry, add black spots, legs, the stripe, and a head.

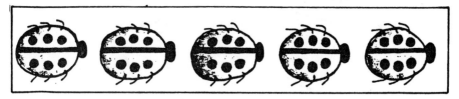

LANGUAGE ARTS

Speaking and listening skills can be developed through making and using puppets. Writing will have more purpose when students plan to publish their work in a variety of ways. Illustrating their work, decorating booklets of poetry, making gifts of writing—all are supportive of the art program as well as the language art curriculum.

Puppetry

Puppetry can consist of the simplest of devices, or it can designate the most complicated string marionette. Puppets can be used and reused in social studies scripts, sociodramas, reporting of books, etc., with only a few changes to make the puppet fit varied roles. Described here are several simple varieties of puppets which are successfully made and used in the classroom.

• Finger puppets are quickly and easily made by primary students but are enjoyd by older students, too. Roll a paper into a cylinder shape that is large enough to contain the index finger (other fingers are used, too). The head for the finger puppet may be cut from a magazine or drawn by the student; it should be on stiff paper that will remain erect when attached to the cylinder. Add yarn hair, eyes, ears, hats, collars, as desired. Arms can also be attached to the cylinder.

• Hand puppets are equally successful and can be quickly made from cloth or paper. Using a pattern like the one pictured here, cut two identical shapes from stiff paper, cotton cloth, or felt. The paper can be stapled together, but will not last as long as when the cloth is sewn together. Eyes, yarn hair, and simple clothing—scarves, aprons, belts, buttons—add to the fun.

• Inventing puppets is another outlet for creativity as students invent new types of puppets to make. Have them make puppets using such materials as bottle caps (bugs with legs painted with enamel) or walnut shells (wrinkled faces). Try some of these materials:

    peanuts in shells (animals with tails, ears, legs added)
    potatoes and other vegetables (animals suggested by shapes)
    wooden spoons (faces painted on back of spoon)
    paper bags (stuff with crumpled newspaper, add features)
    paper plates glued to sticks (add faces)
    squares of cloth (tie knots for head and two hands)

NOTE: No puppet stage? Puppets can be operated behind a reading table. Hang a blanket, sheet, or tablecloth over the front of the table to conceal puppeteers. Or operate puppets without a stage by simply holding them up as they talk; the audience will use its imagination.

Illustrating Poetry

Use the collage technique to share poems. Have each child select one poem (either original or by other poets); this poem can be copied and attached to one corner of the collage or mounted on the back for reference. The student examines the elements of the selection to determine the types of pictures, materials, etc., he or she can use in portraying the poem.

Edward Lear's poem, "The Owl and the Pussy-Cat," for example, contains many pictorial elements—owl, cat, green boat, money, guitar, honey, Bong-tree, pig, ring, shilling, turkey, mince, spoon, sand, moon, dancing—any or all of which can be incorporated in the collage. Some can be clipped from magazine illustrations; others can be drawn. Play money, a ring of wire, a plastic spoon, sand, and so on may also be used. Students can read their poems while showing the class the symbols they have used in their collage, or, students can first show the collage asking if anyone knows which poem is illustrated.

A color collage is suggested by this poem by Christina Rossetti:

What is pink? a rose is pink
By a fountain's brink.
What is red? a poppy's red
in its barley bed.
What is blue? the sky is blue
Where the clouds float thro'.
What is white? a swan is white.
Sailing in the light.
What is yellow? pears are yellow
Rich and ripe and mellow.
What is green? the grass is green
With small flowers between.
What is violet? clouds are violet
In the summer twilight.
What is orange? Why, an orange,
Just an orange!

Published Student Writing

Forms of publication should suit what has been written. Folders, booklets, and framed work to display on the wall stimulate students to think of innovative ways of presenting their work.

Long, slim books for poetry (Oriental design for Haiku)

Shapes of states or countries reported on (Cover and inside
   paper in same shape)
Scrolls for a story or a collection of original poetry
Folders which tie as in these examples:

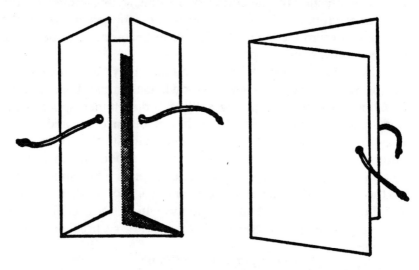

Writing folders made from painted paper techniques as here:

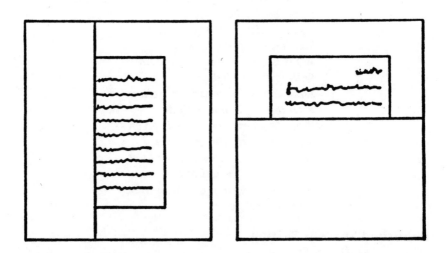

Responding to Books

Reading books offers many opportunities to use art processes.
Students can begin, for example, by sharing books with others.

• A collage of *McElligott's Pool* by Dr. Seuss (New York: Random House, 1947, K-3) would include many interesting fish shapes made from a variety of materials. Fish could be cut from foil, sandpaper, Christmas wrappings, magazine ads, or cloth. The boy could be cut from a magazine, while a thin bamboo strip could add a three-dimensional fishing pole. The student will think of other interesting elements to add—air bubbles cut from waxed paper, other underwater life, stones, etc.

• Let students advertise their favorite books by constructing miniature billboards. They will need to review printing techniques and the spacing and wording required for a poster.

• Mobiles can be used to depict any story, with the student cutting from paper (or other light materials) the figures or symbols appropriate to his or her story. Hang the figures from two stiff hanger wires that are tied with black thread to form an X which is suspended from the ceiling.

• Have each student construct a diorama picturing a dramatic scene from the book he or she is reviewing. Pipe cleaner figures can be made in proper proportion. Buildings, trees, landforms—all add to the telling of the scene being enacted. The making of the diorama serves as a Book Review.

• Give renewed life to old books by having students make jackets for books they have read. Use heavy paper on which the student can draw an illustration that will catch the eye of the next reader. A "blurb" can be printed on the inside flap with a "Word About the Author" on the other flap or on the back of the jacket.

• Have each student sketch the portrait of one of the characters in the book he or she has read. The student uses his or her imagination, guided somewhat by the description written by the author. These portraits can be framed and displayed with names indicated.

Bookmarks

The making of bookmarks stimulates interest in reading as each student makes his or her own bookmark and then uses it. Several simple varieties can be used.

Cut one corner from a discarded envelope to make a functional bookmark that slips over the upper corner of the book page. These markers can be decorated by pasting a cut paper shape over the point

of the corner, so the decoration projects beyond the edge of the book.

Another attractive bookmark that may be used as a Mother's Day gift is made from a strip of colored burlap which is decorated with yarn stitching to form a design. The edges may be painted to add interest.

A Book Party

Let the students of your class plan a BOOK PARTY with each one portraying a favorite character from a book. Each student can make simple costumes using paper, unbleached muslin, or discarded clothing items decorated appropriately with crayon. Have each child enact an interesting part of the book; several children may represent characters from the same book with all sharing in the same short presentation.

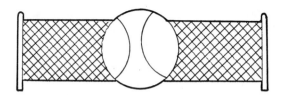

11. Games and Activities: Indoors and Outdoors

Students need activities that provide a change of pace from sedentary work, as well as offer exercise and a chance to be part of a team. Games and activities may take place in the classroom, although movement is more restricted; in the multipurpose room; or on the playground.

SEVENTH INNING STRETCH

Games that permit students to get out of their seats and to move around a bit are important to a good learning situation. Students who have been working on reading and writing activities may need five minutes of physical activity to provide a change of pace.

Calisthenics

A few minutes of fairly rigorous exercise is possible even in a crowded classroom. Ask students to stand beside their desks as they follow your directions:

Touch your toes three times.
Run in place (1 minute).
Stretch your hands as high as possible, then to the side and down.
Stand on tiptoe, then slowly lower yourself.
Put your hands on your waist, then slowly squat (3 times).
Touch your left toe with your right hand; reverse (5 times).

Simon Says

This old favorite offers good exercise for a whole class. The Leader (Simon) directs the students to perform. They perform only when the directions are preceded by the words, "Simon says…" Those who do the described action at the wrong time must be seated. Let different students be the Leader, competing to see who can seat the most people in five minutes. In this way, no one is seated for very long, and several students have a chance to be the Leader.

Weather Vane

This is a good way to combine exercise with learning the directions. The Weather Person calls, "The wind is blowing from the South." All must turn so their arms point North and South like a weather vane. If he or she calls, "The wind is blowing from the Northeast," all must turn with arms extending Northeast-Southwest. If there is a Tornado or Hurricane, all will spin around.

Birds Fly

Birds fly, but do dogs or goats fly? When the Leader says, "Robins fly," everyone flaps his or her wings, but when the Leader says, "Horses fly," they must not fly even though the Leader tries to fool them.

On Command

This calls for rapid moving of seats as the Leader says, "Everybody move one seat to the North," or "Move two seats to the West." The person at the outer edge in these exchanges moves to the end of the row or the opposite side of the room.

Eraser Tag

This is an active game in which two persons balance an eraser on their heads while one attempts to tag the other. The two players are sometimes named CAT and MOUSE. If the eraser falls or one player is caught, that player selects someone to take his or her place.

Batty Balloons

This is a game that involves everyone actively although all remain at their desks. Several inflated balloons are batted back and forth as two teams try to get them to selected goals. Teams may consist of alternate rows with rows 1, 3, and 5 playing against 2, 4, and 6 as one group of players tries to work the balloons to the back of the room while the other tries to bat balloons toward the front.

Musical Activities

A number of action songs provide opportunity for children to stand as they perform active motions to a song. Usually, songbooks include several which the class can learn together, and there are old favorites children can enjoy:

"Did You Ever See a Lassie?"
"Here We Go Round the Mulberry Bush"

Encourage students to write words to familiar tunes, making a point of including material that calls for action. Suggest such melodies as "The Battle Hymn of the Republic," "Ten Little Indians," "The Caisson Song," and "Home on the Range." For "Ten Little Indians," a student might compose the following type of song:

Hop a little, skip a little, turn all around;
Sway a little, bend a little, touch the ground.
Step a little, wave a little, jump with a bound.
Sit without a sound.

Relays

There are many variations of the relay race that work well in the classroom. These games may involve use of the chalkboard or pencil and paper, or they may call for individual action. In any case, the class is divided into several teams of six to eight members.

• "Word Building" requires each child on a team to add a letter to form a word. The first may begin by writing B on the chalkboard, with the second team member adding R, and the next E, and so on. Each must have a longer word in mind. The letters in each completed word are counted at the end of five minutes to determine each team's score.

• "The Scavenger Hunt" is scored by one person who collects information for his or her team. The Leader asks questions like these:

How many people have blue eyes?
How many are wearing something yellow?
How many are girls?
How many have a red pencil?

• "Pass the Ring" is a relay in which all remain in their seats as each team member passes a rubber canning ring (or a large jar lid) to the person behind him or her. The ring must not be touched by the hands but must be picked up with the student's pencil and passed to the next person's pencil without dropping. If dropped, the ring must be recovered by use of the pencil only.

• "Chain Reaction" focuses attention on words, with each child in turn writing a word on the board. If the first team member writes BLACK, for example, the next student must supply a word which begins with K (the last letter in BLACK). If that person writes KITE, then the next one must write a word beginning with E. The emphasis here is on speed. Score can be kept by giving five points to the team finishing first; four to the second, and so on, repeating the contest several times.

• "Follow Directions" can include a variety of actions. All students may, for instance, be requested to untie both shoes. (Those students not wearing tied shoes might be used as scorekeepers.) At the word GO, the first member of each team ties both his or her shoes and touches the shoulder of the next student, who then ties his or her shoes, and so on. Let students invent sets of directions like these:

1. Stand up; spell your first and last names backwards; then touch the next person's right hand.
2. Walk to the front of the room; clap your hands over your head three times; then touch the next person's shoulder.
3. Hop forward to a chair; sit down; repeat "Little Jack Horner"; hop to the last seat in your row.

• "What's Your Name?" requires the first team member to walk to the chalkboard where he or she writes the first and last name of some historical figure. The student then passes an eraser back to the last person in the row who comes up, erases the name from the board, and writes another. The team moves back one seat each time to make room for the player who has just written so he or she can pass the eraser back to the student who is now at the rear of the line.

RAINY DAY RECESS

Teachers need resources to provide for those days when students are unable to go outdoors. We begin here with pencil-and-paper games and move to more active types of games. Once students know a variety of such activities, they can operate more independently in selecting a Leader and getting started.

Games That Teach

Many enjoyable games teach concepts.

• Students enjoy playing "Hangman," a game that involves spelling skills. The Leader decides on a word and draws the "gallows" on the board.

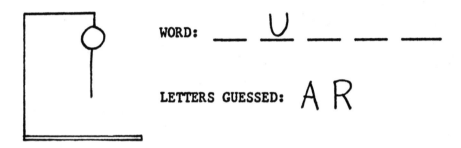

As students take turns guessing letters that might be in the word, the Leader writes wrong guesses on the board or inserts correct letters in place. For each wrong guess, a part of the body is drawn: head, body, two arms, two legs. Talk with students about how to play the game wisely as they share generalizations they have learned through playing, such as, "Every word contains a vowel" or "some letters—s, t, r—appear more frequently than others—b, q, w."

• "A, B, C—Geography!" can be either an oral or written game. For each letter of the alphabet, the student writes a sentence telling where he or she is going—LONDON—and what they plan to do there—LIFT THE CROWN JEWELS. The destination and the action must begin with the same letter. Begin with A, but permit students to skip letters which are difficult for them; they can come back to these later.

I am going to Australia to address a group of kangaroo keepers.
I am going to Boston to browse through historic mansions.
I am going to Chicago to chase gangsters.

• "What Can I Buy?" is a variation of "A, B, C—Geography!" Here, the student is given a destination such as LONDON and asked the question, "What can I buy there?" to which he or she answers as many items as possible, all of which must, in this case, begin with L— lipstick, lace, lilacs, limousines, limes, lighthouses, lollipops.

• "Who Am I?" is the question each student tries to answer. Pin a name of a famous person, a known character in a book, or a figure in history on the back of each student. Each in turn shows the class the name and stands before the class asking questions of specific people in the room such as, "Brad, am I a living American?" "Carol, was I known for writing a book?" Questions asked must require YES or NO answers. See who can identify his or her person through only a few questions.

Individual Activities

Many puzzles lend themselves to individual efforts which can later be shared. Prepare duplicated copies of such activities as crossword puzzles, word brackets, and word finds.

• "The Spotted Giraffe" (or any other animal) requires each student to add spots on the figure of a large giraffe which you have duplicated on sheets of white ditto paper. Before the class begins, you draw several large spots on one copy of the animal. Hang this copy before the class as they try to duplicate exactly the spots you have drawn (without leaving their desks). After a period of time, check the exactness of the spots drawn by laying each paper in turn over your copy held against the window.

• "Rebus" are fun to concoct as well as to unscramble. This type of riddle combiness pictures with letters and numbers. Duplicate several examples on a sheet of paper to acquaint students with this type of puzzle. Then encourage them to make some examples with which to challenge their classmates.

$$\text{☆} + MY - ST = (army)$$

$$ST + \text{◐} - B = (stall)$$

• The versatile game of "Categories" can be adapted to different subject areas or holiday themes.

	Animals	Plants	Names
H	hippo	hyacinth	Harriet
A			
L	lion		
L			
O		onion	
W			Walter
E			
E			
N			

• "Animal, Fish, or Fowl" is a game played by any number of students. The Leader calls the name of a student, then says one of the categories, FISH. He or she then counts rapidly from 1 to 10 trying to reach ten before the designated student can name a fish.

• "My Uncle Went to Bombay and brought me back a rocking chair (begin rocking motion)." The next student repeats, "My uncle went to Bombay and brought me back a rocking chair (begins rocking) and a fan (begins fanning also)." The next person repeats these words and motions and adds a third. All continue the motions until someone forgets something, or a new list may be started with each row of students.

• "Blindfolded Artists" stand before the chalkboard with chalk in hand. The Leader designates something they are to draw, such as a horse. As he or she calls out directions—"draw a body; draw a head; add two ears; put on a tail"—they draw a horse. The results are then admired by all!

Whole Group Games

Ask your class what whole group games they already know. You will be sure to hear some of these favorites:

Dog, Dog, Your Bone Is Gone
Simon Says
Seven Up

I See Something
Fruit Basket Upset
Buzz
Twenty Questions

Introduce new games to increase the group's repertoire from which to draw on a rainy day.

- "Poison" is played with a small wooden block or other object that is passed rapidly from desk to desk. No one wants to be caught with the block as the Leader counts to ten, turns around, and cries, "Poison!" The person on whose desk the block is lying at that time becomes the next Leader. No one gets out of his or her seat except the one who acts as the Leader.
- "Touch and Tag" requires the first person to touch an object in the room, perhaps the door, and then another class member. The person tagged must then tag the door and another object, perhaps the wastebasket, and then a third person. That person must touch the door, the wastebasket, another object, and a fourth person, and so on.
- "Cat and Dog Fight" involves two students who walk rapidly in chase around the room. As the dog chases the cat, the cat can save itself only by standing at the end of a row calling, "Meow, Meow, Meow." All the students in that row move up one position with the person at the head of the row becoming the DOG. The former DOG then becomes the CAT who is being chased.
- "Sherlock Holmes" is the child selected to leave the room. While he or she is gone, another child (or several) is selected to hide in the closet. Other children may change seats to confuse the detective. When Sherlock returns, he or she tries to name the person(s) missing within a given limit of time.
- "Who Stole the Peanuts From the Peanut Can?" is a provocative game in which each student is given a number in order starting with one. Number One acts as the Leader for the group in chanting and clapping the following rhythm:

```
   K   T      O    T    KTO
Who stole the peanuts from the peanut can?
T      K                          T        K    T    KTO
Number SIX (Leader chooses any number) stole the peanuts from the peanut
can.
   T   K
Who me? (Number SIX must answer without breaking the rhythm.)
```

T   O
YES, you! (Group responds in rhythm.)

T   K
Couldn't be! (SIX answers.)

T   O
Then, who? (Group questions.)

                                  T   K   T   K   T   KT
(SIX passes the chant.) Number ELEVEN stole the peanuts from the peanut
O
can. (Then number ELEVEN must answer, and so on.)

K = Slap knees
T = Clap hands together
O = Throw hands out after clapping

The object of this game is to keep the chanting and clapping going without a break; each person tries not to make mistakes so that he or she will move toward the Number One position. If a student is inattentive, he or she will not respond quickly, and the rhythm breaks. The one making the mistake moves to the last position, and everyone else moves up one seat. ALL THE NUMBERS of those who move up will change, which means that each student must be alert to remember new numbers. In beginning the chant, again ONE leads. This game can be played with students in rows, but it works even better if all are seated in a circle. (Have several students work out the directions for this activity, which they can then teach the rest of the class.)

• "I Spy!" involves the "hiding" of a small object (chalk, rubber eraser, small box) in a place where it can readily be seen without the movement of any concealing material. Five students are chosen to leave the room while one person places the object. As the five enter, they look around the room; if they spy the object, they simply sit down at their desks saying, "I Spy!" The others continue to search until all have found it. The person who hid the object may be designated to hint the location by saying, "You're cold," or "You're getting warmer." The student who first spied the object then hides it.

USING THE MULTIPURPOSE ROOM

If the multipurpose room is not being used, students might enjoy occasional recess periods there. Physical education can also be more formally taught during the day in this large area. Teachers who are working with dances from different cultures or teaching students marching skills may require more space in order to work more effectively. Several classes may use this room together as they play circle games or learn volleyball. In this section, we will explore physical activities that demand more space than that offered by the classroom.

Group Games

• "Pom, Pom Pullaway" is an exciting game for a large group. Divide the group in half with each half lining up at opposite sides of the room. One group is called to advance toward the other until the Leader calls, "Pom, Pom, Pullaway." At this signal, the advancing team turns to run back home. The other team runs forward to catch anybody they can; those caught join that team, then the action reverses.

• "Midnight" is a game in which the fox chases the sheep. The Fox's Den (there may be more than one fox) is at one corner of the room. The Sheep's Fold is located diagonally across the room. The Fox and Sheep all go out walking. The sheep repeatedly ask the fox what time it is as they advance closer. The Fox answers, "It's five o'clock," or "It's eight o'clock." When he or she replies, "It's MIDNIGHT!" the sheep run home as the Fox tries to catch them. Those caught are taken back to the Fox's Den.

NOTE: To distinguish one team from another, or the persons who are chasing the group, as in MIDNIGHT, prepare a number of brightly colored sashes of inexpensive cotton cloth that can be tied on players to identify them.

• "Three Deep" (or "Two Deep") is played with groups of three students who stand behind each other with these groups forming a circle. Two players are designated the CAT and RAT (or other titles) who chase each other. The RAT who is being chased can save him- or herself by stepping in front of a group so that the last one of the three must leave. The displaced student must then become the CAT who chases the former CAT.

Tumbling

Mats or inexpensive mattresses are worthwhile additions to equipment for physical education where indoor activity is essential. Students enjoy a variety of simple tumbling activities as well as gymnastics.

Forward roll from a squatting position
Forward roll from a standing position
Backward roll
Cartwheel
Headstand
Tip-up (from squatting position raise body above hands)
Pyramids

• "Indian Wrestling" is started from a prone position with two persons lying side by side with their heads at opposite ends. At a signal, both players raise the leg nearest the opponent and lock it around that of his or her opponent. Without moving from the flat position, they try to turn each other over.

• "Oriental Pushups" are fun both outdoors and in the multipurpose room. Two players sit on the floor or grass back-to-back with arms locked. At a signal, they push against each other trying to stand up. With practice and cooperation, they learn to achieve this tricky feat.

Challenging Competition

Contests add to the excitement and interest of familiar activities. Competitions can be arranged with a small committee keeping scores and conducting the contest for several days. Here are suggestions for competitions:

Who can bounce the ball the most consecutive times?
Who can jump rope individually the most times without missing?
Who can throw a ball (any specified size) the farthest?
Who can run a certain distance the fastest?
Who can broad jump the farthest?

Include such group competitions as a hopping marathon (5 in a group), relay races (teams of 6-8), tumbling performances, and rope jumping.

Relay Teams

Relays are probably used more than any other type of team game, both indoor and outdoor. Students will continue to enjoy them as long as ample variety is ensured. Here is a list of different activities that can be done relay fashion:

Dribble a ball around a specified goal and back
Run while holding ankles
Duck waddle (squatting)
Crab walk (squatting, then tipped back with hands on ground)
Camel walk (walking on hands and feet with knees straight)
Skip, gallop, hop, walk backward
Obstacles around which to run, hurdles to jump or scale
Dribble a basketball and shoot a basket
Hand ball over one player's head and under legs of next
Cartwheels
Three-legged race
Wheelbarrow
Elephant walk (one person atop the toes of another)
Caterpillar (hands on floor, feet inch up to meet hands)

Physical Fitness

Physical fitness tests place stress on the development of physical skill through the use of charts listing varied skills in which each student tries to achieve at least minimum ability. Include some of the following:

Running in place
Regular and modified pushups
Touching toes with both hands
Turning somersaults (backwards and forwards)
Jumping rope
Ball throwing
Knee bends

Marching in Formation

Marching and drilling are of interest to most students. The class can begin with simple marching skills—attention, mark time, keeping time while moving. They can learn to respond to the Halt command by allowing two beats after the command and to get back in step with the group by skipping. After these basic skills are acquired, you can add Right Face, Left Face, Address Right, and Address Left and students can learn to pivot while making a turn.

Have the group march around the outer edge of the room; then direct them to come down the center in twos and then in fours. (You may use this technique for readying the group for relays.) Marching is another good beginning activity for a physical education period.

Lined up at attention, the group can Address Right and count off to break into groups for a game.

Ball Games

• Volleyball is an excellent indoor sport that permits the whole class to participate. Younger students succeed well with a variation which requires the catching of the ball. The person catching the ball immediately puts it back into play without the use of a special serve. Assists are permitted as needed.

• Kickball can be played indoors. This game can also be varied with the batter catching the pitched ball and throwing it rather than kicking it. The rules are the same as those for softball. Rules for games may be obtained from:

> The Athletic Institute
> 209 South State Street
> Chicago, Illinois 60604

• Variations of basketball can be played with a mixed group. Divide the group into two teams. Each team passes the ball ten times (or any specified number). The team possessing the ball tries to score one point by passing without interception. If they succeed, the ball is then given to the other side who tries to complete ten passes for a point.

For practice in shooting baskets, divide the group according to the number of baskets available. Each group lines up before a basket. The first person bounces the ball, approaches the basket, shoots, catches the ball, bounces it to the next person, and goes to the end of the line. This shooting practice moves quickly so that each person has a number of turns.

• "Medic" is appropriate for the upper elementary grades. Each of two teams occupies one half of the playing area. One player on each team is designated as the Medic. The game is somewhat similar to Bombardment: 8 to 10 balls are placed on the center line and, upon hearing the whistle, all individuals rush to gain possession of the balls.

The object of the game is to eliminate opponents by throwing balls at them and hitting them below the waist. A player must sit down immediately on the floor in the playing area when hit. A hit must be direct and not from a floor bounce or wall ricochet. A player possessing a ball can deflect another ball by permitting the oncoming ball to bounce off his or her own ball. If a player catches a ball thrown at him or her, the thrower sits down. The catcher of the ball remains "alive" and in the game.

During the game, the Medic remains behind the baseline to assist his or her "downed" teammates. He or she cautiously advances to a "stricken" member out in the playing area and walks this person back to the baseline. If the Medic is successful, the rescued member can engage in the game again. If hit, the Medic must go behind the opponents' baseline as a prisoner. The Medic can be reclaimed by his or her team only if he or she catches a ball thrown by a teammate from midcourt.

The referee stops the game at the end of a specified period of time. The team with the least number of casualties sitting on the floor is declared the winner.

• In "Four-Corner Relay," divide the class into four squads, each occupying a corner of the gymnasium. A one-foot square is marked off on the floor about six feet out from each corner.

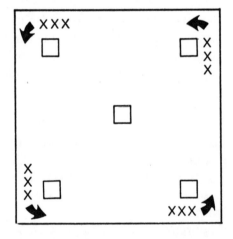

Each squad leader has three Indian clubs and, upon a starting signal, runs around the gymnasium and places a club in each square except his or her own. Upon returning home, the leader tags the next teammate, who runs around the gymnasium and picks up a club from each of the squares other than his or her own. This process continues on an alternating basis until every team member has had a turn either placing or picking up clubs. A runner responsible for any clubs falling down must return to those squares and reset the clubs. The squad finishing first is the winner.

Dancing and Rhythms

Musical activities can be done in lines, circles, or with partners. At least one set of records should be purchased for use in teaching students folk dances. Select a set that includes some of the following:

"Gustaf's Skoal"	"Schottische"
"Virginia Reel"	"Varsovienne"
"Oh, Johnny"	"Minuet"
"Sicilian Circle"	"Hansel and Gretel"
"Patty Cake Polka"	"La Raspa"

Greek line dances are good ways of demonstrating to students that dancing is done and enjoyed by everyone, whether male or female. Invite members of the school community to share their knowledge of dancing with your class. This invitation will make sure that cultures represented in your community are acknowledged by you and your students.

A Dance Festival

After your students have learned a few dances well, invite the members of another class to join you in the multipurpose room. Your class can demonstrate a dance and then teach students from the other class to dance with them. This effort can spread room by room until everyone knows a number of dances.

Plan a Dance Festival, perhaps for an evening performance for parents. Have one or two classes demonstrate specific dances they have learned. Older and younger students can dance together, fun for both age groups.

GOING OUTDOORS

Whenever possible, students should have a chance to play outdoors. Brief recess activities and fresh air provide a healthy change of pace from sedentary classroom work. Students also need opportunities to socialize with other students as they play team sports and have fun together. We begin with a variety of group games that can also be played in the multipurpose room. Activities for snowy days are suggested, as well as ways of stimulating student interest in developing skills.

Favorite Group Games

Students should develop a number of games that they all know how to play. They may decide in the classroom to play, for example, "Bull in the Pen," choosing the first bull and the location for the game while still in class, so no time is wasted in getting started. Occasionally, introduce a new game to the students.

• "Bull in the Pen" calls for one player, the BULL, to be encircled by the class who lock their arms tightly. The BULL charges and tries to break through the pen. If he or she succeeds in getting free, the student runs away with all running after him or her to catch the BULL.

• "Red Light, Green Light" is a well-known game which can be played by any number of children. The group spreads out along a line while the Leader closes his or her eyes and counts to ten, then calls quickly, "Red Light!" Anyone caught moving against the Red Light must return to the starting point. The first child to safely reach the Leader is the winner.

• "Tag" has been a favorite game in varied forms for ages. Introduce students to variations of this versatile activity which includes any number of players.

Stoop tag (you're safe if stooping)
Stork tag (you're safe if standing on one leg)
Statues (you're safe if kneeling with outstretched arms)
Link tag (several children link arms with the two end people able to tag)
Chinese tag (person tagged must hold his or her right hand on place tagged)
Frozen tag (person tagged is frozen in position until a free player touches him or her)
Hop tag (all players hop)
Shadow tag (IT tries to step on shadow of player)

• "Balloon Breakers" necessitates a balloon for each child. The inflated balloon is attached by string to the right ankle. Each student tries to break the balloon of another student while still protecting his or her own. The winner is the person who has an unbroken balloon.

• "Come With Me" is a good game for younger children. One child skips around the outer edge of the circle. He or she tags someone saying, "Come skip with me." They hold hands and skip around. The first child then takes a place in the circle while the second one invites the next child to join him or her, "Come hop with me." The game continues in this way around the circle with each child getting a turn using varied movements.

Hopscotch

Hopscotch is an old game that still delights children today. The court is usually drawn with a stick in the dry earth, but it can also be painted on blacktop outside or on the floor of the multipurpose room.

John Kautz of Davenport, Iowa offers the following information for hopscotch. The play consists of tossing the puck into the areas of the court, following a definite order of progression. Holding the puck in one hand, a player stands on one foot in hopping position behind the baseline of the court.

The first player tosses the puck into the area marked 1 and then hops into this square without putting the other foot down or stepping on a line, picks up the puck, and hops out again. The puck is then tossed into the area marked 2, and this time the player must first hop into 1 and then into 2. Again, the player picks up the puck and retraces the course outward by hopping to 1 and then hopping beyond the baseline.

This continues, with each space taken in order, until the player either fails to toss the puck into the proper space or violates the hopping rule. When this happens, the next participant proceeds as described until a rule is violated. When the player's turn comes about again, he or she begins in the space in which he or she previously failed. The first player to hop successfully into all the spaces and return in the prescribed method wins.

A player loses his or her turn under the following conditions:

If he or she tosses the puck while not in proper hopping position behind the baseline. (Leaning over the baseline is permitted.)

If the puck, on toss, does not come to rest entirely within the designated space and touches any part of a court line.

If the puck, on kick, passes out of the court over a side line rather than the baseline.

If the puck, on kick, comes to rest on any part of a court line.

If the player's foot touches any court line.

If a player is guilty of any other irregularity in the progression.

Using this hopscotch pattern, try these variations in playing the game.

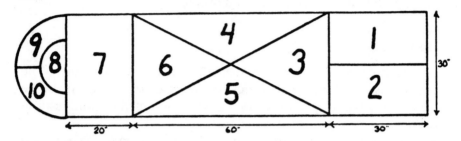

Stunt 1: Toss or drop puck into square 1. Hop into square 1. Take any number of hops in square without touching any line with any part of body. Kick puck out of square over and beyond baseline. Finally, hop out of square over and beyond baseline. Do not step out. If no error is made, proceed to Stunt 2.

Stunt 2: From starting position, toss puck into square 2. Hop into square 1 and then into square 2. Take any number of hops and kick puck directly out beyond baseline.

Stunt 3: From starting position, toss puck into triangle 3. From this position, stand on one foot and leap into squares 1 and 2. Land with right foot in 1 and left foot in 2 at the same instant. Jump from both feet and land on either foot in triangle 3.

When ready, after pushing or sliding puck with hopping foot, kick puck toward or beyond baseline. If it stops in a square of a smaller number without resting on a line, it must be retrieved as follows:

> Return by leaping into squares 1 and 2 with right foot in 2 and left foot in 1 at the same time.
> If puck has reached only one of these squares, raise either foot and, while hopping, kick puck out.
> Hop beyond baseline.

Stunt 4: From starting position, toss puck into triangle 4. Advance as in stunt 3 to triangle 3 and hop into triangle 4. Retrieve puck as in stunt 3. Hop into 3 and return as in stunt 3.

Stunt 5: From starting position, toss puck into triangle 5. Advance as in stunt 4 and hop straight into 5. Retrieve puck and return as before.

Stunt 6: From starting position, toss puck into triangle 6. Advance as in stunt 3 to number 3. Learn to alight with right foot in triangle 4 and left foot in triangle 5 at the same time. Jump from both feet to land on one foot in triangle 6.

Retrieve puck as before. Return by leaping to alight with right foot in 5 and left foot in 4 at the same time. Jump into 3 with one foot only. Leap into 2 and 1 with right foot in 2 and left foot in 1 at the same time. Jump out beyond baseline to land on one foot.

Stunt 7: From starting position, toss puck into rectangle 7. Advance as in stunt 6 and leap to land on both feet at the same time in 7. Walk about in 7, moving puck with foot or feet only until in position to retrieve it by kicking it out over the baseline or into space of a smaller number.

Stunt 8: From starting position, toss puck into semicircle 8. Advance as before to 7. When ready to progress to space 8, raise either foot and hop out of rectangle into semicircle 8, landing on one foot. Retrieve as before. Return by leaping to land on both feet at the same time in rectangle 7. When ready, proceed as in stunt 7.

Stunt 9: From starting position, toss puck into arc 9. Advance as in 8. Retrieve while in hopping position in semicircle by picking up the puck by hand from 9. Return as in stunt 8, carrying puck in hand.

Stunt 10: From starting position, toss puck into arc 10. Advance as in stunt 9 and hop into arc 10. Retrive as in stunt 9. Hop into semicircle 8 and return as before. Stop for a few seconds' rest in space 7 if desired.

Stunt 11: From starting position, without tossing or carrying puck, advance as in stunt 8 to semicircle. Leap to land on both feet at the same time with right foot in arc 9 and left foot in arc 10. About-face and reverse position of feet by leaping into a half-turn. Return by jumping to land on one foot in semicircle and continue out according to stunt 8.

Using this hopscotch pattern, try these variations.

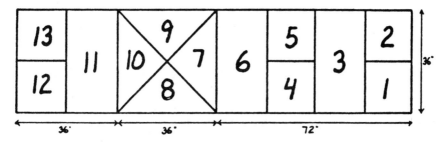

In returning, after the player reaches space 3, he or she may be required to hop and land so the right foot is in space 1 and left foot in space 2. Likewise, when in space 6, the player must land so the right foot is in 4 and the left foot in 5 at the same time. When jumping from space 3, the player must land with one foot in 1 and the other in 2.

In other words, whenever there are two spaces side by side in returning, these spaces must be taken simultaneously, with one foot in each space.

Jumping Rope

Provide both short ropes for individual students and long ropes for group jumping activities that accommodate as many students as possible who want to participate.

Let students share their knowledge of rope activities, and have them try the following:

Touch ground with hands on alternate jumps.
Sparrow hop (jump in bent position).
Jump on all fours.
Two people hold hands and jump together.
Jump in air and touch toes with fingers.
Climb the ladder (jump toward one end and back).

• "High Water" requires student to try jumping over the rope as it is raised higher and higher. When no one can succeed in jumping over the rope, the game begins again.

• "Hot Pepper" requires students to jump as fast as the turners can turn the rope.

• Students can learn to turn two ropes at once. The ropes turn toward the center alternately. Students can learn to time their entry just right as they jump "double dutch".

• Ask students to share jumping songs they know, for example:

Teddy Bear, Teddy Bear,
Turn around.
Teddy Bear, Teddy Bear,
Touch the ground.

Not last night but the night before,
Twenty-four burglars at my door.
I went downstairs to let them in;
They hit me over the head
With a rolling pin!

Fun in the Snow

On cold days, have playground activities that keep your students moving. These can range from whole group activities to individual or small group activities. Remember to check that children are adequately clothed for such outdoor recesses.

• "Fox and Geese" is a must after a fresh fall of snow. The game can quickly be organized if the group follows a Leader who leads them in a large circle. After circling several times to tramp the path well, the Leader can crisscross the circle a number of times to make more paths. A FOX is then selected to chase the GEESE.

• "Snow Sculpture" is a challenging activity for large or small groups. All can work on one large sculptured animal or small groups can develop varied selections. Each classroom can work on one project with a date set for judging THE MOST BEAUTIFUL, THE MOST IMAGINATIVE, etc.

• "A Snowman Army" can be made in areas of heavy snow. Let students work in teams of two or three to construct snowmen in one part of the playground. See how many can be made in one recess period; add to the army as long as the snow and interest last.

• "Follow the Leader" enables the whole group to participate. The Leader can invent a variety of movements to provide exercise.

Hopping, skipping, jumping, galloping
Walking backward; sliding sideward
Winding in toward the center of the circle and out again
Running around an obstacle
Walking by twos, fours
Duck waddle; camel walk
Touching toes three times

• "Snowballing Targets" provides a workout for students' pitching arms as they throw snowballs. If large cardboard targets (similar to those used in archery) are provided, students can compete individually or as teams to see who is the most accurate. Other types of targets can be used—tin cans set along a board supported by wooden horses or a large cowbell hung from an upright support. Measure off 20 feet (adjust to the group's abilities) to mark a place where each participant stands for throwing.

An All-School Play Day

Involve students and parents in planning an all-school Play Day. Activities may be divided into several areas to provide for differences in physical maturity. A variety of contests and activities can be scheduled with each classroom being responsible for one activity. It is helpful if entrants for all events are signed up ahead of time, with each child entering something and the number of entries being limited for any one individual. Listed here are some activities that might be included.

Contests—Running, jumping, throwing (several entrants from each classroom)
Races—Wheelbarrow, three-legged, backward, distances
Relays (selected team representing each room)
Scavenger Hunt (each room as a team)

The room amassing the most points can be awarded a prize that all can share. Make a "gold cup" by inverting a plastic bottle and attaching paper handles. Mount on a block of wood, spray with gold paint, and fill with wrapped candy.

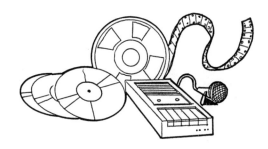

12. Resources for Teaching

Teachers are always looking for new materials and different ideas to spark their teaching. In this chapter are listed a number of resources that will assist the busy teacher.

The directory of publishers' addresses will facilitate your ordering of resources that interest you. When ordering anything, always request a copy of the latest catalog or list of materials published to help you keep up to date.

BOOKS TO EXPLORE

A potpourri of books are recommended for your purchase. Since book prices constantly change, write to the publisher to ask the current price so that you can order items prepaid. This usually saves on handling charges.

Adventuring with Books: A Booklist for Preschool—Grade 6 by Mary Lou White, editor (National Council of Teachers of English, paperback).

Anchor: A Handbook of Vocabulary Discovery Techniques for the Classroom Teacher by Mary E. Platts (Educational Services, paperback). Vocabulary development for the intermediate grades.

Celebrating America by Sharon Belshaw and Candy Carter (Contemporary Press, paperback). A student activity book for reading, language arts, and social studies; integrates American history with language arts.

Change for Children by Sandra Kaplan, JoAnn Kaplan, Sheila Madsen, and Bette Taylor (Goodyear, paperback). Ideas for individualized learning centers.

Children's Literature: Strategies of Teaching by Robert Whitehead (Prentice-Hall). Activities for using books in the classroom.

Content and Craft by Dorothy G. Hennings (Prentice-Hall). Suggestions for working with language arts.

Creative Teaching of the Language Arts in the Elementary School by James A. Smith (Allyn & Bacon, paperback). Creative approaches to speaking, listening, and writing.

Creative Writing Ideas by Sidney and Iris Tiedt (Contemporary Press, paperback). A variety of provocative ideas for stimulating student writing.

Do You Know What Day Tomorrow Is? A Teacher's Almanac by Lee Bennett Hopkins and Misha Arenstein (Citation Press). An almanac of historical events.

Exciting Reading Activities by Sidney and Iris Tiedt (Contemporary Press, paperback). Practical ideas for inspiring students.

Exploring Books with Children by Iris Tiedt (Houghton Mifflin). Ways for using literature in the K-8 grades.

Hooked on Books: Program and Proof by Daniel Fader and Elton McNeil (Berkley Medallion, paperback). Motivating reluctant readers.

Ideas for Teaching English in the Junior High and Middle School by Candy Carter and Zora M. Rishkis, editors (National Council of Teachers of English, looseleaf binder).

Language Arts Activities for the Classroom by Sidney and Iris Tiedt (Allyn & Bacon). Describes all aspects of language arts instruction for K-8 classrooms.

The Language Arts Handbook by Iris Tiedt (Prentice-Hall). An integrated approach to teaching listening, speaking, reading, writing and thinking.

Language Experience Activities by Roach Van Allen and Claryce Allen (Houghton Mifflin, paperback). Resources for creating learning centers.

The Listening Activity Book by Charlene W. Smith (Fearon, paperback). Teaching literal, evaluative, and critical listening in the elementary school.

The Magic If: Stanislavski for Children by Elizabeth Y. Kelly (National Education Press). Imagination exercises for children as a prelude to acting.

Multicultural Teaching by Pamela and Iris Tiedt (Allyn & Bacon). A 353-page handbook of activities, information and resources for introducing concepts across the curriculum.

Pass the Poetry, Please by Lee Bennett Hopkins (Citation, paperback).
More ideas about teaching poetry.

Poetic Composition Through the Grades: A Language Sensitivity Program by Robert A. Wolsch (Teachers College Press, paperback).
Helping students express themselves through poetry.

Poetry and the Child by Flora J. Arnstein (Dover, paperback). Awakening children's ability to write poetry.

Reading Activities for Child Involvement by Evelyn Spache (Allyn & Bacon, paperback). Variety of teaching strategies for developing reading skills.

Reading Aids Through the Grades by Anne Marie Mueser (Teachers College Press, paperback). Presents individualized reading activities for beginning and advanced readers.

Reading Games by Iris M. Tiedt (Contemporary Press, paperback). Games for learning centers and individualized reading programs.

Reading Ladders for Human Relations, 6th edition, edited by Eileen Tway (National Council of Teachers of English, paperback). An extensive annotated listing of books for developing self-esteem and appreciating our diverse cultures.

Reading Strategies by Iris M. Tiedt (Contemporary Press, paperback). Ideas for stimulating reluctant readers and teaching specific skills based on psycholinguistics, Cloze techniques, USSR.

Rose, Where Did You Get That Red? by Kenneth Koch (Random House). Teaching classic poems as models for student writing.

Round-the-Year Puzzlers by Frank and Letha Smith (Contemporary Press, paperback). Activities that add excitement and enjoyment to learning.

Sets of Task Cards (Contemporary Press). (1) Basic Reading Skills: A set of Big Task Cards; (2) Basic Grammar Concepts: A Set of Big Task Cards; (3) Basic Writing Skills: A Set of Big Task Cards; (4) Basic Spelling Skills: A Set of Big Task Cards. Useful large cards for the learning center; helpful directions included.

Slithery Snakes and Other Aids to Children's Writing by Walter T. Petty (Meredith, paperback). Stimulating creative writing.

Smiles, Nods, and Pauses by Dorothy Grant Hennings (Citation). Ideas about teaching writing.

Sparking Words: Three Hundred and Fifteen Practical and Creative Writing Ideas (National Council of Teachers of English, paperback).

Spelling Strategies by Iris M. Tiedt (Contemporary Press, paperback). Activities to get students interested in spelling.

Spice: A Handbook of Classroom Ideas to Motivate the Teaching of Primary Language Arts by Mary E. Platts (Educational Services, paperback). Teaching basic reading skills to primary students.

Tabletop Theatres and Plays by Louise Cochrane (Plays, Inc.). Detailed instructions for constructing theaters and puppets; plays included.

Teaching Human Beings: 101 Subversive Activities for the Classroom by Jeffrey Schrank (Beacon, paperback). Exciting ideas to promote creativity and thoughtful discussion.

Teaching Writing in K-8 Classrooms: The Time Has Come by Iris Tiedt, et al (Prentice-Hall). A composition program described step-by-step by classroom teachers.

TRIP (Theory and Research into Practice) series by various authors (ERIC Clearinghouse on Reading and Communication Skills, paperback). (1) Beginning Reader's Theatre: A Primer for Classroom Performance; (2) Communicating with the Elderly: Shattering Stereotypes; (3) Communication Games and Simulations; (4) Contract Grading in Speech Communication Courses; (5) Development of Functional Communication Competencies K-6; (6) Group Inquiry Techniques for Teaching Writing; (7) Individualized Writing in the Elementary Classroom; (8) Instruction In and About Small Group Discussion; (9) Instruction in Conflict Resolution; (10) Intercultural Communication; (11) Introduction to Film Making; (12) A Learning Center Approach to Basic Communication Courses; (13) Learning to Spell; (14) Listening Instruction; (15) Mainstreaming and the Non-English Speaking Student; (16) Nonverbal Communication in the Elementary Classroom; (17) Observing and Writing; (18) Perception and Communication; (19) Quiet Children in the Classroom; (20) Structuring Reading Activities for English Classes; (21) Teaching Interviewing for Career Preparation; (22) Theater Games: One Way into Drama; (23) Writing About Ourselves and Others.

Values Clarification: A Handbook of Practical Strategies for Teachers and Students by Sidney Simon, et al (Hart, paperback). An outstanding collection of ideas to help children become aware of value and attitudes.

Wishes, Lies, and Dreams by Kenneth Koch (Vintage, paperback). Great ideas for motivating the writing of poetry.

Workjobs by Mary Lorton (Addison-Wesley, paperback). Ideas for the individualized classroom.

The Workshop Way by Grace H. Pilon (Xavier University, paperback). Motivating student learning through a new approach.

Writing Aids Through the Grades by Ruth K. Carlson (Teachers College Press, paperback). A variety of ways to stimulate student writing.

Writing Ideas by Beverly and Frank Deen (Contemporary Press, paperback). Good ideas for the learning center.

BOOKS FOR YOUNG STUDENTS

The following is a list of the latest Caldecott Award winners. Judged outstanding in terms of illustrations, these books are appropriate for preschool and primary grade children.

1978

Peter Spier, illus. *Noah's Ark* translated by Peter Spier. Doubleday.

Honor Book:

Margot Zemach. *It Could Always Be Worse: A Yiddish Folktale.* Farrar, Straus & Giroux.

1979

Paul Goble. *The Girl Who Loved Wild Horses.* Bradbury.

Honor Books:

Donald Crews, illus. *Freight Train.* Greenwillow.
Peter Parnall, illus. *The Way to Start a Day* by Byrd Baylor. Scribner.

1980

Barbara Cooney, illus. *Ox-Cart Man* by Donald Hall. Viking.

Honor Books:

Rachel Isadora, illus. *Ben's Trumpet.* Greenwillow.
Uri Shulevitz, illus. *Treasure.* Farrar, Straus & Giroux.
Chris Van Allsberg. *Garden of Abdul Gaszai.* Houghton Mifflin.

1981

Arnold Lobel, illus. *Fables.* Harper & Row.

Honor Books:

Molly Bang. *Grey Lady and the Strawberry Snatcher.* Scholastic.
Donald Crews. *Truck.* Greenwillow.
Joseph Low. *Mice Twice.* Atheneum.
Ilse Plume. *Bremen Town Musicians.* Doubleday.

1982

Chris Van Allsberg. *Jumanji.* Houghton Mifflin.

Honor Books:

Arnold Lobel. *On Market Street.* Greenwillow.
Maurice Sendak. *Outside, Over There.* Harper & Row.
Nancy Willard. *Visit to William Blake's Inn: Poems for Innocent and Experienced Travellers.* Harcourt Brace Jovanovich.

BOOKS FOR OLDER STUDENTS

Listed here are the latest Newbery Medal winners for outstanding content in books for children. Because the emphasis is on the subject matter rather than illustrations, these books are better suited for students in grades 4-8.

1978

Katherine Paterson. *Bridge to Terabithia.* Harper & Row.

Honor Books:

Beverly Cleary. *Ramona and Her Father.* Morrow.
Jamake Highwater. *Anpao: An American Indian Odyssey.* Lippincott.

1979

Ellen Raskin. *Westing Game.* Dutton.

Honor Book:

Katherine Paterson. *Great Gilly Hopkins.* Harper.

1980

Joan Blos. *A Gathering of Days: A New England Girl's Journal.* Scribner.

Honor Book:

David Kherdian. *Road from Home: The Story of an Armenian Childhood.* Greenwillow.

1981

Katherine Paterson. *Jacob Have I Loved.* Harper.

Honor Books:

Jane Langton. *Fledgling.* Harper.
Madeline L'Engle. *Ring of Endless Light.* Farrar, Straus & Giroux.

1982

Nancy Willard. *A Visit to William Blake's Inn: Poems for Innocent and Experienced Travellers.* Harcourt Brace Jovanovich.

Honor Books:

Beverly Cleary. *Ramona Quimby, Age Eight.* Morrow.
Aranka Siegal. *Upon the Head of a Goat: A Childhood in Hungary 1939-1944.* Farrar, Straus & Giroux.

BOOKS ABOUT WORDS AND LANGUAGE

This list of books is recommended for purchase for the school library. Most of the books in the first section can be used directly by students, as well as provide teaching ideas for the elementary school teacher. The second part of the list includes references for the teacher.

Books for Students

Alexander, Arthur. *The Magic Words.* Englewood Cliffs, New Jersey: Prentice-Hall, 1962.
Applegate, Mauree. *The First Book of Language.* New York: Franklin Watts, 1962.
Asimov, Isaac. *Words from the Myths.* Boston: Houghton Mifflin, 1961.
_____. *Words in Genesis.* Boston: Houghton Mifflin, 1962.
_____. *Words of Science and the History Behind Them.* Boston: Houghton Mifflin, 1959.
_____. *Words on the Map.* Boston: Houghton Mifflin, 1962.
Bach, Mickey. *Word-a-Day.* New York: Scholastic Book Services, 1972.
Basil, Cynthia. *Nailheads & Potato Eyes.* New York: Morrow, 1976.
Batchelor, Julie F. *Communication: From Cave to Television.* New York: Harcourt Brace Jovanovich, 1953.
Cahn, William, and Rhoda Cahn. *The Story of Writing from Cave Art to Computer.* Irvington-on-Hudson, New York: Harvey House, 1963.
Cataldo, John W. *Words and Calligraphy for Children.* New York: Van Nostrand Reinhold, 1969.
Denison, Carol. *Passwords to People.* New York: Dodd, Mead and Co., 1956.
Dugan, William. *How Our Alphabet Grew.* New York: Golden Press, 1972.
Epstein, Samuel and Beryl. *The First Book of Words.* New York: Franklin Watts, 1954.

_____. *The First Book of Printing.* New York: Franklin Watts, 1955.

_____. *What Is Behind the Word?* New York: Scholastic Book Services, 1964.

Ernst, Margaret S. *In A Word.* New York: Knopf, 1939.

_____. *Words.* New York: Knopf, 1936.

_____. *Words: English Roots and How They Grew.* New York: Knopf, 1937.

Evans, Bergen. *Comfortable Words.* New York: Random House, 1962.

Fadiman, Clifton. *Wally the Wordworm.* New York: Macmillan, 1964.

Ferguson, Charles. *The Abecedarian Book.* Boston: Little, Brown, 1964.

Folsom, Franklin. *The Language Book.* New York: Grosset and Dunlap, 1963.

Friend, M. Newton. *Words: Tricks and Traditions.* New York: Scribner, 1957.

Funk, Charles. *Heavens to Betsy.* New York: Harper & Row, 1955.

_____. *Hog on Ice and Other Curious Expressions.* New York: Harper & Row, 1948.

_____. *Thereby Hangs a Tale.* New York: Harper & Row, 1950.

Funk, Charles E., and Charles E. Funk, Jr. *Horsefeathers and Other Curious Words.* New York: Harper & Row, 1958.

Funk, Wildfred. *Word Origins and Their Romantic Stories.* New York: Grosset and Dunlap, 1950.

Hansen, Carl F., et al. *A Handbook for Young Writers.* Englewood Cliffs, New Jersey: Prentice-Hall, 1965.

Hanson, Joan. *Antonyms.* Minneapolis: Lerner, 1972.

_____. *Homographs.* Minneapolis: Lerner, 1972.

_____. *Homonyms.* Minneapolis: Lerner, 1972.

_____. *Synonyms.* Minneapolis: Lerner, 1972.

Hofsinde, Robert. *Indian Sign Languages.* New York: Morrow, 1956.

_____. *Indian Picture Writing.* New York: Morrow, 1959.

Hogben, Lancelot T. *Wonderful World of Communication.* New York: Garden City, 1959.

Hudson, Peggy, comp. *Words to the Wise.* New York: Scholastic Book Servces, 1971.

Hymes, Lucia, and James M. Hymes. *Oodles of Noodles.* Glenview, Illinois: Scott, Foresman, 1964.

Jacobs, Frank. *Alvin Steadfast on Vernacular Island.* New York: Dial, 1965.

Juster, Norton. *The Phantom Tollbooth.* New York: Epstein and Carroll, dist. by Random House, 1961.

Kaufman, Joel. *The Golden Happy Book of Words.* New York: Golden Press, 1963.

King, Joyce, and Carol Katzman. *Imagine That!* Pacific Palisades, California: Goodyear Publishing, 1976.

Laird, Charlton, and Helene Laird. *Tree of Language.* New York: World, 1957.

Lambert, Eloise. *Our Language.* New York: Lothrop, Lee and Shepard, 1955.

Lambert, Eloise, and Mario Pei. *Our Names: Where They Came From and What They Mean.* New York: Lothrop, Lee and Shepard, 1960.

Mathews, Mitford M. *American Words.* New York: World, 1959.

Merriam, Eve. *A Gaggle of Geese.* New York: Knopf, 1960.

Moorhouse, Alfred C. *The Triumph of the Alphabet: A History of Writing.* New York: Abelard-Schuman, 1953.

Morris, William and Mary Morris. *Dictionary of American Word Origins.* New York: Harper & Row, 1963.

Ogg, Oscar. *The Twenty-Six Letters.* New York: Thomas Y. Crowell, 1948.

O'Neill, Mary. *Words Words Words.* New York: Doubleday, 1966.

Osmond, Edward. *From Drumbeat to Tickertape.* New York: Criterion Books, 1960.

Partridge, Eric. *A Charm of Words.* Boulder, Colorado: Hamilton, dist. by Chapter & Cask (Glenshaw, Pennsylvania), 1960.

Pei, Mario. *All About Language.* Philadelphia: Lippincott, 1954.

_____. *Our National Heritage.* Boston: Houghton Mifflin, 1965.

Provensen, Alice, and Martin Provensen. *Karen's Opposites.* New York: Golden Press, 1963.

Radlauer, Ruth S. *Good Times with Words.* Chicago: Melmont, 1963.

Rand, Ann, and Paul Rand. *Sparkle and Spin.* New York: Harcourt Brace Jovanovich, 1957.

Reid, Alastair. *Ounce, Dice, Trice.* Boston: Little, Brown, 1958.

Rogers, Frances. *Painted Rock to Printed Page.* Philadelphia: Lippincott, 1960.

Roget, Peter M. *New Roget's Thesaurus of the English Language.* New York: Putnam's, 1961.

Rossner, Judith. *What Kind of Feet Does a Bear Have?* Indianapolis, Indiana: Bobbs-Merrill, 1963.

Russell, Solveig P. *A Is for Apple and Why.* Nashville, Tennessee: Abingdon, 1959.

_____. *Peanuts, Popcorn, Ice Cream, Candy, and Soda Pop and How They Began.* Nashville, Tennessee: Abingdon, 1970.

Sage, Michael. *Words Inside Words.* Philadelphia: Lippincott, 1961.

Schaff, Joanne. *The Language Arts Idea Book.* Pacific Palisades, California: Goodyear, 1976.

Schwartz, Alvin. *A Twister of Twists, a Tangler of Tongues.* Philadelphia: Lippincott, 1972.

Shipley, Joseph T. *Playing with Words.* Englewood Cliffs, New Jersey: Prentice-Hall, 1960.

_____. *Word Games for Play and Power.* Englewood Cliffs, New Jersey: Prentice-Hall, 1962.

_____. *Word Play.* New York: Hawthorne Books, 1972.

Sparke, William. *Story of the English Language.* New York: Abelard-Schuman, 1905.

Spector, Marjorie. *Pencil to Press: How This Book Came to Be.* New York: Lothrop, Lee & Shepard, 1975.

Vasilu. *The Most Beautiful Word.* New York: John Day, 1970.

Waller, Leslie. *Our American Language.* New York: Holt, Rinehart & Winston, 1960.

White, Mary S. *Word Twins.* Nashville, Tennessee: Abingdon, 1961.

Wilbur, Richard. *Opposites.* New York: Harcourt Brace Jovanovich, 1973.

Yates, Elizabeth. *Someday You'll Write.* New York: Dutton, 1962.

Zim, Herbert S. *Codes and Secret Writing.* New York: William Morrow, 1948.

Books for Teachers

Adams, J. Donald. *The Magic and Mystery of Words.* New York: Holt, Rinehart & Winston, 1963.

Brewer, E. Cobham. *Brewer's Dictionary of Phrase and Fable,* revised by Ivor Evans. New York: Harper & Row, 1970.

Carothers, Gibson, and James Lacey. *Slanguage.* New York: Sterling, 1979.

Chapman, Bruce. *Why Do We Say Such Things?* New York: Miles-Emmett, 1947.

Collins, V.H. *A Book of English Idioms.* Bristol, England: Longmans, 1956.

_____. *A Second Book of English Idioms.* Bristol, England: Longmans, 1958.

_____. *A Third Book of English Idioms.* Bristol, England: Longmans, 1960.

_____. *A Book of English Proverbs.* Bristol, England: Longmans, 1959.

1811 Dictionary of the Vulgar Tongue, edited by Captain Francis Grose. Chicago: Follett, 1971 (originally compiled in 1796).

Eisiminger, Sterling. "Colorful Language." Verbatim, vol. VI, no. 1. Summer 1979, 1-3.

Ernst, Margaret. *In a Word.* Great Neck, New York: Channel, 1939.

Evans, Bergen, and Cornelia Evans. *A Dictionary of Contemporary American Usage.* New York: Random House, 1957.

Flexner, Stuart Berg. *I Hear America Talking.* New York: Simon and Schuster, 1976.

Frazer, Sir James G. *The Golden Bough*, abridged edition. New York: Macmillan, 1922.

Freeman, William. *A Concise Dictionary of English Idioms*. New York: Thomas Y. Crowell, 1951.

Funk, Wilfred. *Word Origins and Their Romantic Stories*. New York: Wilfred Funk, 1950.

Holt, Alfred H. *Phrase Origins*. New York: Thomas Y. Crowell, 1936.

Jacobs, Noah Jonathan. *Naming-Day in Eden*. New York: Macmillan, 1958.

Mencken, H.L. *The American Language*. New York: Knopf, 1937, and Supplement II, 1948.

Morris, William, and Mary Morris. *Morris Dictionary of Phrase and Word Origins*. New York: Harper & Row, 1977.

The Oxford English Dictionary. 12 vols. Oxford: Clarendon, 1933.

Partidge, Eric. *A Dictionary of Catch Phrases*. New York: Stein and Day, 1977.

_____ *Dictionary of Clichés*. New York: Macmillan, 1940.

Radford, Edwin. *Unusual Words and How They Came About*. New York: Philosophical Library, 1946.

Radford, Edwin, and Mona A. Radford. *Encyclopedia of Superstitions*, edited and revised by Christina Hole. London: Hutchinson, 1961.

Standard Dictionary of Folklore, Mythology, and Legend, edited by Maria Leach. New York: Funk & Wagnalls, 1972.

Webster's New World Dictionary, second college edition. New York: World, 1972.

Wentworth, Harold, and Stuart Berg Flexner. *Dictionary of American Slang*. New York: Thomas Y. Crowell, 1975.

RECOMMENDED FILMS
FOR THE ELEMENTARY CLASSROOM

These films will be useful in promoting visual literacy. They also stimulate oral language development and can be used to motivate reading and writing.

Primary and Intermediate

Title	*Producer*	*Running Time*
"Clown"	Learning Corp.	15 min.
"Cow"	Churchill	10
"Creating a Children's Book"	ACI	12

Primary and Intermediate

Title	Producer	Running Time
"Fable"	Xerox	18
"Fun with Words: Word Twins"	Coronet	11
"Fun with Words: Words That Name & Do"	Coronet	11
"Glass Marble"	Modern Learning Aids	9
"Hailstones & Halibut Bones, Part I"	Sterling	6
"Hailstones & Halibut Bones, Part II"	Sterling	7
"The Happy Owls"	Weston	10
"Let's Write a Story"	Churchill	11
"Little Mariner"	Ency. Britannica	20
"Open Sea"	Frith	5
"Pigs"	Churchill	15
"Poetry for Beginners"	Coronet	11
"Poetry for Me"	Grover	15
"Rainshower"	Churchill	15
"Red Balloon"	Brandon	34
"Tikki Tikki Tembo"	Weston	10
"Treehouse"	BFA	9

Upper Elementary

Title	Producer	Running Time
"Adventures of an *"	Contemporary	10 min.
"Building Better Paragraphs"	Coronet	12
"Building Better Sentences"	Coronet	13
"A Chairy Tale"	IFB	10
"Chest" (Story Starter)	Discovery	5
"Clubhouse Boat"	Churchill	19
"Golden Fish"	Brandon	20
"Jail Door Went Clang"	Churchill	16
"Kite Story"	Churchill	25
"Ladder" (Story Starter)	Discovery	5
"Loon's Necklace"	Ency. Britannica	11
"Magic of Communicating"	Shaw	11

Upper Elementary

Title	Producer	Running Time
"Man Who Bought Monday Nite"	Churchill	16
"Mean, Nasty, Ugly Cinderella"	Churchill	16
"Paper Drive"	Churchill	15
"Poems We Write"	Grover	15
"Rock in the Road"	BFA	6
"Spelling Is Easy"	Coronet	11
"Story of a Book"	Pied Piper	11
"Storymaker—Don Freeman"	Churchill	14
"Trick or Treat"	Churchill	15
"We Discover the Dictionary"	Coronet	11
"What's Riding Hood without the Wolf?"	Churchill	16
"Wheels—Wheels—Wheels"	BFA	11
"Writing a Report"	Coronet	11
"Zlateh the Goat"	Weston	27

Advanced

Title	Producer	Running Time
"Abyss" (Rock Climbing)	Phoenix	17 min.
"Brown Wolf"	Weston	27
"Catch the Joy"	Pyramid	14
"Climb"	Churchill	22
"Current Events— Understanding and Evaluating Them"	Coronet	11
"Dream of Wild Horses"	McGraw-Hill	9
"Ezra Jack Keats"	Weston	27
"English Language—How It Changes"	Coronet	11
"Genius Man"	ACI	3
"Help! My Snowman's Burning Down"	McGraw-Hill	10
"In a Spring Garden" (Haiku)	Weston	10
"Journey"	Wombat	10
"Moods of Surfing"	Pyramid	15

Advanced

Title	Producer	Running Time
"Newpaper Layout"	Oxford	13
"Refiner's Fire"	Doubleday	6
"Robert McCloskey"	Weston	24
"Short Story"	Grover	20
"Sixty Second Spot—Making of a TV Commercial"	Pyramid	25
"Solo"	Pyramid	15
"Story of a Newspaperman"	Sterling	25
"Story of a Writer" (Ray Bradbury)	Sterling	25
"String Bean"	McGraw-Hill	17
"Talking Ourselves into Trouble"	Indiana U.	29
"Why Man Creates"	Pyramid	29
"Words That Don't Inform"	Indiana U.	29

ADDRESSES OF PUBLISHERS

This handy directory of companies that publish books and other instructional materials will help you in requesting publishers' catalogs and specific items of interest.

Abelard, Schuman, Ltd. 666 Fifth Avenue, New York, NY 10019.

Abingdon Press, 201 Eighth Avenue South, Nashville, TN 37202.

ACI Films, 35 West 45 Street, New York, NY 10036.

Addison-Wesley Publishing Co, Reading, MA 01867.

Aims Instructional Media Services, P.O. Box 1010, Hollywood, CA 90028.

Allyn & Bacon, Rockleigh, NJ 07647.

American Heritage Press, 1221 Avenue of the Americas, New York, NY 10020.

American Library Association, Publishing Services, 50 E. Huron Street, Chicago, IL 60611.

Appleton Century Crofts, Hartford, CT 06101.

Association for Childhood Education International, 3615 Wisconsin Avenue, N.W., Washington, D.C. 20016.

Atheneum Publishers, 122 East 42 Street, New York, NY 10017.

Avon Books, 959 Eighth Avenue, New York, NY 10019.

Barr Films, P.O. Box 7-C, Pasadena, CA 91104.

Beacon Press, 25 Beacon Street, Boston, MA 02108.

Bell & Howell, 2201 West Howard, Evanston, IL 60202.

Bobbs-Merrill Company, 4300 W. 62 Street, Indianapolis, IN 46268.

Stephen Bosustow Productions, 1649 11th Street, Santa Monica, CA 90404.

The R. R. Bowker Company, Xerox Education Group, 1180 Avenue of the Americas, New York, NY 10036.

Bowmar Publishing Corporation, 622 Rodier Drive, Glendale, CA 91201.

Bradbury Press, 2 Overhill Road, Scarsdale, NY 10583.

Brigham Young University, Motion Picture Department, M.P.S., Provo, UT 84602.

Centron Educational Films, 1621 West Ninth, Lawrence, KS 66044.

Changing Times Education Service, 1729 H Street, N.W., Washington, D.C. 20006.

Children's Book Council, Inc., 67 Irving Place, New York, NY 10003.

Children's Press, 1224 W. Van Buren Street, Chicago, IL 60607.

Churchill Films, 662 North Robertson Boulevard, Los Angeles, CA 90069.

Citation Press, 50 W. 44 Street, New York, NY 10036.

Clearvue, 666 North Oliphant Avenue, Chicago, IL 60631.

William Collins & World Publishing Co., 2080 West 117 Street, Cleveland, OH 44111.

Columbia University Press, 562 W. 113 Street, New York, NY 10025.

Contemporary Press, Box 1524, San Jose, Ca 95109.

Coronet Instructional Media, 65 East South Water Street, Chicago IL 60601.

Council on Interracial Books for Children, 1841 Broadway, New York, NY 10023.

Coward, McCann & Geoghegan, 200 Madison Avenue, New York, NY 10016.

Thomas Y. Crowell Co., 666 Fifth Avenue, New York, NY 10019.

Corwell-Collier Press, 640 Fifth Avenue, New York, NY 10019.

Crown Publishers, 419 Park Avenue South, New York, NY 10016.

The John Day Co., 666 Fifth Avenue, New York, NY 10019.

Delacorte Press, 1 Dag Hammarskjold Plaza, 245 East 47 Street, New York, NY 10017.

The Dial Press, 1 Dag Hammarskjold Plaza, 245 East 47 Street, New York, NY 10017.

Dilton Press, 106 Washington Avenue North, Minneapolis, MN 55401.

Walt Disney Educational Materials, 800 Sonota Avenue, Glendale, CA 91201.

Dodd, Mead & Co., 79 Madison Avenue, New York, NY 10016.

Doubleday & Co., 245 Park Avenue, New York, NY 10017.

Doubleday Multimedia, 1371 Reynolds Avenue, Santa Ana, CA 92705.

E. P. Dutton & Co., 201 Park Avenue South, New York, NY 10003.

Educational Development Corporation, 202 Lake Miriam Drive, Lakeland, FL 33803.

EMC Corporation, 180 East Sixth Street, St. Paul, MN 55101.

Encyclopaedia Britannica Educational Corporation, 425 North Michigan Avenue, Chicago, IL 60611.

M. Evans & Co., 216 East 49 Street, New York, NY 10017.

Farrar, Straus & Giroux, 19 Union Square West, New York, NY 10003.

Far West Laboratory, 1855 Folsom Street, San Francisco, CA 94103.

F. W. Faxon Company, 15 Southwest Park, Westwood, MA 02090.

Fearon Teacher Aids, 6 Davis Drive, Belmont, CA 94002.

The Feminist Press, Box 334, Old Westbury, NY 11568.

Follett Publishing Co., 1010 West Washington Boulevard, Chicago, IL 60607.

Four Winds Press, 50 West 44 Street, New York, NY 10036.

Funk & Wagnalls, Inc., 53 E. 77 Street, New York, NY 10021.

Garrard Publishing Company, 1607 N. Market Street, Champaign, IL 61820.

General Educational Media, 350 Northern Boulevard, Great Neck, NY 10021.

Golden Gate Junior Books, 1247½ North Vista Street, Hollywood, CA 90046.

Golden Press, (Western Publishing Co.), 850 Third Avenue, New York, NY 10022.

Goldsholl Associates, 420 Frontage Road, Northfield, IL 60093.

Allan Grant Productions, 808 Lockearn Street, Los Angeles, CA 90049.

Grosset & Dunlap, 51 Madison Avenue, New York, NY 10010.

Guidance Associates, 41 Washington Avenue, Pleasantville, NY 10570.

G. K. Hall & Company, 70 Lincoln Street, Boston, MA 02111.

Harcourt Brace Jovanovich, 1250 Sixth Avenue, San Diego, CA 92101.

Harper & Row, Publishers, 10 East 53 Street, New York, NY 10022.

Harvey House, 20 Waterside Plaza, New York, NY 10010.

Hastings House Publishers, 10 East 40 Street, New York, NY 10016.

Hawthorn Books, 260 Madison Avenue, New York, NY 10016.

Holiday House, 18 East 56 Street, New York, NY 10022.

Holt, Rinehart & Winston, 383 Madison Avenue, New York, NY 10017.

Horn Books, Inc., 585 Boylston Street, Boston, MA 02116.

Houghton Mifflin Co., 2 Park Street, Boston, MA 02107.

International Reading Association, 800 Barksdale Road, Newark, DE 19711.

Alfred A. Knopf, 201 East 50 Street, New York, NY 10022.

Learning Corporation of America, 711 Fifth Avenue, New York, NY 10022.

Learning Resources Company, P.O. Box 3709, 202 Lake Miriam Drive, Lakeland, FL 33803.

Learning Tree Filmstrips, 934 Pearl Street, P.O. Box 1590, Dept. 105, Boulder, CO 80302.

Lerner Publications Company, 241 First Avenue North, Minneapolis, MN 55401.

Libraries Unlimited, Box 263, Littleton, CO 80120.

J. B. Lippincott Company, 521 Fifth Avenue, New York, NY 10017.

Little, Brown & Co., 34 Beacon Street, Boston, MA 02106.

Lothrop, Lee & Shepard Company, 105 Madison Avenue, New York, NY 10016.

Macrae Smith Company, Lewis Tower Building, 225 S. 15 Street, Philadelphia, PA 19102.

Macmillan Publishing Co., 866 Third Avenue, New York, NY 10022.

McGraw-Hill Book Co., 1221 Avenue of the Americas, New York, NY 10020.

David McKay Company, Publishers, 750 Third Avenue, New York, NY 10017.

Charles E. Merrill Publishing Co, 1300 Alum Creek Drive, Columbus, OH 43216.

Julian Messner (A Division of Simon & Schuster), 1 West 39 Street, New York, NY 10018.

Miller-Brody Productions, 711 Fifth Avenue, New York, NY 10022.

William Morrow & Co., 105 Madison Avenue, New York, NY 10016.

National Council for the Social Studies, 1201 Sixteenth Street N.W., Washington, D.C. 20036.

National Council of Teachers of English, 1111 Kenyon Road, Urbana, IL 61801.

National Council of Teachers of Mathematics, 1906 Association Drive, Reston, VA 22091.

National Instructional Television, Box A, Bloomington, IN 47401.

Thomas Nelson, 407 7th Avenue South, Nashville, TN 37203.

Newsweek, 444 Madison Avenue, New York, NY 10022.

New York Library Association, Children and Young Adult Services Section, 230 W. 41 Street, Suite 1800, New York, NY 10036.

New York Office of State History, State Education Department, 99 Washington Avenue, Albany, NY 12210.

J. Philip O'Hara, 20 E. Huron Street, Chicago, IL 60611.

Oxford Films, 1136 North Las Palmas Avenue, Los Angeles, CA 90036.
Oxford University Press, 200 Madison Avenue, New York, NY 10016.

Pantheon Books, 201 East 50 Street, New York, NY 10022.
Parents' Magazine Press, 52 Vanderbilt Avenue, New York, NY 10017.
Parker Publishing Company, Inc., West Nyack, NY 10995.
Parnassus Press, 4080 Halleck Street, Emeryville, CA 94608.
Pathescope Educational Films, 71 Weyman Avenue, New Rochelle, NY
    10802.
S. G. Phillips, 305 West 86 Street, New York, NY 10024.
Pied Piper Productions, P.O. Box 320, Verdugo City, CA 91046.
Pitman Learning, Inc., 6 Davis Drive, Belmont, CA 94002.
Plays, 8 Arlington Street, Boston, MA 02116.
Platt & Munk, Publishers, 1055 Bronx River Avenue, Bronx, NY 10572.
Prentice-Hall, Inc., Englewood Cliffs, NJ 07632.
Psychology Today, Del Mar, CA 92014.
G. P. Putnam's Sons, 200 Madison Avenue, New York, NY 10016.
Pyramid Films Corporation, P.O. Box 1048, Santa Monica, CA 90406.

Q-ED Productions, P.O. Box 1608, Burbank, CA 91507.

Rand McNally & Co., P.O. Box 7600, Chicago, IL 60680.
Random House Educational Media, Order Entry Department-Y, 400
    Hahn Road, Westminster, MD 21157.
The Reilly & Lee Co., 114 W. Illinois Street, Chicago, IL 60610.
The Ronald Press Co., 79 Madison Avenue, New York, NY 10016.

St. Martin's Press, 174 Fifth Avenue, New York, NY 10010.
Salinger Educational Media, 1635 12th Street, Santa Monica, CA 90404.
Scarecrow Press, 52 Liberty Street, Box 656, Metuchen, NJ 08840.
Schloat Productions, 150 White Plains Road, Tarrytown, NY 10591.
Schmitt, Hall & McCreary Co., 110 N. Fifth Street, Minneapolis, MN
    55403.
Scholastic Magazines, Audiovisual and Media Department, 50 West 44
    Street, New York, NY 10036.
Scott, Foresman & Co., Educational Publishers, 1900 E. Lake Avenue,
    Glenview, IL 60025.
Screen Education Enterprises, 3220 16th Avenue West, Seattle, WA
    98119.
Charles Scribner's Sons, 597 Fifth Avenue, New York, NY 10017.
Scroll Press, Publishers, 129 East 94 Street, New York, NY 10028.
The Seabury Press, 815 Second Avenue, New York, NY 10017.
See Hear Now! Ltd., 49 Wellington Street East, Toronto M5E 1C9
    Canada.
Simon & Schuster, Publishers, 1230 Sixth Avenue, New York, NY
    10020.

Steck-Vaughn Co., Division of Intext Publishers Group, Box 2028, Austin, TX 78767.
Sterling Publishing Co., 419 Park Avenue South, New York, NY 10016.

Teaching Resources Films, Station Plaza, Bedford Hills, NY 10507.
Technicolor, 299 Kalmus Drive, Costa Mesa, CA 92626.
Troll Associates, 320 Route 17, Mahwah, NJ 07430.

University of Chicago Press, 5801 Ellis Avenue, Chicago, IL 60637.
University of Pittsburgh Press, 127 N. Bellefield Avenue, Pittsburgh, PA 15213.

The Vanguard Press, 424 Madison Avenue, New York, NY 10017.
Van Nostrand-Reinhold Co., 450 W. 33 Street, New York, NY 10001.
The Viking Press, 625 Madison Avenue, New York, NY 10022.

Henry Z. Walck, Publishers, 19 Union Square W., New York, NY 10003.
Walker & Co., 720 Fifth Avenue, New York, NY 10019.
The Ward Ritchie Press (Anderson, Ritchie & Simon), 3044 Riverside Drive, Los Angeles, CA 90039.
Frederick Warne & Co., 101 Fifth Avenue, New York, NY 10003.
Ives Washburn, 750 Third Avenue, New York, NY 10017.
Franklin Watts, 730 Fifth Avenue, New York, NY 10019.
Westminster Press, Witherspoon Building, Philadelphia, PA 19107.
Weston Woods, Weston, CT 06880.
Albert Whtiman & Co., 560 West Lake Street, Chicago, IL 60606.
The H. W. Wilson Co., 950 University Avenue, New York, NY 10452.
Windmill Books, 201 Park Avenue South, New York, NY 10003.
World Publishing Co., 2080 W. 117th Street, Cleveland, OH 44111.

Xerox Films, 245 Long Hill Road, Middletown, CT 06457.

Young Scott Books, Reading, MA 01867.

Index

A

Acting out, 117-118
Activities (*see* Games and activities)
Addition, 145-146
Addressing a group, 57
Alike and different, words, 59
Alphabet activities, 102-104
Art:
  across curriculum, 243-256
    language arts, 251-256
    science, 249-251
    social studies, 244-249
  April, 240-241
  calligraphy, 110-112, 203, 245
  chalks, 229
  collage, 200, 244-245
  color, techniques, 227
  crayons, 225-226
  December, 234-236
  enhance writing, 88
  February, 237-238
  fingerpainting, 229-230
  January, 236-237
  June, 242-243
  March, 239-240
  May, 241-242
  November, 233-234
  October, 232-233
  painting, 227-228
  presenting a lesson, 224-225
  prints, 228-229
  scientific facts, 176-177

Art (*cont'd.*)
  September, 231-232
  tempera, washable, 226
  through school year, 231-243
  uses, 230-231
  watercolors, 226
Attention span, 20

B

Ball games, 269-270
Behavior problems, 21-22
Bilingual students, 58-63
Block letters, 31
Book fair, 135
Bookmarks, 255-256
Book party, 256
Books:
  choosing, 114-115
  featuring handicapped children, 128-129
  reporting, 130-131
  responding, 71, 131
  reviewing, 128
  science, 167
  teaching resources, 279-289, 292-297
  writing, 89
Brainstorming:
  problem solving, 159-160
  writing topics, 27
Breaks, 20
Bulletin board displays:
  backgrounds, 32

DATE DUE

APR 1 2 1990		
MAY 8 1992		
MAR 31 1993		
MAY 7 1993		
Sent 10-1-93		
NO 2 '93		
NO 30 '93		
SEP 22 1994		
FEB 20 1995		

GAYLORD   PRINTED IN U.S.A.